Bu ... g
Research Design
in Education

Tara Jakes

Building Research Design in Education

Theoretically Informed Advanced Methods

Edited by Lorna Hamilton and John Ravenscroft

BLOOMSBURY ACADEMIC
LONDON • NEW YORK • OXFORD • NEW DELHI • SYDNEY

Bloomsbury Academic
Bloomsbury Publishing Plc
50 Bedford Square London WC1B 3DP UK

BLOOMSBURY, BLOOMSBURY ACADEMIC and the Diana logo are
trademarks of Bloomsbury Publishing Plc

First published in Great Britain 2018

Cover design: Anna Berzovan
Cover image © AVTG / iStock

A catalogue record for this book is available from the British Library.

ISBN: HB: 978-1-3500-1950-8
          PB: 978-1-3500-1949-2
        ePDF: 978-1-3500-1952-2
       eBook: 978-1-3500-1951-5

Typeset by Integra Software Services Pvt. Ltd.
Printed and bound in Great Britain

To find out more about our authors and books visit www.bloomsbury.com
and sign up for our newsletters

For Lorna's daughter Katie
and
For John's family, Elaine and Euan

Contents

List of Figures

List of Tables

Contributors

Pete Allison is Associate Professor of Values and Experiential Learning in the College of Health and Human Development, The Pennsylvania State University, USA. He is interested in moral development, values education, outdoor and experiential leadership and wilderness expeditions.

Ellen Boeren is Lecturer at the Moray House School of Education, University of Edinburgh, UK. She is programme director of the MSc Educational Research and course organiser of Comparative Analysis in Education and Designing Educational Research. She is the Edinburgh team lead on the Horizon 2020 project ENLIVEN: Encouraging Lifelong Learning for a Vibrant & Inclusive Europe.

Jane Brown is a qualitative researcher with extensive experience of undertaking research in schools, family homes and youth settings. She has a long-standing commitment to researching topics which impact on the lives of children and young people, including youth violence. In the last ten years, her work has focused on pupil participation and citizenship.

Katie Cebula is Senior Lecturer in Developmental Psychology at the Moray House School of Education, University of Edinburgh, UK. Her research focuses primarily on relationships and experiences within families who have a child with a developmental disability.

Lorna Hamilton is Senior Lecturer in Education Research at the University of Edinburgh, UK. Her research focuses on the nature of identity in relation to current educational issues: professional identity and early professional learning in the face of educational reform and pupil sense of self and potential for agency in modern classrooms.

Luke Eric Lassiter is Professor of Humanities and Anthropology and Director of the Graduate Humanities Program at Marshall University, USA. His books on ethnographic theory and practice include *The Chicago Guide to Collaborative Ethnography* and (with Elizabeth Campbell) *Doing Ethnography Today*.

Andrew Manches, based at the University of Edinburgh, UK, is a Learning Scientist concerned with the relationship between action and cognitive development, focusing on the role of hands-on learning in the early years STEM and the design implications for early learning technologies. Andrew is an invited member of the Royal Society of Edinburgh's panel of Education.

Christina McMellon is a research fellow based at Strathclyde University, UK. She completed her MSc and Ph.D. in Childhood Studies at Edinburgh University, UK. Christina is particularly interested in participatory research with young people and service users, research ethics, young people's participation, community engagement and subjective well-being.

Mary Mitchell has a professional background in social work and community work. She has worked extensively in the voluntary, non-government and government sectors in both Australia and Scotland. Her research focus is on investigating outcomes for looked after children and their families. She is also Teaching Fellow (Social Work) for the University of Edinburgh, UK.

Fiona O'Hanlon is Chancellor's Fellow in Languages Education at Moray House School of Education, The University of Edinburgh, UK. Her research focuses on Gaelic-medium education, and on the teaching of modern languages in English-medium education. She uses mixed-methods approaches in her own research, and supervises mixed-methods postgraduate projects.

John Ravenscroft is Professor of Childhood Visual Impairment at the University of Edinburgh, UK. His research focuses on the nature of representation, cerebral visual impairment and the incidence and prevalence of children with visual impairment. Professor Ravenscroft is also keenly interested in understanding knowledge through virtue epistemology and relating this to pupil learning and teacher education.

Jen Ross is Senior Lecturer in Digital Education at the University of Edinburgh, UK, co-director of the Centre for Research in Digital Education and Deputy Director (KE) of Research and Knowledge Exchange in the School of Education. She teaches about research methods on the fully online MSc in Digital Education, and on a new Massive Open Online Course (MOOC) on Social Research Methods.

Dimitra Tsakalou is Teaching Fellow in Educational Studies/Initial Teacher Education at the University of Edinburgh, UK, with a strong research background in inclusive education and educational studies. She has an MSc in Inclusive and Special Education as well as a Ph.D. from the University of Edinburgh, UK. The latter focused on the nature of inclusive communities in Greece.

Introduction

Lorna Hamilton and John Ravenscroft

There is nothing more rewarding than conducting your own research. Every step of the process should be exciting, full of anticipation and one that is built upon a series of decisions that you as a researcher will have made, in order to find an answer to your research questions. Doing research, without doubt, is a learning experience and the more you do it, the more understanding you develop in research methodology and methods. It is also the case that the more you do, the more you learn about differing approaches to the same and/or differing research questions. Understanding how to address a particular problem is key, and as experience grows we find that there are perhaps more keys that open the doors of differing research methodologies than perhaps once thought at the beginning of the research journey.

In approaching any attempt to explore and investigate the nature of the world that we live in and how we try to capture it, a profound but simple idea needs to be considered – 'researcher know thyself'. By this, we mean that it is your own beliefs about the nature of knowledge and how it can be known which will shape how you move forward with your research endeavours. Creating a robust design should involve researchers in reflection on world views and associated theories that underpin them, but often we note that these theoretical assumptions that drive the design may be *an absent presence* within research proposals. Implicit assumptions about the nature of the world and how it is knowable may inform researcher decisions in an ad hoc way but don't necessarily lead to an explicit, transparent and rigorous decision-making process. This book tries to address this *absent presence* and hopefully provides insights to achieve a better understanding of educational research design.

In doctoral study, students often find themselves having to complete a proposal prior to acceptance that often concentrates on the practicalities of a literature review and the nature of the data collection tools to be used. It can then be a shock for doctoral students to have to take several steps back from this process in order to wrestle with the big questions of ontology and epistemology and just what their own beliefs might be, about knowledge and knowing.

Of critical importance within advanced study of research methods and the creation of meaningful and rigorous research projects is the researcher's ability to understand and justify fully their choice of methodology, grounded in clear ontological and epistemological positioning. Through insights gained from authors' experiences as supervisors and teachers of research methods as well as through their own research and theoretical research positions, we have harnessed a wide range of researchers to share their insights into their own particular philosophical position. It is through the lens of other researchers that we can sometimes best understand the nature of research design and its underpinning values, principles and ways of thinking. Of note, however, is that we do not simply use broad brushstrokes in structuring this book, and essential paradigmatic positions, although acknowledged and engaged with, are not the key organizing mechanism. Instead we sought to invite authors from a range of backgrounds and research preferences who would initiate discussion around diverse, sometimes innovative and, for some, even radical knowledge positions. Jen Ross's chapter (Chapter 10) is a beautiful example of a challenge to conventional thinking around research, while Eric Lassiter's work on collaborative ethnography (Chapter 8) highlights both the difficulties for the researcher in this kind of collaborative working, where the traditional power imbalances may be swept away, and the quality and richness that can be achieved when aspiring to build a different kind of relationship between researcher and researched. In challenging any traditional hierarchical notion of the researcher as expert, the co-construction of research becomes a real and meaningful possibility. However, it is not just the range and diversity of approaches to research that are important here; it is in the ways that researchers share their personal theoretical journeys and consequently engage in research that provides confident starting points for novice researchers to begin to know themselves more fully.

As this book is designed to be an advanced text we do assume a basic knowledge of social research and social research terminology within education. Although most contributors to this book are based in the School of Education at Edinburgh University, they represent a rich tapestry of nationalities, research experiences and outlooks. John Ravenscroft from Edinburgh University and Pete Allison from the The Pennsylvania State University, the United States, have drawn on their work and teaching in research methods to engage with the fundamental ideas that need to be discussed around ontology and epistemology. They set out the key concerns and issues for reflection when beginning to delve into theoretical frameworks. The opening chapter, therefore, where the difference between 'ontology' and 'epistemology' is discussed, is deliberately placed first. We note that doctoral students unfamiliar with philosophical content find these two terms particularly challenging at times. The chapter also introduces the reader to philosophical discussions of 'what is knowledge', and that knowledge was once thought to be akin to justified true belief. This classic view of knowledge has had to be re-examined as a result of the work of Edmund Gettier who by illustrating various examples, contained in the chapter, highlighted instances where this account of knowledge can be satisfied but yet we would not identify the user as having knowledge. We have included these accounts in the chapter as they enable the reader to start to consider the very epistemological issues of what is knowledge, and how as a researcher we need to be aware of the knowledge we are creating and eventually disseminating.

The second chapter by Ellen Boeren starts our journey into some of the methods researchers use and draws on her European experiences to inform her work at Edinburgh University. It provides insights into the different types of quantitative surveys students or researchers can use to collect and analyse data. This chapter discusses the different steps when carrying out survey research, from defining the objectives for the research to analysing and reporting the result. Many doctoral students we have supervised have used surveys in their work and therefore we have asked Ellen to theoretically position and to specifically distinguish between cross-sectional and longitudinal data, which she has explained and is backed up in the chapter by a number of specific examples of these types of surveys which, we hope, readers will find useful.

Katie Cebula is a developmental psychologist at Edinburgh and she considers the positioning of experimental and quasi-experimental work in education research and the possible theoretical stances that might form part of that approach. This chapter provides for us a very interesting discussion on the epistemological assumptions that have been highlighted in Chapter 2. She very carefully examines some of the concerns raised around the use of experimental and quasi-experimental research design and helpfully provides the reader with a view to understanding how these can be addressed. Of particular note within this chapter is the discussion Katie brings around validity, causation and replication, of which these key concepts in research design are often confused and misused.

Jane Brown's chapter moves us smoothly away from quantitative methods to more qualitative methods, where we see that with such an approach, relationships between the researcher and researched begin to be debated, raising ethical issues. It also continues the theme of justification that is paramount to good education research design. We have positioned this chapter quite early in the book as we wanted the reader to think more deeply about the implications of qualitative research design and about ethics in research as being more than a technical submission to the various ethics committees for approval.

Continuing from the previous chapter on qualitative research is Lorna Hamilton and Dimitra Tsakalou's chapter that draws on their experiences with case study work and their approach to critically framing and developing it. They challenge the often-atheoretical and ad hoc use of case study and highlight the importance of positioning case study as a deliberate choice and as theory informed. As you have come to expect within each of the chapters by now, Lorna and Dimitra take note of what was discussed in Chapter 2 and suggest some possible ontological and epistemological stances that might be used in order to ground case study in a theoretically robust frame. They also consider the ways in which multiple case study design can be used effectively through the use of specific theoretical frames (e.g. interpretivist and sociocultural grounding) and multidimensional analysis across past, present and future axes.

Also at Edinburgh, Fiona O'Hanlon focuses on an increasingly popular mixed-methods approach where harmonizing theoretical positioning may involve thoughtful compromises. Apart from the extremely useful rationale and justification for mixed methods that Fiona highlights in the chapter, she writes for us an extremely helpful philosophical framing section which is rarely found in other mixed method texts. One cannot, and should not, escape the ontological and epistemological lens through which we view our research and Fiona helps us to contextualize this through the mix method approach.

We return to Ellen for our next chapter on comparative methods and, as she notes herself, chapters on comparative methods are often absent from methodological textbooks so we felt it was important to correct this. It is interesting to consider why there has been this lack of admission, for we know that governments from all over the world take very seriously comparative approaches in education. Look, for example, at the Scottish government's reaction to triennial international surveys which aim to evaluate education systems worldwide by testing the skills and knowledge of fifteen-year-old students, commonly known as the Programme for International Student Assessment (PISA). The current deputy first minister of Scotland and the cabinet secretary for education and skills is quoted as saying, "There is great strength in Scottish education but these results underline the case for radical reform of Scotland's education system. The [PISA] results undoubtedly make uncomfortable reading but they contain a plain message: we must continue to make the changes that are necessary to strengthen Scottish education" (www.holyrood.com/articles/news/scotland's-schools'-pisa-scores-drop-lowest-level). We do not think that Scottish deputy minister is the only government official across the world to react in this way to their own country's PISA results. If comparative approaches can have such an impact on senior political figures, then we believe it is important to understand such approaches within education research and hence the inclusion into our book is not only warranted, but is essential.

We are also delighted to have a colleague from Marshall University in Virginia, the United States, to contribute a memorable chapter on a challenging approach, collaborative ethnography. Eric Lassiter is author of seminal works on collaborative ethnography and uses his research experiences on substantial and significant projects in the United States to help other researchers understand the strengths and challenges of such work while making it accessible to different kinds of researchers, both academic and community. The richness of such work is highly desirable but the issues of power, textual ownership and decision-making highlight that this is a challenging option for any researcher.

Continuing on from this theme of co-construction of research, we have two researchers who have a great deal of experience in working with young people, Cristina McMellon and Mary Mitchell. Building on their own work in this area, they consider Participatory Action Research (PAR) and the implications for theory and practice. This chapter starts with describing PAR as an approach rather than as a prescriptive process for they argue that PAR is not a fixed process but rather it is a research practice 'that is made up of a dynamic interaction between inquiry, participation, action, and reflection'. This dynamic interaction is of real interest to academic researchers who perhaps do not hold to traditional models of research methods. The values and biases of the researchers are not only acknowledged but also embraced within the research design. Bias has been seen in past research books as something that should be avoided and mitigated against, but we see in this chapter how bias and research values are key components and, by utilizing these, PAR breaks down the assumed hierarchies between academic, professional and personal knowledge.

We end this book with two different approaches to research that we believe may become as mainstream as the others described above but are as yet considered new and innovative approaches, particularly in education research. Both chapters have at their core a focus on being in a digital world, where research into digital processes and the role of modern technology in the lives of children are explored by Jen Ross (Chapter 10) and Andrew Manches (Chapter 11). Jen engages with speculative method as a means of framing digital research. This is really quite an exciting approach, for speculative method treats the world as 'ongoing', in the sense that it does not see the world as a static entity. The speculative method, as Jen outlines it, can be a powerful approach to generating and examining new perspectives and questions, and to helping understand and shape complex topics, especially those that deal with the future. Epistemologically speaking, this chapter is of real interest to researchers who have difficulty with more traditional approaches that have been outlined in some of the chapters discussed. But actually, this chapter also challenges the way we deal with uncertainty through qualitative approaches, too. What Jen brings to the discussion in her chapter is her critique of the, perhaps, overly technical application of research methods within education and her discussion of what is considered evidence. This again ties nicely with the themes and concepts that run through this book that focus on the ontological and epistemological divides that occur in education research.

Our final chapter in the book, at first glance, appears to be a bit of an outlier, an odd inclusion into a methods book of education research. However, we have included this chapter because Andrew provides us with an interesting way of how to define knowledge, which is a very traditional epistemic question. Andrew asks us to consider how technology itself may be integral to our definitions of knowledge and learning. This is not asked elsewhere in the book and it is a question that we find very interesting. Andrew also asks us to consider 'learning' and to define exactly what learning is, as he, in this chapter, considers the challenge of defining learning relative to technology. Defining learning and knowledge is clearly the aim of all research and hence is a fitting way to end this book.

Once you have read this book, we hope that you will better understand your possible ontological position, which will lead to your understanding of the nature and sources of knowledge as an epistemological foundation. No one chapter has primacy over another, but understanding different approaches is a key element in making informed choices and arguing successfully for your own particular research approach. Having this essential grounding in ontological and epistemological positioning assures that research can develop from a robust framework and can inform theoretically sound decisions during the research process. We have focused on this sometimes difficult part of the research process in order to stimulate thinking around the fundamental foundations of research and the impact that ideas about the nature of the world can have upon the research design, process and outcomes when the *absent presence* is brought to the fore. *Nosce te* (the motto of our School of Education at Edinburgh) – Know thyself – is then the starting point for your research journeys.

1

Building a Research Design: Thinking about Knowledge and What It Means to Education Research

John Ravenscroft and Pete Allison

Key points

- Positioning/stance: Capturing complexity within education research design.
- Locating yourself within theoretical positions: Struggling for clarity at the start of the research process.
- Identifying key theoretical positions: Where do I belong?
- Building theoretical and conceptual frameworks.

Introduction

To understand the fundamental aims and ideas of education and educational research, we believe that one needs to have an understanding of what knowledge is. Through having this understanding, we are well placed to recognize knowledge and, subsequently, enhance the research process. It is from this position that this chapter and indeed this book will introduce philosophical, ontological and epistemological perspectives that inform the aims and practices of social and, in particular, educational research. A significant part of the chapter is concerned with recognizing the value of different research approaches in relation to the substantive literature in various fields of practice. Through this process, it is possible to recognize strengths, weaknesses and gaps in the literature of these fields. As such this chapter will introduce readers to:

- theories of the nature of knowledge and their relationship to educational research.
- relationships between research, theory and practice in educational research.
- the relationship between methods and methodologies.
- epistemic preference as a driver for research questions.

Considering where to start

To achieve this, a discussion of the main debates of educational epistemology such as what counts as knowledge will be necessary. Our starting point is a conversation that we often have with doctoral students starting their research that goes along these lines …

Student: I want to do a survey.
Professor: Very good, tell me what you are going to ask people.
Student: I am not sure yet; I have not got that far.
Professor: That is fine; tell me about who you are going to survey.
Student: Well I am not sure about that yet either … I was thinking of an internet survey as that will improve the validity and I will be able to get a lot of responses from people.
Professor: OK. So can you tell me about the research questions or the research aim? What is it that you are interested in?
Student: Yes, well I am interested in teaching for citizenship and how that happens in schools throughout the country.
Professor: OK. Why don't you have a seat … I think we will need a bit of time to work out your research plan so better to be comfortable.

This is a fictional story but it is based on many years of experiencing similar discussions with students embarking on their thesis or dissertation research. There are many factors at play in this dialogue but one of the main points we want to make is that the starting point is confusing; starting with the method rather than the question is a common error and secondly what we often see at doctoral level is that in creating a research proposal students often assume that they only need to consider the pragmatic applied aspect of their research and not the underlying concepts and beliefs. We find that some students come to us having created what looks like a detailed proposal and so very quickly want to move into data collection and yet without dealing with the significant building blocks of understanding what is knowledge and their ontological positioning which will ensure that their research has a solid foundation. We soon see (if we let it continue) the 'hurry to data collection student' research run into difficulty due to something akin to building a house on rock versus rushing to build it on sand.

We are interested in how we can teach research understanding to address this and encourage people to try and step back from the methodology and methods discussion until they have thought about the questions they are asking, why they are asking them and then we can work from there. This, therefore, raises further questions. For example, it immediately raises questions about (1) the motivations to do research and (2) about the intended audience for the research when completed. Let's examine these two questions to start with.

Researchers are attracted to questions that interest them. This starts in early choices about what to study and then develops as interests are nurtured and experiences contribute to refining interests and undertaking research. Our own journeys both involved early experiences that focused our research in later life. One of us had several wilderness experiences in early life that then emerged into a lifelong interest in experiential learning and became a potential source of contributions to values education. The other author came from a more traditional psychological route but has been heavily influenced by philosophical conceptions of the nature of representation and animal thought. These examples illustrate what we know across many fields of research – that people undertake research into things that interest them. This has both advantages and disadvantages. Of course, it means that people want to know about a given subject and so spend time and energy researching this subject to learn more about it. Unfortunately, it also means that people often influence their research findings as it is human nature to focus on information that confirms our beliefs (confirmation bias). This means that researchers may find information that confirms their expectations/theories however implicit or explicit they may be. For this reason, we often ask students to argue the opposite to their natural inclination. For example, we might ask a student who is convinced that small class size is an indication of greater student attainment to argue the opposite and look at literature which is counter-intuitive. Our experience is that this activity helps students to examine topics from different angles and become more aware of their own assumptions. Similar to this example, we are delighted when research brings up unexpected results and is reported as such – as this demonstrates a commitment and openness to evidence or what we might describe as a 'spirit of enquiry'. It is inevitable that researchers have some inherent bias around areas we are interested in and therefore reflexivity is an important personal characteristic for educational researchers to nurture. Research is, of course, also shaped by its purpose, sociopolitical context and the proposed audience.

Activity 1.1

Outline a different counter-theory or argument to one that you make in your research proposal using a different perspective.

Who is research for?

In addition to asking what motivates someone or some people to undertake some research, we also find it useful to think about whom the intended research is for – who is the audience for research. Sometimes there are multiple audiences but in a broad sense we believe there to be three large categories to consider: policy, practice and theory. While some research is of interest to more than one of these three, it is normally focused mainly on one of these audiences. It is normally worth spending some time thinking about what kinds of evidence the audience listen to and/or are likely to be convinced by. For example, policy makers (politicians) normally need evidence that will stand up to critique from their opposition – which typically means large sample sizes and very clear recommendations, findings presented in a visually easy-to-consume format. Education practitioners often do not need answers based on large sample sizes but often require a clear answer to different 'so what should I do differently then?' type questions. We find Stake (1995) to be helpful in this respect – he identified three different types of generalizations in case study research: petite, naturalistic and grand. Briefly, petite are made to very similar situations; naturalistic are based on a rich understanding by the reader of the context and which enable application;

and grand are 'law like', similar to those often found in natural sciences and are rare in educational research/social sciences.

One must be aware that doctoral students have a very distinct academic audience who will be examining and assessing the quality of several components, that is, theory, engagement with literature, methodological rigour, critical analysis and, most importantly, a clear contribution to knowledge. This 'audience', the examiner, will be particularly demanding regarding the coherence and quality of the theoretical framing of the study and the rigour of method, and for this reason we encourage researchers to begin with exploring what Hager and Halliday (2009) refer to as their 'epistemic preferences'. This is preferable to starting with research methods and planning logistics.

Activity 1.2

Describe the 'foundation' your research proposal is based on. Detail your epistemic preferences, your understanding of what knowledge you are expecting to find and what theoretical justification you have for this foundation.

Assumptions we make

The problem we may have in education research, as highlighted by Pring (2000), is that very often those that commission and use research, such as governments, can view education research as 'different' or even 'inferior' from other realms of research. How can the contributions of wilderness and adventure trekking or thinking about animal thoughts be aligned with and put on the same research compendium as medical randomized control research, the type of research we find in the Cochrane Review library?[1]

---

[1]The Cochrane Review library is a collection of six databases that contain different types of independent evidence to inform healthcare decision-making. Articles in the databases are often systematic reviews which attempt to identify, appraise and synthesize all the empirical evidence that meets pre-specified eligibility criteria to answer a given research question. The major premise is that systematic reviews use explicit methods aimed at minimizing bias (Cochrane Library, 2017).

There is a history to this perception of education research and it could possibly be even linked to the first issue of the *Education Review* in 1891 where the very first article by Royce asked 'Is There a Science of Education?' (Royce, 1891). This predominance of viewing scientific research as the gold standard and other research such as political, aesthetic, feminist and action research, to name some differing approaches, as secondary shows no sign of slowing down and is a topic that is found in most education research books and even here it is mentioned but thankfully not dwelled upon. The reason why we do not focus on this debate in this book is twofold: one is that it has been comprehensively discussed in other education research method books such as Arthur et al. (2012) and Cohen et al. (2011); the other reason is that part of the misunderstanding we see about education research is the misunderstanding about knowledge and the assumptions we make about the world and the nature of knowledge – it is this latter reason that we focus upon. It does seem pertinent to note that this history of viewing scientific research as the gold standard illustrates a narrow conception of science which we believe to be unhelpful in progressing educational research and in encompassing relationships between research, theory and practice to a more nuanced and sophisticated understanding.

These misunderstandings, as you may have guessed, are ontological and epistemological ones that we quite often see (education) researchers shy away from. However, addressing the ontological and epistemological assumptions we make of the world must be the top of our research priorities, whether we are about to set off on a trek through the Antarctic or to examine the reading ability of five-year-old children. To be clear what we are advocating is that the doctoral researcher should not start by generating a series of research questions, for this is often the first fundamental error a naive or inexperienced researcher makes. The researcher when meeting their supervisor for the first time should come prepared with answers to the two sets of the following questions:

i   What assumptions about the world do I make?
ii What assumptions do I make about the nature of knowledge?

As researchers, we make assumptions about the world we share, we all have conceptual views on being and how this relates to form in the social world; its existence, whether it is subjectively or objectively understood, or it is internally or externally verified. Our ontological position effects how we perceive our social reality (Basit, 2010). Or as Carr (2006) explains, 'understanding is never simply "given" in any perception or observation but is always "prejudiced" by an interpretive element that determines how perceptions and observations are understood' (Carr, 2006: 429). If our ontological position effects how we perceive reality, then clearly it is argued here that it must also affect how we do research. It must not be the other way around. As we will see in the book, our research methods should not drive our ontological positions, outcomes from research can, and they can help us move and change our ontology, but choosing methods simply because they are fashionable or current, without understanding their relationship to epistemology and ontology, is an unwarranted intrusion into educational research.

So what does all this mean? Here is an example which might be helpful in illustrating the point: an education researcher, let us give her the name 'Ingrid', could have an assumption that social reality is independent of herself and phenomena in that social reality are real. Ingrid will also assume that there is an objective truth which is independent from her in that Ingrid's own values and beliefs do not effect this discoverable truth. She is a realist, in the sense everyday objects and their properties cannot be said to be dependent on anyone's linguistic practices, conceptual schemes or whatever (Miller, 2016).

All Ingrid has to do then as a researcher is to find the objective truth(s) and the (independent of Ingrid) relationships or properties that connect them. Ingrid will also have an assumption that these truths are discoverable through research hypothesis and experimentation and that there are universal laws which are causal, and these laws lie at the foundation of these truths which are also discoverable through a series of experimental educational trials (Shrag, 1992). Ingrid and perhaps other educational researchers would call themselves a positivist researcher, although Ingrid does not call herself this due to the stigma this term has within some educational establishments. What matters is that Ingrid has a definite realist view of the world and this view shapes the type and form of research questions that she will generate in order to construct her research frame prior to conducting her research through a series of experiments.

Duncan, on the other hand, does not share Ingrid's ontological assumptions of the world. Duncan believes that knowledge is subjective and is not independent of himself. He views his own beliefs and values as being core to his research. He sees himself as anti-realist about truth in that a theory should never be regarded as a truth but more as a temporary guiding idea or concept.

Duncan recognizes his biases and rather than try to eliminate these, as Ingrid would do, he acknowledges them and will even make them part of his research design by explicitly stating his biases (e.g. that he is a white, middle-class male with certain prejudices) in the research proposal. Duncan is an emancipator, such that he believes that his research can transform the lives of people he researches through constant interaction between himself and the participants of his research whether exploring the wilderness of Yellowstone National Park or the mathematical abilities of children of working-class mothers. Duncan, rather than focus on causality, will focus on such individually perceived concepts of power and inequality and will often but not always try to generate holistic answers to the research questions he asks, by identifying and recognizing a range of inclusive factors that are inextricably linked to the answers he is seeking. Duncan calls himself an interpretivist but he can also be called a constructivist or even a post-modernist but again for this explanatory example these distinctions are not important. The point is the way both Ingrid and Duncan ontologically perceive the social word in different ways of being.

Each of their own ontological and epistemological approaches will intertwine, creating for each of them a holistic view of how knowledge is understood and how they see themselves in relation to this knowledge, and the methodologies that are used to underpin their research and their research objectives forming the background that their own research questions will be based on. Of course, Ingrid and Duncan are extremes but one can easily see as Phillips (2005) does that these differing positions are contested, and that often sides are taken (Gage, 1989; Guba and Lincoln, 2005). However, we believe that the question of which ontological position is correct is the wrong question to ask. Rather than ask this, the question should be around the researcher's relationship to knowledge and how epistemic knowledge is acquired. Therefore, we move onto the second issue of what is knowledge.

Activity 1.3

Do you think there are such things as ultimate objective truths?
If there is no such thing as objective truth, do we have shared realities?

What is knowledge?[2]

As highlighted above, before any in-depth research investigation begins it is important that we understand, as a researcher, what knowledge may be considered to be and what is our relationship to knowledge. The definition of what is knowledge has been the concern of philosophers for centuries, and yet we have still not arrived at a definition that has been widely accepted. A classic philosophical view of knowledge and one that we have often found student education researchers hold, which is interesting as this is the same view as Plato,[3] is that knowledge is something that is justified, true and believed and all three components are needed for knowledge. This is known as the justified true belief (JTB) account of knowledge (Sosa, 1991) and goes something like this. Mary knows that polar bears can be white ('Polar bears can be white' is a proposition and can be written as 'p', Mary is an agent so Mary can be written as 'S') so we can write S knows that p. But Mary (S) only knows this if and only if S believes p and that S's belief that p is true and that S's belief that p is justified. Perhaps an illustration is needed to clarify. Breaking this down, we see knowledge demands belief. If you know that polar bears are not green with yellow spots, then you believe this. If you know something, then you have to believe it but believing something does not mean you know it. For example, I believe, as many Japanese people do, that there is a rabbit in the moon that makes *mochi* or rice cakes, but I do not know this. I do not actually know if there is a real rabbit in the moon making rice cakes, but I can certainly believe it. Another example may also be helpful. Peter believes that Glasgow is the capital of Scotland. All his friends tell him so; he lives and works in Glasgow and as such Peter has come to believe that Glasgow is the capital of Scotland. But, we would not accredit Peter with the knowledge that Glasgow is the capital of Scotland, as it is not true. We are happy to acknowledge that Peter believes that Glasgow is the capital and not Edinburgh, but we do not want to say he has the knowledge of 'what is the capital of Scotland'. So clearly what we believe about the world may not equate with how the world really is and so within the classical theory of knowledge there is a distinction between belief and truth

---

[2]When we talk about knowledge in this chapter, we are talking about propositional knowledge, that is, the know-that-something-is-so knowledge, in contrast with other kinds of knowledge such as the procedural knowledge or knowledge by acquaintance or direct awareness (see Moser, 2002; Zagzebski, 2004; Steup, 2005; Pritchard, 2009).

[3]Plato in his work *Theaetetus* gives an answer to what knowledge is: 'Knowledge is true opinion accompanied by reason' (Plato, *Theaetetus* 202c).

and in order to know something it must be true. This relationship between truth, belief and knowing the world lies at the heart of this book – for different research methodologies such as experimental and quasi-experimental designs this relationship is fixed and unshakable; however, for some constructivist approaches we will see that they completely oppose this relationship. However, as with all relationships, especially those with truth, one should not always see it as a polar distinction.

Back to Mary, Mary is justified in believing that polar bears are white because Mary is an Arctic explorer, has done experiments on polar bear fur and has found out that polar bear fur is in fact transparent and hence reflects the light from the snow and hence polar bears can be white. Mary also knows that polar bears can be black, as their skin is black or that polar bears can take a light yellow colour if the polar bear has eaten a lot of seals.

Conversely, we would not say that Peter would be justified in his belief to claim Glasgow is the capital of Scotland even when overnight the Scottish government has secretly moved the capital from Edinburgh to Glasgow. Peter's belief that Glasgow is the capital of Scotland has come true, but it has only come true because of luck. It is lucky that the Scottish government decided to move the capital in the first place and then secondly move it to Glasgow. As Peter does not know the Scottish government has moved the capital to Glasgow (as it was done secretly), he is not justified in his belief, as we are sure that Mary is justified in hers.

Knowledge based on the justified true belief definition appears to warrant justification over and above simply needing to be true; when we talk about knowing something, we expect to be able to support what we are saying and provide evidence. Someone who cannot provide this or provide justification for their claim, we would say they do not have knowledge and hence their claim would be untrue.

The JTB account of knowledge is attractive, and has been seen as a main account of knowledge from Plato's time (Fine, 2003) up to the latter part of the twentieth century and hence useful as a guiding theory for education research. But in 1963 this all stopped as Edmund Gettier (1963) showed in his short three-page paper where he argued that the JTB account of knowledge is not sufficient for a full account of knowledge.

Gettier's argument is based on examples that show that beliefs appear to be both true and can be justified but are examples of something we would not want to attribute 'knowing' to the person. There are many Gettier examples in the literature, but our two favourite examples which demonstrate how Gettier challenged the justified true belief argument stem from various farm yard instances.

Example 1.1: Sheep in the field (a variation of the original presented by Chisholm, 1966, 1977)

Farmer John is a farmer, and one day when he was doing his rounds looking after his animals he drives in his tractor past one of his fields. Farmer John sees something that looks like a sheep, and therefore Farmer John has a belief that there is a sheep in the field. This belief is true as there are sheep in the field but Farmer John is not looking at a sheep but rather a hologram (Snyder and Feit 2003) of a sheep, [here you can substitute a big hairy white dog, or large amounts of cotton wool etc.] as unknown to Farmer John all of the sheep are over the hill in a dip and out of sight.

Clearly, Farmer John has a justified belief that there is a sheep in the field, for it is also true there are sheep in the field, but they are over the hill and in a dip out of sight. The JTB account would say that Farmer John has knowledge that he has a sheep in the field as he satisfies all the conditions of knowledge, in that he has a justified true belief. However, Farmer John's belief that there is a sheep in the field was based on luck, that it was lucky for Farmer John that the sheep were actually in the field making his belief true. But knowledge cannot be based on satisfying a luck condition as well; therefore, his belief is unwarranted and knowledge seems to require more than only justified true belief.

Example 1.2: Barns in Fields (a variation of the original presented in Goldman, 1976)

Farmer John has not been doing very well and he is struggling to make both ends meet. However, in order to deceive tourists who come to see his farm, Farmer John decides to erect three barn façades for every genuine barn. So when tourists come to see his farm they will see lots of barns, some are real barns, but the majority are fake façades of barns. This way the tourists will think Farmer John is really a successful farmer. Tourist Tom decides to take a trip to see Farmer John's farm and Tourist Tom sees what looks like a fine barn. Tourist Tom therefore believes that he sees a fine barn. Actually Tourist Tom does see a genuine fine barn, it is a real barn and not one of the false façade barns.

Here the JTB account of knowledge says that Tourist Tom has a justified true belief that he is looking at a fine barn, and therefore has knowledge of this fine barn that is in the field right in front of him. But again what we see here is that Tourist Tom has been incredibly lucky that his belief (that this is a fine barn) is true. If he looked at one of the false façade barns, then he would also not have knowledge as in the Farmer John and his sheep example. Tourist Tom's true belief that there is a field of fine barns is not warranted, even though it is justified, and as such Tourist Tom does not have knowledge as again his justified true belief is only true because of luck.

The above examples are just an introduction to the problem of analysing knowledge; there have been many attempts to resolve Gettier case examples (see Lycan, 2006, for a historical review of attempted Gettier solutions). Interestingly enough Gettier offers no solution to defining what is knowledge, and like Gettier we too offer no solution but the debate still continues with education and epistemology (Hetherington, 2016; Kotzee, 2013, 2016; McCain, 2016).

Activity 1.4

What do you think the aim of education is? And how does this aim fit in the JTB account of knowledge?

So why is this brief epistemological journey into the nature of knowledge important to education and particularly to education researchers? We think the answer to this lies in what you as a researcher fundamentally believe is the aim of education. You could believe, for example, like Goldman (1999) that the *fundamental aim of education, like that of science, is the promotion of knowledge* (1999: 349) and for Goldman, knowledge is simply a variant of the justified true belief account of knowledge. But surely as educationalists and education researchers, we find ourselves in agreement with Pritchard (2013) in that we do not want education to solely provide children with a body of true beliefs that when needed can be called upon. However, some of you may disagree with Pritchard's further contention that education should in fact provide children with the cognitive skills to be able to determine truths for themselves (Prichard, 2013: 236). Some of you may hold a more postmodernist view in that there is no such thing as truth for education to transmit, such that education should not be about getting children to believe specific truths but that children should be able to think critically and reflectively for themselves. A starting position to this could be to adopt (Harding's, 1987) feminist methodology as this provides a different set of 'epistemic preferences', which suggests that the traditional starting point for knowledge comes from a dominantly held position which does show distorted accounts of reality.

We would be remiss if we were not to, at least briefly, make mention of Thomas Kuhn and his seminal work on the structure of scientific revolutions and of the trap of paradigm wars.

Kuhn and the structure of scientific revolutions

In his seminal text, Kuhn provides a commentary and analysis of the way in which science progresses and how revolutions occur. The work is all based on the natural sciences but the lessons are just as useful for the social sciences. Recognizing that shared understanding or paradigms explanation is essential for science to progress, he notes that as paradigms develop and general agreement emerges so do methodological traditions that dominate research practices within fields of research. This inevitability also means that as paradigms emerge they also tend to create self-fulfilling empirical evidence cycles where the empirical work provides evidence that reinforces the dominant paradigmatic thinking. Good science then builds on prior work and inherits the thinking embedded within that research and tends to reproduce confirmatory findings or findings that make small incremental developments in understanding. This research progresses at a glacial speed in what he refers to as 'normal science'. In Kuhn's (1967: 16–17) words 'no natural history can be interpreted in the absence of at least some implicit body of intertwined theoretical and methodological belief that permits selection, evaluation, and criticism'. He characterizes normal science as matching facts with theory and puzzle solving. In doing so, he shows how the development of paradigms leads to competing theories and conceptualizations fading into the background and one theory or paradigm dominating. One of the most obvious examples of this is the shift from the belief that the world is flat to the now widely accepted view that the world is spherical. What is interesting for this chapter is the subsequent stages that Kuhn identified when paradigms change – through discovery or crisis. Discovery happens when research identifies anomalies that are acknowledged and become interesting – this provides a novelty for researchers to study. As researchers study the anomalies, theories have to be adjusted to make sense of the anomaly … to account for it in the theory and once this is completed the anomaly becomes predictable and a part of the theory which sits within the paradigm. This is important for both reading and undertaking research as it highlights the importance of paying attention to anomalies and exceptions.

Crisis happens when a theory fails to explain a phenomenon. Repeated failure of theory to solve puzzles is normally something that is long-standing. This is important as it helps to create a climate for a general loosening or blurring of strong paradigm stereotypes and an openness of different understandings, interpretations and theories. Kuhn then identifies three possible paths: (1) the previous paradigm remains as it manages to accommodate the new information, (2) the problem resists and is labelled and left to one side or future generations to study or (3) a new paradigm emerges and the specifics of that paradigm are then 'fought out' until general agreement is reached. Researchers who understand how knowledge and understanding evolve over time can understand their work in a much wider context and see the relevance of their and others' work.

Of course, the work of Kuhn is more complex than these few paragraphs can do justice to and we recommend reading the original text. However, for the purposes of this chapter the above summary is sufficient to lead to the next issue which is what happens as new paradigms emerge – paradigm wars.

Paradigm wars

As new paradigms emerge, researchers debate and contest them until they reach general agreement and sometimes very specific agreement (Guba, 1990). However, in educational research this is further complicated as education is an area of study by people who come from different disciplines (e.g. philosophy, sociology, psychology) and subsets of these, in addition to subject specialists (e.g. geographers, mathematicians). This means that those studying education come from a wide range of backgrounds/training and thus respective research traditions or paradigms. One result of this is that researchers get caught up in paradigm wars that can be distracting. Our view on this is a resigned inevitability to these paradigm wars but we encourage educational researchers to transcend these paradigm wars and it is our intention that we encourage all researchers to transcend or otherwise disrupt these traditional paradigmatic boundaries and not to stay within them. There may be benefit in multiple paradigmatic perspectives on educational practice, theory and policy. This is illustrated by glancing through the last five issues of any quality educational research journal. Readers interested in this area are encouraged to read Pring (2000) and Guba (1990), while keeping in mind that, in our experience, research rarely unfolds the way it is planned. Even with the best of intentions and planning, educational research is influenced by multiple factors. And given that people are normally involved, there is unpredictability to research so we tend to characterize it as planned messiness, which involves ongoing choices throughout the research process.

Conclusions

We have in the chapter tried to get across the idea that understanding our ontological and epistemological position matters to education research. This is not a debate about qualitative or quantitative methods, but rather this is about enabling ourselves to get into the right conditions so that we understand the how and the why we are generating the research questions in such an epistemic way. Whatever position you take as an educational researcher, the relationship with knowledge, understanding what knowledge is and how you obtain knowledge is critical. We believe that meeting these criteria is helpful throughout the research process when questions arise and various, often unpredictable, decisions have to be made. We advocate that we should disassociate ourselves from the paradigm wars we see in the education literature. Find your ontological stance, know how to justify it and build appropriate research questions and methodologies around it. Finally, no one position in education research is 'better than' any other, although some may be more appropriate than others for certain questions.

Chapter key points

- Establish your position with regard to the nature of knowledge – what it is and how it can be obtained.
- Maintain coherence of your research by using your acknowledged theoretical position to inform your decisions about your research design and processes.
- Engage critically with other positions while avoiding giving primacy to one or the other.

Recommended reading

Bechhofer, F., & Paterson, L. (2000). *Principles of Research Design in the Social Sciences*. Oxford: Routledge.
This book summarizes considerations for research design that avoid the binary conceptions of qualitative versus quantitative methods but rather addresses methods, methodology and the kinds of claims that will or will not be possible as a result of various decisions through the research process.

Hirst, P., & Carr, W. (2005). Philosophy and Education. A Symposium. *Journal of Philosophy of Education*, 39(4): 615–632.
This is an interesting article that we get our students to look at when they start their courses; it debates the use of philosophy in education. It can be quite a difficult read but well worth persevering as it sets the frame for why this discussion is important in education research.

Pring, R. (2000). *Philosophy of Educational Research*. London: Continuum.
A balanced summary of the issues surrounding educational research by a very capable thinker and writer. Essential reading for anyone serious about understanding and learning how to think about research in education.

Pritchard, D. (2009). *Knowledge*. Basingstoke: Palgrave Macmillan.
An excellent introduction to the theory of knowledge, written by an extremely accessible author.

Pritchard, D., Haddock, A., & Millar, A. (2012). *The Nature and Value of Knowledge: Three Investigations*. Oxford: Oxford University Press.
This book explores more the value of knowledge and in particular the thesis that perhaps it is not knowledge we are after but understanding. The three authors all discuss the value of knowledge from their own perspective.

Silverman, D. (2000). *Doing Qualitative Research*. London: Sage.
A very accessible text for those interested in qualitative methods. The book is structured in such a way as to be used as a reference or to be read cover to cover. Lots of useful sections for masters and Ph.D. students alike.

Stake, R. E. (1995). *The Art of Case Study Research*. London: Sage.
A clear and concise read to introduce case study research and explain the aims and purposes.

Advanced reading

Anyon, J. (2008). *Theory and Educational Research: Toward Critical Social Explanation*. London: Routledge.

Boyle, D. (2000). *The Tyranny of Numbers: Why Counting Can't Make Us Happy*. London: HarperCollins.

Crotty, M. (1998). *The Foundations of Social Research: Meaning and Perspective in the Research Process*. London: Sage.

Pritchard, D. (2005). *Epistemic Luck*. Oxford: Oxford University Press.

Taleb, N. (2007). *The Black Swan: The Impact of the Highly Improbable*. New York: Random House.

Web links

National Centre for Research Methods
https://www.ncrm.ac.uk/
Podcasts, brief papers and lots more of interest for doctoral students in social sciences

Socialtheoryapplied.com
An interesting website by Dr Mark Murphy and colleagues exploring issues of epistemological, operational, analytical imperatives and practices through the lens of social theory.

Stanford Encyclopaedia of Philosophy
https://plato.stanford.edu/
A starting point for any venture into philosophical discussion. An extremely useful resource.

Part I

Building Quantitative Research Designs

2

Cross-Sectional and Longitudinal Surveys

Ellen Boeren

Key points

- Survey research is generally defined in relation to quantitative methods, drawing on positivist and realist epistemic preferences, with the aim to reveal the objective truth.
- Survey research has to be carefully planned as it starts from a fixed research design which needs a finalized questionnaire before the start of data collection.
- Surveys can be longitudinal and cross-sectional in nature and differ in the opportunities they offer.
- Collection of data can be carried out through face-to-face, telephone, postal or online surveys, each having its own advantages and disadvantages.
- Analysing survey data starts with univariate and bivariate inspection of the data.

Introduction

This chapter discusses the use of surveys in educational research and focuses on both cross-sectional and longitudinal survey designs. It starts with the discussion of background information and definitions of surveys, including its predominantly positivist and realist epistemologies, aiming to establish an objective and independent reality through the application of a mainly scientific approach. The chapter focuses on the different steps to undertake when designing your own survey project. Strengths and weaknesses of cross-sectional and longitudinal surveys are explored and attention is paid to the issue of sampling. A specific section provides examples of different types of survey questions and modes of surveys are discussed as well, distinguishing between face-to-face, telephone, postal and web-based surveys. Finally, a brief section provides ideas on how to analyse survey data.

Survey definitions

The use of surveys in social sciences research is not new and it is therefore difficult to provide a straightforward answer to the question, 'what is a survey?' (Ornstein, 2013; Andres, 2014). In certain regions of the world, such as Scandinavia and North America, census data have been collected since the beginning of the nineteenth century and Charles Booth's work – which focused on unemployment and poverty in London – has often been labelled as 'foundational empirical work' in the social sciences (O'Day and Englander, 1993). It is interesting to note that Booth's research approach was rather wide and included the analysis of existing data, as well as the gathering of new qualitative data, topographical work based on maps and observations of the poor. The way his work has been described as a 'survey' is interesting, as nowadays definitions of surveys are much narrower in focus, mainly emphasizing the collection of factual data that are meant to provide an objective perspective on a certain problem, in such a way it is quantifiable and generalizable, thus more likely to be positioned in a positivist epistemological tradition, drawing on an ontology of objective reality (see e.g. Fink, 2003; Bryman, 2004; Cohen et al., 2007).

Other ways of defining surveys include elements of discovering patterns of association based on quantitative data (Bryman, 2004), the description of a population (Sapford, 2007) or the quantitative description of a sample group representing the research population (Fowler Jr., 2013). It is thus clear that survey research nowadays has been very much discussed in relation to quantitative research, although it can be argued that a survey with many open questions can equally generate more in-depth qualitative data (Boeren, 2015). Within this chapter, however, the main focus will be on surveys carried out using structured questionnaires generating quantitative data, but with a focus on the differences between cross-sectional and longitudinal surveys. Before explaining the differences between these two types of surveys (cross-sectional and longitudinal), more information will be provided on the different steps to undertake when planning your own survey project.

Planning survey research

As discussed in the previous chapter on 'knowledge', the design of a new research project logically flows from the researcher's 'epistemic preferences' and their 'relationship to knowledge'. These aspects come also in play in the first stages of planning your survey project. Authors who have been referred to above have also focused on the different steps to undertake in planning a survey project, which is important as survey research follows a fixed research design and the entire research procedures need to be set out before data collection starts (Robson, 2011). Among the literature on survey planning (see e.g. Robson, 2011; Ornstein, 2013; Andres, 2014), work by Cohen et al. (2007) has been selected here to engage in a discussion on the different steps to undertake. Cohen et al. (2007: 257) discuss that researchers/research students need to consider three aspects before they start designing survey research. First of all, they need to carefully work out the purposes of their research and make sure they formulate a central aim that is as specific as possible. This first consideration is also important to generate some more information on what exact information should be collected during the data gathering phase. It is within this first stage there will be a logic combination of ontological, epistemological and methodological aspects. It is also at this point in the survey design cycle that researchers/research students can start considering which survey modes they will be using (e.g. face-to-face surveys versus a web-based survey). Secondly, researchers/research students need to decide on their research population. A sampling framework will therefore need to be set up. Thirdly, Cohen et al. (2007: 58) argue that it is very important to make a sound judgement on the financial cost of carrying out survey research. Researchers/research students will have to work on designing the questionnaire, sampling, piloting the survey, coding and analysing data. All these aspects tend to be time-intensive. When conducting face-to-face surveys, it is important to pilot the questionnaire and become familiar with the entire process. Additionally, while designing the survey project, researchers/research students will have to take ethical consideration into account and ask for ethical approval of their research institutions.

While Cohen et al. (2007) mention these three overarching considerations, they also define fourteen more detailed stages to follow when planning a survey (Table 2.1). As stated above, but not mentioned in Table 2.1, it is important to plan the ethical approval process before you start piloting and collecting your data.

Fink (2003: 2) focuses on similar steps to take into account when designing survey research and identified six features: (1) survey research needs to start from 'specific, measureable objectives', (2) the research design needs to be sound – for example, selecting between a cross-sectional or longitudinal design given the objectives of the research study, (3) the research team needs to define the population and construct a sound sampling framework, (4) they need to develop 'reliable and valid instruments', (5) analyse the data in an appropriate way, and finally (6) report on the findings in an accurate way. While description of these stages are thus written down in different forms by different authors – too many to discuss them all in detail – it is clear that they all focus on the importance of certain general stages, such as choosing the design, engaging in sampling, constructing the data collection instrument, and collecting and analysing data.

Table 2.1 Fourteen stages of survey planning

1. Define the objective.
2. Decide the kind of survey required (e.g. longitudinal, cross-section, trend study, cohort study).
3. Formulate research questions or hypotheses (if appropriate): the null hypothesis and alternative hypotheses.
4. Decide the issues on which to focus.
5. Decide the information that is needed to address the issues.
6. Decide the sampling required.
7. Decide the instrumentation and the metrics required.
8. Generate the data collection instruments.
9. Decide how the data will be collected (e.g. postal survey, interviews).
10. Pilot the survey instruments and refine them.
11. Train the interviewers (if appropriate).
12. Collect the data.
13. Analyse the data.
14. Report the results.

Source: Cohen et al. (2007: 259)

In order to provide a more detailed discussion on these steps, the following sections discuss these aspects more in detail, starting with providing insight into the differences between cross-sectional and longitudinal surveys.

> ## Activity 2.1
>
> Create a timeline outlining your survey project, reflecting on and using the fourteen steps of survey research design as discussed in Table 2.1.

Cross-sectional versus longitudinal surveys

In discussing the different designs of surveys, a distinction is often made between cross-sectional and longitudinal surveys, although Johnson and Christensen (2014: 402) wrote about 'retrospective' designs as a way of comparing between the different time dimensions of research. Cross-sectional surveys are therefore described as providing a snapshot of the current situation, retrospective surveys look back into the past and longitudinal surveys run over an extended period of time. As explained above, the choice for a longitudinal or cross-sectional survey flows from your research aims and objectives. As a doctoral or postdoctoral researcher, you might not always have the time to set up an entire survey yourself, but even if you choose to use existing secondary data, it is essential that you familiarize yourself with the aims of the study, the sampling frame and the data gathering methods used. In this section, I start by focusing on longitudinal surveys and give some examples of existing longitudinal studies relevant for educational research.

It can be argued that many surveys that are being repeated on a regular basis are longitudinal in nature, proving insights into a range of trends, either at individual or societal level (Cohen et al., 2007; Robson, 2011; Boeren, 2015). However, longitudinal surveys are often defined as cohort or panel studies in which a single sample gets followed through during different survey waves. In a cohort study, people from a specific group are being followed up over time, for example, those born in a specific year. Examples include the National Child Development Study which follows people born in March 1958 – they were further surveyed at ages 7, 11, 16, 23, 33, 42, 46, 50 and 55 (see www.cls.ioe.ac.uk/ncds) – the 1970 British Cohort Study following people born in 1970 collecting information about their education, health, economic and social circumstances (see www .cls.ioe.ac.uk/BCS70), and the Millennium Cohort Study which includes people who were born in 2000 and 2001, thus a newer study compared to those that started in 1958 and 1970. The Millennium Cohort Study has also collected more detailed information about early childhood and followed them during the compulsory school system compared to the older cohort surveys (see www.cls.ioe.ac.uk/page.aspx?sitesectionid=851). The 1958 and 1970 cohort studies follow around 17,000 people, while the Millennium Cohort Study follows 19,000 young people. Panel studies install specific units that are being surveyed regularly, for example, households, but they do not belong to a specific cohort or group. A well-known example is the British Household Panel Survey set up in 1991, following around 5,000 households in Britain, although in 2001 Northern Ireland joined the study as well. Nowadays, the Panel Survey is part of the larger Understanding Society project (see https://www.understandingsociety.ac.uk). A range of questions in the survey map the education and employment history of respondents as well as their individual and neighbourhood demographics. Data can be used for research purposes and are thus relevant for use in educational research. As with cohort studies, the same respondents are being tracked over time. Going back to the earlier discussions about the nature of knowledge, it can be said that longitudinal surveys are interested in capturing the objective truth, but with a specific focus on how this truth changes over time.

These cohort and panel studies are thus distinct from cross-sectional surveys. As with the latter ones, cross-sectional surveys can also take place more than once over a given time period, but they do not follow the same sample and for each wave, another sample is being selected (Cohen et al., 2007; Field, 2013; Boeren, 2015). Famous examples of cross-sectional survey projects, which can be considered for use in doctoral or postdoctoral research in the field of education include PISA – the OECD's (Organisation for Economic Co-operation and Development) Programme for International Student Assessment (see http://www.oecd.org/pisa/), the Trends in International Mathematics and Science Study (TIMSS) and the Progress in International Reading Literacy Study (PIRLS) (see http://timssandpirls.

bc.edu/). PISA is undertaken with fifteen-year-olds every three years and the survey includes a background questionnaire as well as tests to map skill levels of these young people, traditionally focusing on mathematics, science and reading. In 2015, seventy-two economies (mostly countries, but sometimes separate regions in countries) took part in PISA, representing around 28 million fifteen-year-old pupils. More than half a million of them completed the PISA questionnaire and test. As PISA focuses on fifteen-year-old pupils, every three years, a new selection of respondents is being used. TIMSS and PIRLS use a similar cross-sectional design and focus on assessing pupils, but instead of selecting them by age, they select them based on the school grade they are currently at, not taking into account their age (e.g. someone who had to repeat a grade can participate in TIMSS and PIRLS if they are in the sample grade, but a sixteen-year-old who is in groups with fifteen-year-olds cannot participate in PISA).

Both longitudinal and cross-sectional survey designs have their advantages and disadvantages which need to be carefully considered before making a decision on which choice to make. Longitudinal surveys are useful to make stronger causal inferences (is B the result of A?), while cross-sectional data are limited to discovering correlational patterns (is there a relationship between A and B?) (Field, 2013). Making causal interpretations is helpful to come up with strong recommendations, for example, for interventions to be undertaken by policy makers or practitioners. Although working with longitudinal data thus generates a range of advantages, it has to be acknowledged that it is likely to be time consuming and expensive. Furthermore, longitudinal studies have to deal with the problem of attrition as respondents decide to drop out from the study which reduces the sample size wave after wave. Additionally, working with longitudinal data requires advanced quantitative skills which you might not have mastered during previous undergraduate and/or postgraduate studies. Undertaking a cross-sectional survey is therefore likely to be a less complex task and is relatively cheap to undertake.

Research population and sampling

Survey research nowadays pays much attention to the desirability to generate objective and generalizable results, as being discussed in most research textbooks focusing on survey research, linking back to the ontological position of the availability of an objective truth and an epistemic preference for positivist and realist approaches, drawing on scientific methods. In order to achieve this, it is recommended to work with a probability sample (see e.g. Robson, 2011; Valliant et al., 2013). Probability sampling strives towards representativeness and gives everyone in the research population an equal chance to be included in the study through random assignment of participants. This approach is often used in big national surveys or surveys carried out by big international organizations. However, many surveys are rather small-scale and it might therefore limit the opportunities for random sampling. Non-probability sampling, for example, purposive sampling (targeting those most useful for the study) or convenience sampling (asking those who are available and immediately approachable), can then be made instead. The researchers/research students need to acknowledge that this is affecting their opportunities for generalizations and have to be realistic about how far the sample can be used to draw conclusions that go beyond the people in their sample. Authors in the field tend to recommend trying to set up probability sampling frames, but whether this is feasible depends on the research population you are working with. It is therefore important during the design cycle of your survey project that you come up with a detailed description of your research population and the ways through which you can reach them. If you succeed in doing that, you can draw a random sample from within.

Apart from deciding on the sample size and the representativeness of the sample, researchers also need to consider how they have access to these people (see Robson, 2011; Boeren, 2015). This is especially important when working with hard-to-reach groups such as those who do not speak the dominant language or those in care who need to be approached through services. Furthermore, not everyone who was initially selected as part of the sample will wish to take part in the study and it is therefore needed that researchers make themselves familiar with the issue of non-response. Unit non-response happens when people received a questionnaire but did not complete, while item non-response relates to respondents skipping certain questions (Field, 2013). In reaching people, it is thus important to pay attention to the tone and style of the initial approach, for example, through a very accessible introduction letter which clearly outlines the aims and objectives of the study as well as the time it will take for respondents to participate in the study. Furthermore, once respondents start filling in the questionnaire, the format/accessibility/length of survey of questions can also influence their preparedness to take part.

Constructing a survey questionnaire

While examples of existing surveys have been mentioned above, it is also possible to design your own survey questionnaire and collect data yourself. Cohen et al. (2007), based on work by Sellitz et al. (1976), mention four important decisions to undertake when constructing a survey questionnaire. First of all, researchers need to decide on the specific content of the questions and need to provide an overview of what exact information they will need. This is important, as information collected through the questionnaire will be used to answer the research questions and to fulfil the research aims. Secondly, researchers need to decide on how to formulate and word their questions and thus translate their decisions about content into questions that can be easily understood by respondents. Thirdly, the research team needs to be aware of the different formats of questions being used in survey research and select those forms of questions that are most suitable for collecting the information they need, of which examples have been provided below. Finally, decisions about the sequence of questions are important as well. Questions measuring personal information such as age, gender and income categories or questions formulated in a more complicated way at the beginning of the survey might frighten respondents and increase the dropout rate.

In focusing on the format of questions, examples are introduced here to help you determine what might be most useful for you in building your survey. Distinctions are made between two-way questions, Likert scales, semantic differential scales, checklists and rankings. An overview can be found in Table 2.2.

The example of the 'two-way' question makes clear that there are only two answers possible to this question and that the two answering categories are mutually exclusive. Likert scales, developed by Likert (1929), are used to measure respondents' attitudes towards a given topic. The format of the Likert scale is often a five-point scale with the categories 'totally disagree', 'disagree', 'neither agree nor disagree', 'agree' and 'totally agree'. Semantic differential scales are often compared to Likert scales, although they are not the same. The semantical scale uses specific words with opposed meanings at the end of the scale, and does not work with item statements which can then be ticked according to agreeing or disagreeing with them. Checklists contain a range of items with the question to respondents to tick all of them that are relevant to them. Rankings differ from checklists as an additional layer of importance is being introduced through asking the respondent which items are more important than others and rank them according to their preferences or opinions.

Table 2.2 Examples of survey question formats

Two-way questions	Have you ever spoken English with a native speaker outside of school? YES/NO
Likert scale	My native English teachers have been/are proficient English teachers. Strongly Disagree/Disagree/Not Sure/No Opinion Agree/Strongly Agree
Semantic differential scale	Please rate the variety of English on the scale 1 5 Unattractive Attractive
Checklists	What skills do you value in your English teachers? Please tick as appropriate: ☐ Knowledge of English grammar ☐ Good pronunciation ☐ Kind ☐ Native-like accent ☐ Ability to create interest ☐ Sense of humour ☐ Pleasant appearance ☐ Approachable ☐ Enthusiastic and motivating ☐ Experience abroad ☐ Other
Ranking	What skills do you value in your English teachers? Please put a number next to the five most important (1=most important) ☐ Knowledge of English grammar ☐ Good pronunciation ☐ Kind ☐ Native-like accent ☐ Ability to create interest ☐ Sense of humour ☐ Pleasant appearance ☐ Enthusiastic and motivating ☐ Experience abroad ☐ Other

Source: McGeown (2013)

Apart from the 'closed' questions explained above, it is also possible to work with 'open-ended' questions in surveys (see Boeren, 2015). Close-ended questions let respondents choose between a number of predetermined answers, but open-ended questions give them the opportunity to formulate their own answers. Saris and Gallhoger (2007: 103) discussed that open-ended questions might be useful when it is important to map answers that are difficult to describe in strict reference frameworks, for example, personal opinions. Half-open questions can also be introduced in surveys as means to give respondents the option to explain why they ticked the category 'other', instead of going with the predefined categories. While open-ended questions thus provide opportunities to collect additional data from a more qualitative nature, surveys are generally interested in gathering quantifiable data and dealing with textual data might therefore be time consuming. Often, the researcher will have to explore these data and recode them into existing or new additional categories. The combination of quantitative and qualitative aspects of educational research will be discussed in more detailed in the chapter on mixed-methods research.

Activity 2.2

Focus on your own interest and formulate a range of survey questions using different formats as shown in Table 2.2.

Modes of data collection: Face-to-face, telephone, postal or web-based

Deciding on the mode of data collection is an important stage in the planning of a survey project. The literature distinguishes between more traditional modes such as face-to-face, telephone and postal surveys as well as more recent modes such as web-based surveys. Detailed information on the different modes of data collection can be found in Fink (2003). Cohen et al. (2007) also provide a rather detailed overview on modes of data collection, as does Robson (2011). These sources are recommended reading for everyone planning to collect data using survey research.

Face-to-face surveys are carried out by interviewers or the researcher/research student him-/herself who sit together with the respondent. It is generally accepted that face-to-face survey interviews generate a high response rate. Especially with groups who experience difficulties in reading and writing, completing a survey guided by an interviewer/researcher/ research student will not exclude them from participating in the study. Answering cards can be shown to respondents so that they do not have to remember all answering categories and additional explanations can be provided in case the respondent has difficulties understanding the question. Nowadays, the process of interviewing face-to-face is also made easier for by using CAPI software (Computer Assisted Personal Interviewing). However, there are also a range of potential pitfalls when carrying out face-to-face surveys. Respondents might feel more reluctant to provide sensitive information. Discussing answering options with a stranger can only take place when the interviewee trusts the interviewer. High-quality training is needed to decrease interviewer effects such as suggesting specific answers or generating high levels of item non-response and it is important to make interviewers/researchers/research students aware of the need to collect standardized and reliable information.

Telephone surveys are generally cheaper than face-to-face surveys as there are no travel costs involved. Affordable telephone rates are available to survey a wide geographical area. While telephone surveys might at first sight seem similar to face-to-face surveys, a number of disadvantages have to be discussed. The lack of opportunities to use answering cards is a huge limitation and basically requires respondents to memorize answering categories. It is also difficult to keep concentrating during a telephone survey and the recommendation is therefore not to choose for a telephone survey if it would take more than fifteen minutes to fill in the questionnaire. Furthermore, questions need to be formulated in a short and very precise way in order to avoid confusion among respondents. Careful training before conducting a telephone survey is thus recommended, including their use of CATI software (Computer Assisted Telephone Interviewing). Choosing telephone interviews is nowadays made more difficult as many, especially younger people, do not have landlines anymore and do not have their mobile phone numbers recorded in phone directories, which might limit the opportunities for random sampling.

Postal surveys are known to suffer from lower response rates and need a very clear introduction letter as well as a pre-stamped envelope with the address details of the research team. As no interviewers are involved, it is very important that the wording of the questions follows a standardized format for which there is limited risk of participants misinterpreting the question. Instructions for skipping questions need to be very clear. The quality of the questionnaire needs to be prioritized in order to reduce item non-response. One of the advantages of postal surveys is the fact that the respondent does not have to work with an interviewer, which will help some people to overcome the barrier of providing information on sensitive topics.

Web-based surveys have become increasingly popular in the last decade and are replacing postal surveys. Similar to using postal modes, no interviewers are involved and the respondent is asked to self-complete the questionnaire, for example, through the Bristol Online Survey tool. Web-based surveys have the advantage that they can deal with skipping non-applicable questions through programming and are stricter in capturing answers to specific categories as there is no space to write down additional comments when open-ended boxes are not available. However, such surveys can contain open-ended/qualitative questions. Item non-response therefore tends to be lower in web-based survey, but the general response rates remain low. Furthermore, people might be sceptical about the information being sent with their completed survey, such as their IP or email address. When opting for web-based surveys, it will be important to explore software packages available to construct questionnaires and to use formats with appealing layouts and clear instructions. As with postal survey questionnaires, questions need to be formulated in a clear way, reducing the risk for misunderstanding and misinterpretation.

Activity 2.3

Make an informed choice based on your research aims and sample, balancing advantages and disadvantages on whether to use a face-to-face, telephone, postal or online survey.

Analysis of data

Analysis of survey data can be undertaken at different levels and space is limited here to provide a detailed overview. Therefore, this section will focus on basic descriptive statistics. For more detailed but accessible information, reading of Andy Field's work is recommended (see e.g. Field, 2013). Data can be analysed using statistical software packages such as SPSS, although descriptive analyses can also be performed in Excel and within survey programmes, such as Bristol Online Survey.

In this section, a distinction is being made between univariate and bivariate analyses. Univariate analyses focus on frequency distributions and means, while bivariate analyses can be used to undertake cross-tabulations between two variables or to compare means. Simple regression analyses with one independent variable are also an example of bivariate analyses. Multivariate analyses include multiple regression analyses and a range of other more advanced techniques. Before deciding on which analyses to undertake, it is important to understand the different measurement levels of variables (Field, 2013). Nominal variables are categorical and the 'values' within the variable are equal. Examples include the colour of hair of eyes. Some people have blue eyes, while others have brown eyes. One is not better or more valuable than the other. Ordinal variables are categorical as well, but present a certain rank. Letting people choose between good, better and best is an example of an ordinal variable. Likert item scales are also ordinal in nature, although researchers tend to analyse them as scale variables as well. Scale variables represent a continuous level of values, for example, age, examination marks or weight.

When conducting univariate analyses, data gathered within the survey will be examined one by one. Variables that are categorical in nature – nominal or ordinal – will be presented using frequency tables, but can also be presented through graphs, for example, bar charts or pie charts. In the (hypothetical) example, a survey has been conducted with 1,000 pupils. During the analysis of data, it becomes clear that 480 of them were boys (48 per cent of the total group) and 520 were girls.

Table 2.3 Example of a frequency table

	Boys	**Girls**
Percentage of boys versus girls who participated in the survey	480 (48%)	520 (52%)

Table 2.4 Example of a mean and standard deviation

	Mean	**Standard Deviation**
Pupils' mathematics score	500	100

Scale variables will mostly be described through inspection of their mean and standard deviation. The mean represents the average score, while the standard deviation focuses on the spread around the mean. The example demonstrates that among the pupils who have undertaken a mathematics test, the average score was 500, but with a spread around the mean of a score of 100. This means that – in case of a normal distribution – 68 per cent of pupils will have a score between 400 and 600. For those who want to read more details on the normal distribution, it is recommended to consult Field (2013). It is useful to know that PISA tests scores are being standardized using the 500 as the mean and 100 as the standard deviation.

Bivariate analyses are undertaken when researchers are interested in exploring the possible relationship between two variables, often as a means to confirm or reject a hypothesis and as a result to establish an objective truth, obtained through a scientific method. Techniques used for bivariate analyses depend on the measurement levels of the variables. If both variables are categorical, it is recommended to start exploring the data through cross-tabulation. Statistical software will be able to produce both row and column percentages and the chi-square test is often undertaken to indicate whether there are significant differences between the groups taken into account in the analysis. In the example, a cross-tabulation is made between gender and whether the pupil is a member of an after school club. Within the groups of boys, 42 per cent are members versus 37 per cent of girls. The chi-square test will use the underlying data to calculate whether this difference is significant.

When the variable of interest is at scale level, but the groups the researchers want to control for are categorical, a t-test or F-test can be used. Comparing mean tests score for boys and girls can be done using a t-test, but when more than two groups are involved in the comparison, an analysis of variance with the computation of an F-test can give more insight into whether significant differences between these groups exist. The example demonstrates the differences in means between mathematics test scores for boys versus girls and demonstrates boys scored, on average, higher than girls. The t-test is then used based on underlying data to calculate whether these scores are significantly different from each other.

A correlation analysis explores whether there is a strong relationship between two scale variables. Scores are always between −1 and +1, with 0 indicating there is no relationship at all, −1 indicating there is a 100 per cent negative overlap and +1 meaning there is a 100 per cent positive overlap. In this example, the correlation between pupils' mathematics test score and reading test score is 0.831, which is a positive correlation (above 0) and

Table 2.5 Example of a cross-tabulation

Total

	Boys	Girls
Member of after school club	200 (42%)	190 (37%)
Not a member of after school club	280 (58%)	330 (63%)

Table 2.6 Example of comparing means

	Boys	Girls
Pupils' mathematics score	515	487

Table 2.7 Example of a correlation

	Pupils' mathematics score
Pupils' reading score	0.831

indicates there is a strong relationship between the two. Pupils who scored high on reading were also likely to score high on mathematics and vice versa.

In relation to multivariate analysis, examples include multiple regression analysis. This technique allows researchers to explore whether there is a relationship between a dependent scale variable and a set of categorical and/or scale variables. Instead of controlling for variables one by one, independent variables are controlled for together. As this goes beyond the basic descriptive level of exploring survey data, regression analysis is not being dealt with in this chapter. However, a detailed guide on how to conduct regression analyses can be found in Field (2013).

While a distinction has been made between univariate, bivariate and multivariate analyses, it is important to mention that data analyses is best undertaken starting from the univariate inspection of data, analysing them one by one before finally analysing them together.

Activity 2.4

Outline the possible univariate and bivariate analyses you could undertake when you have data available for the variables Home/EU and overseas students and final dissertation mark.

Conclusions

This chapter started with a discussion on the quantitative nature of today's survey definitions and focused on the different stages to undertake when designing your own survey project, including the positivist and realist epistemological dominance, aiming to establish an objective truth, obtained through scientific approaches and independent from the researcher him-/herself.

Chapter key points

- Identifying and planning your survey.
- Consider the dominant theoretical stances with regard to survey and reflect on others.
- Selection of a longitudinal versus cross-sectional designs.
- Selection of sample from the research population.
- Formulation of survey questions, different modes of data collection and examples of data analysis techniques.
- The use of fourteen steps of survey design as a useful checklist when designing your own survey project.

Recommended reading

Cohen, L., Manion, L., & Morrison, K. (2007). *Research Methods in Education.* London: Routledge.
This is a bestseller core text on research methods in education and is one of the best resources on the market for educational researchers and postgraduate students wanting to increase their knowledge on methodological issues. The chapters on survey methodology and the construction of questionnaires are extensive. This book also helps in further understanding the theoretical underpinnings of research.

Field, A. (2013). *Discovering Statistics Using IBM SPSS Statistics.* London: Sage.
This book helps researchers and postgraduate students to understand statistics and to apply them in a very accessible and humorous way, drawing on the software package IBM SPSS.

Fink, A. (2003). *They Survey Handbook*. Los Angelos: The Langley Research Institute.
Fink has produced a very comprehensive survey handbook which focuses on a wide range of aspects researchers and postgraduate students need to take into account when doing survey research, from start to finish.

Saris, W. & Gallhofer, I. (2007). *Design, Evaluation and Analysis of Questionnaires for Survey Research*. Hoboken, NJ: Wiley.
This book engages in discussions on the optimization of survey research and helps researchers and postgraduate researchers to increase the reliability and validity of their questionnaires with a range of practical advices.

Advanced reading

Andres, L. (2014). *Designing and Doing Survey Research*. London: Sage.
An interesting source that will further help in understanding the process of survey research, from planning and designing the research to analysing and reporting your data.

Ornstein, M. (2013). *A Companion to Survey Research*. London: Sage.
This book helps researchers and postgraduate students with research procedures to follow in survey projects and also focuses on the history of survey research.

Robson, C. (2011). *Real World Research*. Chichester: John Wiley & Sons.
Real World Research is an important methodological textbook for social scientists and includes useful information on quantitative research, questionnaire design and data collection.

Sapsford, R. (2007). *Survey Research*. London: Sage.
This book will help students and postgraduate students to further understand the aims of survey research and provides specific information on the analysis of survey data.

Web links

www.cls.ioe.ac.uk/ncds
This is the main website for the National Child Development Study (NCDS) which follows the lives of over 17,000 people born in England, Scotland and Wales in a single week of 1958. Also known as the 1958 Birth Cohort Study, it collects information on physical and educational development, economic

circumstances, employment, family life, health behaviour, well-being, social participation and attitudes.

www.cls.ioe.ac.uk/BCS70
This is similar to the above but it follows the lives of more than 17,000 people in a single week in 1970.

www.cls.ioe.ac.uk/page.aspx?sitesectionid=851
This is the link for the Millennium Cohort Study which follows the lives of around 19,000 children born in the United Kingdom in 2000–2001.

https://www.understandingsociety.ac.uk/
This provides the link to the Understanding Society dataset. It is an innovative world-leading study about twenty-first-century UK life and how it is changing. It captures important information about people's social and economic circumstances, attitudes, behaviours and health. The study is longitudinal in its design.

http://www.oecd.org/pisa/
This is for the Programme for International Student Assessment (PISA).

3

Experimental and Quasi-Experimental Research Design in Education

Katie Cebula

Key points

- Experimental and quasi-/experimental design in education often represents a dialogue with psychology.
- Quasi-/experimental studies are often either to advance understanding of children's development/learning or to evaluate educational policies, approaches and interventions.
- A range of concerns require consideration in relation to this research design, including those around philosophical issues; validity and causation; the use of experimental design in evaluation research; and replication.
- Quasi-/experimental research design has much to offer across a range of important areas of education, but rigorous design, measurement of potential mediating variables, high-quality replication and careful interpretation of results are vital.

Introduction

This chapter focuses on experimental and quasi-experimental design in educational research. It briefly explores the key methodological elements of experiments, before going on to look at the place, epistemological assumptions and value of experimental design in educational research. Some of the concerns raised around the use of this research design are then explored, with a view to understanding how these can be addressed. Examples of experimental research are considered, both those used to advance understanding of child developmental processes, and those used in the evaluation of educational policies, approaches and interventions. This allows consideration of the extent to which experimental studies, in these two areas, are associated with different issues in relation to theory, design and generalizability. Overall, quasi-/-experimental research design has much to offer across a range of important areas of education, but rigorous design and careful interpretation of findings are key. First, though, let's begin with an example of a recent study:

The ability of children and young people to understand the thoughts, feelings and beliefs of others (known as their 'theory of mind': Premack and Woodruff, 1978) is crucial for their engagement in a range of educational and social experiences: reading fiction, collaborative learning, peer relationships and friendships can all involve the ability to think about the mental states of others. Theory of mind (ToM) develops through childhood and adolescence (Devine and Hughes, 2016), so an important question is whether teachers can boost this ability through classroom-based teaching. If so, this would be particularly important for the support of pupils who have poorer theory of mind. This was recently explored by Bianco and Lecce (2016), who researched the effectiveness of a 'mental state conversation' intervention, delivered by teachers in Italy. Seventy-two pupils (eight- to nine-years old) in four classes, from four separate schools participated. Each class was randomly assigned to a mental state conversation 'experimental' group (who received four lessons of a ToM intervention, involving discussion and inferences about mental states) or a 'control' group (who received four lessons, involving discussion and inferences about physical rather than mental states). ToM ability was measured pre-test, and again post-test one week after the end of the intervention programme. The researchers who gathered the pre- and post-intervention data were blind to the group to which the child had been allocated. At pre-test the groups did not differ on ToM ability, or a range of other variables known to be related to ToM, such as age, verbal ability and family affluence. Although both the experimental and the control group improved significantly in ToM ability between the pre- and post-test, by post-test the experimental (intervention) group significantly outperformed the control group, a difference which was maintained at a follow-up assessment 2 months after the end of the programme. The authors suggest that these results show that teachers of eight - to nine-year-old pupils can promote ToM development during regular classroom-based teaching.

Experimental studies, such as this, often reflect a dialogue between psychology and education. Increasingly such experimental studies are conducted in classrooms, rather than in lab settings. But pupils, teachers and educational settings do not always operate in a uniform or predicable manner: they are all wonderfully and necessarily complicated, offering a rich abundance of variables. Is the tightly controlled experimental study a truly realistic pursuit in an educational context?

Key elements of experimental and quasi-experimental design

The Bianco and Lecce study illustrates some of the key components of experimental design, and its use within educational contexts. A detailed account of experimental design is beyond the scope of this chapter (see Sani and Todman, 2006; Whitely and Kite, 2013 for excellent overviews), but in brief, an experiment is used to test a hypothesis: in the example above, the hypothesis was that the children in the experimental group who received the ToM intervention would show enhanced ToM ability compared to children in the control group who had not received the intervention. The researcher then manipulates an independent variable – here, whether the class received a ToM intervention or not – to assess the effect on a dependent variable (here, the pupils' ToM ability). This example study is relatively straightforward, with two 'conditions' (in other words, two levels of treatment of the independent variable – here the experimental ToM condition and the control condition). Other experiments use multiple independent and dependent variables, and more than two conditions (see Clark-Carter, 2004 for detailed discussion). There are also various types of experimental design. The ToM example is a 'between group' design, as each condition of the independent variable was experienced by only one group of participants. In a 'within group' design each participant experiences all levels of the independent variable. In our ToM example this would have involved, for example, the children receiving the control lessons followed by the ToM intervention.

A final important distinction is between a 'true' experiment, in which the researcher randomly allocates participants to conditions and determines the levels of the independent variable, and a 'quasi-experiment', which retains many of the features of a well-controlled experiment, but in which the researcher does not randomly allocate participants to groups or does not have full control over manipulation of the independent variable (Campbell and Stanley, 1963). In practice, quasi-experiments are used in situations where random allocation is not possible, not ethical or not practical. Quasi-experiments may also take the form of 'natural experiments' where the researcher examines 'naturally occurring conditions', and extracts from it an independent variable and an assumed dependent variable (e.g. Torche's (2011) study of the effect of prenatal maternal stress on birthweight, with earthquakes as the source of stress).

A nice example of a 'true' experiment is Fletcher-Watson et al.'s (2016) randomized control trial of an intervention for children with autism using an iPad™ app to support the development of social communication skills. Here fifty-four preschool children with autism were randomly assigned to either an intervention or a control condition. The independent variable (receiving use of the iPad™ app) was systematically manipulated, such that the intervention group received a two-month trial of the iPad™ app and the control group did not have use of the app, receiving only 'treatment as usual'. In contrast, Remington et al. (2007) provide an example of a quasi-experimental design. Here again, the study was an evaluation of an intervention for preschool children with autism. However, in this case it was for an intensive home-based behavioural intervention, which parents used for 25+ hours per week for at least two years. Remington et al. also compared child developmental outcomes (language ability, social behaviour etc.) in an intervention and a control condition. However, Remington et al. did not randomly allocate children to the two different groups. Instead they located families who had already opted to use the approach (intervention group) or were receiving 'treatment as usual' (control group). In evaluations of long-term intensive home-based interventions such as this, quasi-experimental design is often more appropriate, in part because of the ethical concerns around randomly allocating families to such a demanding intervention, or conversely of denying them access to an intervention which might be helpful for their child's development.

The dividing line between quasi-experiment and non-experiment can, in practice, be hard to define. Group difference studies – in which the independent variable has been *selected* (e.g. male/female differences in reading ability) rather than *manipulated* – are usually not regarded as quasi-experimental studies because the independent variable has not been 'controlled' at all by the researcher (Coolican, 2004): they therefore lack a central feature of experimental design.

Activity 3.1

Design a study to evaluate a school-based intervention to reduce risk-taking behaviour in adolescents. Would you use an experimental or a quasi-experimental research design? Which factors would influence your decision? How might your choice of design affect validity in the research?

The place, epistemological assumptions and value of quasi/-experimental design

Experimental designs have a relatively long history within medicine, where they are viewed as the 'gold standard' in establishing the effectiveness of new medication in drug trials (Goldacre, 2013). Quasi/-experimental designs have also long been used across numerous branches of psychology (Goodwin, 2008). Within educational contexts, quasi/-experimental design studies have typically taken the form of (i) psychology studies on pupils' learning and development and (ii) evaluation of educational policy, teaching approaches or other educational interventions.

Experimental design is associated with the positivist paradigm, which holds that an external world exists independent of human experience and that objective knowledge about the world can be obtained through scientific methods such as experimentation (see Fishman, 1991 for a full discussion). A more moderate position, the post-positivism paradigm, is also relevant to discussion of experimental methods. This holds the same ontological position as positivism – that objective reality exists – but contends that we can only know this reality imperfectly, that there are differences between the social and natural sciences and that the researcher may influence what is observed. Indeed, Rosenthal and Rosnow (2009), for example, describe how an experimenter's identity (e.g. sex and age), behaviour and expectations can all – if not carefully addressed in study design – influence the outcomes of experiments. As discussed in Chapter 1, realist ontology is relevant to experimental design. Although there are many varieties of realism, broadly it holds that a definite world with particular phenomena and properties exists independent of what people say or think about them (Maxwell and Delaney, 1990). Importantly, though, one might be realist with respect to some theories/phenomena and not others (Maxwell and Delaney, 1990).

In terms of the value of experimental design, there is debate, for example, in the North American literature, about the extent to which quasi/-experimental design is 'the only show in town' when it comes to making decisions around education. Some (e.g. Sadoff, 2014) acknowledge the value of a range of approaches in educational research but argue that, when it comes to the delivery of strong causal evidence on 'what works', well-designed randomized experiments should be the 'gold standard' for policy makers. Others raise concerns about the weight given to findings produced via quasi- but particularly via experimental design. Howe (2004), for example, criticizes what he describes as the methodological frameworks of 'neoclassical experimentalism' (a view that in determining 'what works', educational research should rely exclusively on randomized experiments) and 'mixed-methods experimentalism' (a view which acknowledges the place of qualitative approaches, but again places more value on randomized experimental studies in educational research). His concern with both of these frameworks is that experimental design is seen as primary, with qualitative-interpretivist methods devalued.

Experimental design studies do, if well designed and executed, bring with them a level of objectivity about whether a particular change in practice is associated with a change in outcome. However, there is a danger that blind faith in experimental design leads to the results from such studies being accepted rather uncritically when in fact, as we shall see, they demand the same level of scrutiny as any other form of research. Furthermore, affording such weight to a single research design can prevent the researcher from identifying situations where other approaches are better suited to the questions to be answered.

So, is quasi/-experimental design a research approach that has 'found its place at the table' of educational research, or is there scope for it to make itself even more useful? Discussion here centres around some common concerns raised about this particular research design, and how/whether these can be overcome. These concerns can be broadly divided into four areas: philosophical concern; concerns around validity and issues of causation; concerns around the use of experimental design in evaluation research; and replication.

Philosophical concern

Clearly, to consider using a quasi-experimental design in research, such a design must, as discussed in Chapter 1, align with one's ontological and epistemological position. Beyond this, though, in Cook's (2003) view, the chief philosophical concern with experimental design centres on the relationship of experiment to theory (specifically, its relationship to the verification of theory). Popper (1968) advanced the notion of empirical falsification – the idea that 'whilst a theory can never be proven it can be falsified'. Cook, though, argues that the post-positivist work of Kuhn (1970) specifies that theories can never be formulated explicitly enough to be definitively tested and falsified. The concern, then, is about the extent to which experiments might allow us to gain objective knowledge about the world.

Cook argues that even if we cannot establish truth beyond doubt, once a theory has been supported across a range of experimental contexts, it can be confidently treated as 'fact-like'. Similarly, he argues, if a theory is not supported in an experiment, this would not necessarily falsify that theory; it may simply suggest that it should be tested under a different set of conditions or perhaps the theory amended (indeed, Popper acknowledged that, in practice, single conflicting findings are seldom sufficient to falsify a theory: Maxwell and Delaney, 1990). Cook argues that once a theory is shown to be ineffective under a range of different conditions, the underlying theory still would not be conclusively falsified, but would rather have 'run out of steam'.

Cook's argument that experiments are useful in demonstrating the 'fact-like' nature of theories does seem to hold. Some theories, such as Bruner's theory of the scaffolding of learning (e.g. Wood et al., 1976), have been so well replicated across a range of different experimental contexts with a range of different participants that it would seem safe to describe them as 'fact like', even if we might not wish to say they were true in all circumstances.

With regard to the falsification of theory, here McKelvie and Low's (2002) investigation of the 'Mozart effect' provides a useful example. This is the theory that listening to Mozart has a short-term enhancing effect on our ability to perform certain spatial tasks. If such a theory were correct, there would be obvious merit in teachers playing Mozart prior to maths lessons which involve spatial activities. McKelvie and Low tested the Mozart effect experimentally with eleven- to thirteen-year-old pupils, comparing the spatial ability of pupils before and after listening to either Mozart or to repetitive dance music. Neither type of music was found to enhance spatial ability. This was one in a series of studies which failed to replicate the Mozart effect; successful replications had only been achieved in a very narrow set of conditions. McKelvie and Low conclude that the effect is extremely difficult to demonstrate empirically, and that 'It is time for the final curtain to fall on the Mozart effect' (p. 256). This obviously does not preclude the existence of other positive effects of music on children's development, but it does seem to exemplify Cook's point: when there is a body of well-designed research which fails to replicate an effect under a range of conditions, the underlying theory is simply discredited, rather than objectively shown to be false. In practical terms, an effect which can be replicated only under a very narrow set of conditions is in any case of little benefit to teachers.

As Cook (2003) notes, this philosophical concern – that experiments can seldom be used to definitively test a theory – does not rule out experiments as a means of developing usable knowledge. Indeed, the discussion sits well with the post-positivist stance that we can only know reality imperfectly.

What do these philosophical concerns mean in practical terms for experiments in education? Here the semantic distinctions between 'truth' and 'fact-like', and between 'falsified' and 'run out of steam', seem less important than the more substantive point about the need to: identify the place of theory in your quasi/-experimental design (e.g. are you seeking to verify a theory, refine an existing theory etc.?); test theories across a range of conditions in order to understand the limits of generalizability; and recognize when there is a sufficient body of evidence to consider that a theory is discredited. Furthermore, a decision to discard a theory may not lie with experimental evidence alone: a theory which promotes educational practices which place a heavy burden of time and finance on a school, or a theory which is also discredited by other forms of evidence (e.g. neuroscience) may face a lower threshold of experimental study opposition before it is abandoned.

Validity and issues of causation

Aside from philosophical issues, a second set of concerns around quasi/-experimental design is around threats to validity. Internal validity, described by Campbell and Stanley (1963: 5) as the 'sine qua non' of experimental design, is the extent to which a change in the dependent variable is real and has truly been caused by manipulation to the independent variable. Threats to internal validity – extraneous variables – must be held constant to rule these out as explanations for any change in dependent variables. In the Bianco and Lecce ToM intervention example described earlier, this was done by ensuring that the experimental and control groups were matched on key variables such as age, verbal ability and socio-economic background.

Concerns around internal validity may be greater in quasi-experiments than experiments. This is because participants in quasi-experiments have not been randomly allocated to conditions, so there is a greater risk that participant groups differ on some extraneous variable which may influence outcome. For example, in the Remington et al. (2007) autism intervention study, it may have been the case that parents who chose to use an intensive intervention also differed from the control group in other important ways (e.g. the way they played with their child), which may have influenced the dependent variable. That said, experimental design is not immune to threats to internal validity, and must be designed with equal care.

Central to validity is the issue of causation: experiments are tasked with establishing whether a change in the independent variable *causes* a change in the dependent variable. How easy is it to do this in an experiment conducted with human participants, in a complex social setting? Romich (2006) explores the issue of internal validity and causation within an ecological framework, such as that of Bronfenbrenner (1979), who posited that the child develops within a series of nested 'systems', from the 'microsystems' which they directly experience (such as family, school) to the 'macrosystem' in which they live (e.g. race or culture). Romich explains that in well-designed 'micro level' studies, which focus on the child and their immediate environment, it is *relatively* straightforward to assess whether a change in the independent variable truly causes a change in the dependent variable. For example, the Bianco and Lecce (2016) ToM intervention was conducted within the microsystem of the school. It was therefore relatively straightforward to assess how the manipulation of the independent variable (use of the ToM intervention) related to a change in the dependent variable (the child's

ToM ability). That said, even in a seemingly straightforward micro-level experimental study such as this, although many extraneous variables were controlled, it is nonetheless possible that additional, unforeseen extraneous variables contributed to the outcome (e.g. effects of the teachers learning about ToM, as opposed to the specific ToM intervention per se). Quasi-experimental studies conducted at the microsystem level then, though relatively straightforward, are not immune to threats to internal validity.

As Romich describes, in experiments which are several steps removed from the child, such as 'macro' level policy experiments, it becomes even more difficult to ascertain whether a change in the independent variable (e.g. a particular educational policy) causes change in micro level dependent variables, such as child outcomes. For example, if we were to test whether a policy to provide free books to preschool children leads to a change in levels of childhood literacy, we could set up a quasi-experimental study comparing childhood literacy in a region which provides the books, with a region which does not provide them. However, there are so many possible extraneous variables (such as availability of libraries, quality of preschools) that it would be challenging to establish that the change in policy has caused the change in outcome. Doing so would require identification and measurement of potential extraneous variables in order to control for them, either through matching the regions, or statistically in the analysis. Indeed, there may be some macro level research topics where analysis of existing large-scale longitudinal cohort data is more effective than novel researcher-designed experimental studies in relating a policy change to child outcome.

Further to the issue of identifying *whether* an experimental manipulation is responsible for causing a change in the dependent variable, is the issue of *how* it has done so – the causal mechanism. Indeed, it is often noted that an experiment can show *that* something has changed but that it may be less illuminating on *how* or *why* it has done so (e.g. Goldacre, 2013). Similarly, Howe (2004) suggests that experiments only provide a 'black box' of relationships, but not the detail on precise causal mechanisms. As Goldacre notes, though, even within experimental design it is possible to develop some understanding of causal mechanisms. One such example is by Bianco et al. (2016) whose experimental ToM intervention study was specifically designed to examine causal mechanisms. Bianco et al. looked not only at *whether* conversations about mental states benefit children's ToM abilities, but *how* they might do so – that is, the causal mechanism. Bianco et al. randomly assigned children either to a two-week mental state conversation intervention or to a control condition, and measured their ToM ability before and after the intervention. They were interested in two possible causal mechanisms: perhaps mental state conversations improve children's ToM abilities because they increase children's *awareness and use of* mental state terms *or* perhaps they work because they increase children's capacity to *accurately reason about* mental states. The researchers measured both of these potential mechanisms and then used mediation analysis (a statistical technique to investigate whether the change in the independent variable is associated with a change in the dependent variable via a third variable) to show that it was the ability to accurately reason about mental states and not a simple awareness of mental states that appeared to be the critical mechanism. However, even within a 'micro' level experiment, such as this, simple ideas about causal mechanism may not always suffice. Indeed, Bianco et al. note that there may have been additional causal mechanisms which they did not measure. Something else to bear in mind is the oft-repeated 'correlation does not equal causation', and the need for longitudinal studies in order to more fully understand causal mechanisms.

Another issue with causal mechanisms is again, to some extent, one of ecological level, with Romich (2006) noting the particular difficulties in identifying the causal mechanisms responsible for micro-level outcomes in macro level experiments. She also notes the importance of identifying potential mediators, so that the hypothesized 'causal chain' from 'macro' policy to 'micro' child can be explored; measurement of variables at both macro and micro-level pre- and post-intervention; and ensuring large sample sizes to allow investigation of outcomes and causal mechanisms among different groups of children.

Potential causal mechanisms have to be identified in advance, if they are to be measured and included in the analysis, and this is not always easy to do. While straightforward experiments in the natural sciences might be sufficient to demonstrate that 'A causes B', real world educational contexts are made up of a range of nonlinear, reciprocal factors which may be difficult to fully untangle, measure and understand in an experimental context. As Cook (2003) notes, we may no longer be looking at 'A causes B' or even – as in the Bianco et al. (2016) study described above – 'A causes B causes C', but something far more complex. While experimental design may be at its best when investigating simple causal mechanisms in studies with only a modest number of variables, it is important to find ways to maximize the utility of this approach for answering more complex questions involving more complex causal mechanisms. In situations where causal mechanisms cannot be readily anticipated, other approaches, both quantitative and qualitative, are likely to prove invaluable. Another aspect to consider, as Wong et al. (2012) note, is that mechanisms are not always inherent to the intervention, but may also be a function of particular participants and context.

External validity is another area of concern. There is a constant tension between external validity (the extent to which the results of the experiment can be generalized to other settings, people and times – known as ecological, population and temporal validity, respectively) and internal validity in experimental research, and a balance must be struck between the two. An example of this comes from my own research (Cebula et al., 2017). In order to investigate emotional understanding in children with Down's syndrome, we used an experimental study design, with photo stimuli of 'regular' and 'exaggerated' emotional expressions, in order to investigate whether the children identified the emotions more accurately when they were exaggerated (if so, this might suggest that using exaggerated expressions is useful in supporting children with Down's syndrome who have difficulty in recognizing emotions). Clearly there are concerns around external validity in this study – using static photo images does not represent the dynamic displays of emotion which children usually experience, and findings may not therefore generalize well to other settings. However, using these particular images gave us confidence that the manipulation of the independent variable (regular versus exaggerated emotion) did lead to change in the dependent variable (number of emotions identified), that is, it increased internal validity. This was because it allowed us to rule out some extraneous variables. For example, it may be that when people exaggerate their emotions in real life they also vocalize more, or hold their expression still for longer. Using static photos enabled us to exclude these variables. The next step is to look at the value of exaggerated emotions using more naturalistic stimuli and settings.

The discussion above perhaps emphasizes, more than anything, the care that must be taken at the design stage of any piece of quasi/-experimental research: assessing the proposed design in terms of levels of internal and external validity, and considering the extent to which causal mechanisms can be understood within the proposed research design. While experimental design can, on the surface, appear to be a straightforward manipulation of one variable and a measurement of change in another variable, clearly there is far more to consider if we are to produce a robust and worthwhile design.

Activity 3.2

Re-read some of your favourite experiments in educational research (look at the references in this chapter if you don't have a favourite!) As you read, think about the possible threats to internal validity. Could these have been avoided? Consider also external validity: are there limits to the extent to which the findings of the study could be generalized to other people, settings and times?

Concerns around the use of experimental design in evaluation research

Turning to our third area of concern, we focus for a moment specifically on the use of experimental design to evaluate policies, interventions and approaches. Is quasi-/-experimental design something which falls apart when faced with evaluations of interventions delivered within complex everyday educational contexts?

Numerous experimental approaches to evaluate long-term interventions taking place in 'variable-rich' complex social settings have been conducted, such as Green et al.'s (2010) randomized control trial of the Preschool Autism Communication Trial, a parent-mediated communication-focused intervention for children with autism. On the face of it, there does not seem to be a de facto need to restrict experimental design only to short, simple and discrete interventions, provided that study design, sample size and methods provide a good 'fit' with the field of inquiry. For example, in a complex intervention taking place over a long period of time it may be necessary to build in measures of fidelity to the intervention, to assess this aspect of internal validity.

However, according to Pawson and Tilley (1997), the randomized control trial – no matter how well designed – is not king when it comes to evaluation of social/educational interventions. Indeed, they describe experimental-design evaluation research as a 'heroic failure' (1997: 8) which has not, to date, sufficiently lived up to its promise of improving the world. This is because, they explain, experimental design is driven by a one-dimensional focus – that change in the independent variable causes change in the dependent variable – with everything else often seen as an extraneous variable. In their view, other factors are simply seen as 'noise', which – in order to maintain high levels of internal validity – must be controlled, either in statistical analysis or via a matched control group. In implementing such control, Pawson and Tilley suggest, the researcher is coming at evaluation from the wrong angle, often 'writing out' the very mechanisms which need to be understood.

Pawson's alternative (Pawson and Tilley, 1997; Pawson, 2013) is the *realist evaluation* approach. Driving this approach is not a focus on cause and effect, but instead a focus on mechanism and context alongside outcome – that is, not only 'what works', but a look inside the mythical black box to establish 'what kinds of … interventions will tend to work, for what kinds of … [people], in what kinds of contexts, to what degree, and what explains such patterns' (Wong et al., 2012: 93). Behind their approach is realism, which is described in this context as a philosophy of science which sits between positivism and relativism/constructivism (Wong et al., 2012). Here realism is defined as 'a view that there is an objective real world, but that our understanding of this reality is influenced by real world constraints' – something which has much in common with the post-positivist stance discussed earlier. Pawson and Tilley's particular *realist evaluation approach* (not simply an ontological/epistemological position, but a whole approach to evaluation) draws particularly on scientific realism's emphasis on the mechanics of explanation – the need to understand *how* something works, in order to move science forwards. They draw a strong analogy with the aspect of the natural sciences which stress the *mechanisms* of change (*why* something led to change) and the context of change (*the conditions* in which the mechanisms led to change) – issues they feel are often inadequately considered in experimental design studies. Pawson and Tilley (1997) do not consider that the social world and the natural sciences are the same, but for them, there is continuity because both begin by thinking about mechanism and context.

So how does experimental design fit with the realist evaluation approach? Those using a realist evaluation approach adopt both quantitative and qualitative methods, often using a mixed-method approach. The approach can therefore include experimental study design (Pawson and Tilley, 1997; Marchal et al., 2013). However, the objection is to experiments used within a strict cause-effect mentality which ignore the 'black box'. Further, those writing on the realist evaluation approach hold that pure experimental design (such as randomized control trials), drawing on a positivist philosophy of science, cannot fit with a realist evaluation approach, not least because the 'stability' required by experimental design cannot be found in a real world educational context:

> What experimental logic treats as stable and identical experimental and control conditions are actually complex and ceaselessly changing social systems. (Pawson, 2013: 49)

Pawson argues that randomized control trials do not sufficiently acknowledge or explore the rich complexity of interacting causal mechanisms and context. While those working in the field are 'cautiously supportive of quasi-experimental designs' (Marchal et al., 2013: 127), they suggest that a realistic evaluation offers a much broader approach, to allow a full exploration not only of outcome, but of context and mechanism.

There is obvious value in considering approaching the issue of evaluation from a 'context, mechanism, outcome' perspective, rather than a 'cause-effect' stance. It is also important to emphasize that the realist evaluation approach is not a wholesale rejection of quasi-experimental design, and exploring a mixed-methods approach may aid exploration of some of these more complex questions about why interventions work, and for whom and in which circumstances. Seeking ways to broaden randomized control trials to allow some measurement of mechanism and contextual factors may also be beneficial. Finally, even the most effective educational interventions rarely produce positive outcomes in every single participant, and a realistic evaluation approach may help develop a better understanding of why this is the case.

What can the student, embarking on an evaluation of an educational intervention, take from all this? It is tempting to offer the easy 'horses for courses' way out: that randomized control trials are appropriate in some research situations, particularly those in which one is interested in outcome and might realistically be able to achieve high levels of internal validity, while realist evaluation approaches (including quasi-experiments) are appropriate in other, more complex settings. However, choice of research design should also be influenced by one's fundamental beliefs around what particular knowledge can and should be developed through educational evaluation research.

> ## Activity 3.3
>
> Your school has decided to implement a new programme, in which all pupils get an extra 15 minutes' physical activity a day (see Ryde et al., under review). Design a study to evaluate the impact of the programme on pupils' cognitive development and attention in the class. How would you investigate outcome? What about mechanism and context?

Replication

A more recent concern raised around experimental psychology research has been the number of high-profile studies which have reported a failure to replicate statistically significant research findings from original studies (Pashler and Wagenmakers, 2012; Maxwell et al., 2015). This replication failure phenomenon is neither unique to psychology nor to experimental design (e.g. Hirschhorn and Altshuler, 2002), though much writing is focused on these areas.

There is now a number of failures to replicate education-relevant experimental phenomena (e.g. Panero et al.'s (2016) failure to replicate the finding that reading segments of literary fiction led to a significant and immediate increase in participants' ToM ability). The 'replication crisis' has led to a concern about the reliability of extant research findings, and more broadly about the credibility of the field (Pashler and Wagenmakers, 2012). Why has there been a failure to replicate important study findings? One reason may be that academic journals appear to have a preference for publishing studies with statistically significant findings (Pashler and Wagenmakers, 2012). Hence while there may be nine examples of an experiment with non-significant findings, it will be the tenth example of the experiment with significant findings which is the only one published and available to the public.

Despite these concerns about the reliability of some existing findings, replications are rare, with submission of replication studies rarely encouraged by journals (Martin and Clarke, 2017). This is perhaps because replication studies are seen as less 'prestigious' than original research (Earp and Trafimow, 2015), and perhaps because the need for replication does not sit well with those seeking 'quick answers' (Maxwell et al., 2015).

What does this mean for experimental work within education? Rather than throwing the whole enterprise of quasi/-experimental research into doubt, it emphasizes the need for multiple replication studies. While we may be excited by educational intervention findings, such as the ToM study of Bianco and Lecce (2016), replication is essential before schools set aside time and resources for wider implementation. Maxwell et al. (2015) and Simons (2014) note a number of recent collaborative initiatives to systematically conduct and record replication efforts. These are invaluable in maintaining the credibility of existing quasi/-experimental research across a variety of contexts, including education. For students and researchers undertaking novel experimental studies, this discussion highlights the importance of a well-designed study and the need to interpret findings cautiously, perhaps including a call for replication of any key findings. Study registration (publication of research predictions and methods prior to beginning an experimental study) is also increasingly emphasized in the field, in a bid to enhance transparency and rigour, and this should also be considered. Further, there is the need for educators and policy makers to be provided with the time and resources necessary to base decisions on a whole body of research, rather than the latest eye-catching significant finding from a single study. This discussion also suggests the difficulty in searching for incontestable 'truths', and instead advocates time spent in considering the confidence we have in any particular body of experimental research (Earp and Trafimow, 2015).

Case studies 1 and 2 available online

As discussed previously, the use of quasi/-experimental research in educational contexts has tended to take the form of psychology studies on child developmental/learning processes, and studies used to evaluate educational policies, approaches and interventions. Exploring examples of each of these can help us to consider the extent to which they are associated with different issues in relation to theory, design and generalizability.

An example of an experimental study used to understand the development of children and young people was undertaken by Dumontheil et al. (2010), who explored ToM development in adolescence. Discussion of this can be found online at: www.bloomsbury.com/uk/building-research-design-in-education-9781350019515/. A second function of quasi-experimental study designs is to evaluate educational policies, approaches and interventions. One such example comes from Holmes and Gathercole (2014), who explored whether a school-based computerized intervention to support the development of pupils' working memory led to improved academic performance in English and maths. Discussion of this can be found online at: www.bloomsbury.com/uk/building-research-design-in-education-9781350019515/.

Conclusions

This chapter explored a range of concerns with quasi/-experimental research design, and the ways in which these might be overcome. Examples of experimental studies were outlined to explore these concerns and to consider the potential value of this research design in education. It is clear that quasi/-experimental research design is firmly established within, and has much to offer, education research. However, careful and thoughtful design is required, with particular attention paid to issues of validity, causation and replication. Only then will we be able to say that quasi-/experimental design is not only welcome at the education party, but has stayed late to help with the washing up.

Chapter key points

- Quasi-/experimental research design has much to offer educational research, particularly around advancing understanding of child development and evaluating educational approaches and interventions.
- However, attention must focus on ensuring that the worth of this research design is realized through rigorous planning and design.
- The complex issues inherent in appropriately interpreting experimental findings and translating these into education practice must also be considered.

Acknowledgements

Many thanks to Dr Gale Macleod and Dr Josie Booth for helpful comments on an earlier version of this chapter.

Recommended reading

Campbell, D. T., & Stanley, J. C. (1963). *Experimental and Quasi-Experimental Designs for Research*. Boston: Houghton Mifflin.
A classic text covering definitions, different types of design and issues around validity.

Clark-Carter, D. (2004). *Quantitative Psychology Research: A Student's Handbook*. Hove: Psychology Press.
Chapter 4 details different types of experimental design and is very useful if you are planning to use experimental design.

Sani, F., & Todman, J. (2006). *Experimental Design and Statistics for Psychology: A First Course*. Oxford: Blackwell.
Aside from the suggestion that psychologists are not 'ordinary people' (!) this is a very straightforward introduction to some of the main concepts in experimental design and a great place for the newcomer to begin.

Whitely, B. E., & Kite, M. E. (2013). *Principles of Research in Behavioural Science*. New York: Psychology Press.
In addition to looking at ethics, this includes a really thorough, and very readable, consideration of internal and external validity and steps that the experimenter can take to strengthen their design.

Advanced reading

Howe, K. R. (2004). A Critique of Experimentalism. *Qualitative Inquiry*, 10(1): 42–61.
Addresses concerns with a perceived over-reliance on experimental evidence in education.

Pawson, R., & Tilley, N. (1997). *Realistic Evaluation*. London: Sage.
Before going on to Pawson's more recent writing, this is a good place to begin in order to understand the principles of realistic evaluation.

Romich, J. L. (2006). Randomized Social Policy Experiments and Research on Child Development. *Journal of Applied Developmental Psychology*, 27(2): 136–150.
A great read for those seeking to use experiments to understand how changes in policy impact on children's development and well-being.

Rosenthal, R., & Rosnow, R. L. (2009). *Artifacts in Behavioral Research: Robert Rosenthal and Ralph L. Rosnow's Classic Books*. New York; Oxford: Oxford University Press.

Brings together three classic books, providing a wealth of information on experimenter and participant effects and strategies for considering these in experimental design.

Web links

Education Endowment Foundation
https://educationendowmentfoundation.org.uk/
A charity focused on closing the attainment gap through the provision of research evidence on what works to improve teaching and learning (see also the 'What Works Clearinghouse' at: https://ies.ed.gov/ncee/wwc/).

British Psychological Society: Origins
http://origins.bps.org.uk/
A great multimedia timeline, with information about the history of experimental psychology, and classic experimental studies.

The Reproducibility Project
https://osf.io/ezcuj/wiki/home/
Facilitated by the Center for Open Science to attempt to reproduce a set of experimental psychology findings.

Part II

Building Qualitative Research Designs

4

Qualitative Research Design: Principles, Choices and Strategies

Jane Brown

Key points

- A robust and well-planned research design is fundamental to a well-executed, ethically informed study.
- Careful attention to the justification, sequencing and interrelationships between methods is integral to sound research design.
- Research questions should be clear and explicitly stated, as well as practical and doable.
- Managing uncertainty from a research position of openness and responsiveness is key to building qualitative research design, particularly at the early stages.
- Researchers require a raised level of ethical awareness and this should be embedded into their research practice from the embryonic stage of planning and beyond.

Introduction

The broad purpose of this chapter is to identify critical stages in the process of undertaking qualitative research, addressing some of the decisions that are necessarily made over the course of the research enterprise. Given the limited space available, the use of texts and documents, observational methods and ethnographic approaches, some of which will be briefly mentioned, are not a prime focus of this chapter. Instead, the emphasis here is on the theoretical positioning and research design decisions which are significant parts of the research process. Discussion will concentrate on the challenges faced in developing research design as a result of theoretical and conceptual framing and the ways in which significant points in the evolution of a research project provide opportunities for reflection on the coherence of a research project.

I will draw on my own qualitative work to consider the need for conceptual clarity in relation to research design. More pragmatic aspects of this chapter will include topics such as honing the research focus, formulating research questions and selecting and combining methods. Strategies for the analysis of data will also be discussed, specifically in terms of justifying the trustworthiness of qualitative research findings. The critical importance of understanding research ethics and the relevance of a 'situated perspective' for research design (Hammersley and Traianou, 2007; Brooks et al., 2014) are emphasized based on an interpretivist understanding of the social reality. It therefore follows that it is necessary to incorporate ethical integrity into the entirety of the research process given the embedded role of the researcher assumed in this position and the rejection of the traditional distinction made between the researcher and the researched. In order to locate this discussion of qualitative research design, the first concern will be to explore some of the principles of a qualitative approach. In doing so the critique of the misleading dichotomy made between interpretivist and positivistic positions is acknowledged and, in particular the argument made earlier by Hammersley (1989). He argued that the act of describing a qualitative, informed position can set up a distorted opposition between research paradigms which underplays some of the overlaps and points of convergence between them.

Principles of qualitative informed research

Qualitative research is a 'broad church' of many approaches, as well as variants of approaches, most of which could be comfortably subsumed under the generic category of a qualitative position (O'Reilly and Kiyimba,

2015). In order to tackle this complexity, Barbour (2014) focuses on the main influential approaches in the qualitative research tradition, and includes symbolic interactionism, phenomenology, ethnomethodology and variations of discourse analysis in her consideration of qualitative research design. While the list can appear endless – further complicated by innovations in the field – core elements of a qualitative approach can be identified. How we come to know and understand the social world is integral to understanding qualitative research design and particular principles underpinning its practice. This emanates from a philosophical position which could be broadly labelled 'interpretivist', which is based on the way in which the social world is experienced, understood and interpreted (Mason, 1996). Sensitivity to social context and understanding relationships in time and place, as well as paying attention to the micro geographies of research sites (e.g. the layout and design of school buildings, the organization of space in classrooms), is fundamental to this kind of approach. According to Mason a qualitative position is 'based on methods of analysis and explanation building which involve understanding of complexity, detail and context' (Mason, 1996: 4). Both the language and conceptual framework of qualitative research privilege the research process and the fact that meaning is negotiated, not only through interaction and dialogue but also through observing the material culture of research settings. Thus it is recognized that the researcher is socially situated and is part of the social world they study. The implication of this is that the researcher uses their awareness reflexively in order to inform the process of research. Moreover, participants are construed as active and knowing agents and in variants of an interpretivist approach, participants may be viewed as experts and/or co-producers of knowledge as in action research as well as feminist positions (see Chapters 9 and 8). The nature of a research relationship and the way in which it is constituted are therefore dependent on the epistemological stance and position taken. One example of this in educational research is that of 'pupil voice' and participation. The starting point of this established and growing field is seeing children and young people as active and capable citizens (Fielding, 2004; Whitty and Wisby, 2007; Brown et al., 2017), informed by theoretical advances in childhood studies where the starting point is that children are viewed as competent social actors who are experts regarding their own lives. This position is driven by empirical knowledge about the social worlds of children, and increasingly knowledge about their relationships and interactions with teachers and other significant adults. The present focus on theorizing the relational aspects of children's lives and building an empirical knowledge base informed the research design of a recent research project (Brown et al., 2017). Broadly, this study examined children and young people's understanding of participation and opportunities for decision-making at school. Given present concerns in Childhood Studies we also explored the role of adults and peers as both facilitators and barriers to participation at school.

Activity 4.1

Look at the research design of the research project: 'Pupils as citizens' study (see references). Given the current interest in the relational aspect of children's and young people's participation where is evidence of this concern in the research design of this study?

The centrality of robust research design

The importance of a well-thought-through research design cannot be underestimated. A finely tuned research design provides a solid framework for any study. Consequently a study with a poor design (i.e. the methods proposed are unable to answer the research questions) would be unlikely to produce reliable and worthwhile findings. The question of 'weak design' is closely intertwined with that of research ethics because it is unproductive on a number of levels. Here the argument made is that badly designed research is unethical because it wastes the time of research participants and intrudes unnecessarily in their lives (Brooks et al., 2014: 60). It also misuses the resources of funding bodies and undermines the credibility of the research community and their institutions. Researchers working in educational settings, such as nurseries and schools, need to be very mindful of the fact that fellow researchers will follow in their footsteps so how they conduct themselves may well have implications for the success of subsequent projects. Some time ago while undertaking observation in nursery playrooms, I had to be sensitive to, and work with suspicion I encountered among some early years specialists who said they had felt uncomfortable when a previous research student had used a stop watch to time their interactions with children.

Kelly and Ali (2004: 130) locate the principles of a sound research design in two main ways in that there is a 'clearly conceived question or problem', and that accepted and desirable ethical practice is assimilated into all phases of the study, including the early design phase (BERA, 2011). Schwartz-Shea and Yakow (2012) conceive research design as a 'signalling device', in that it tells the reader about the overall quality of the project, whether research planning is timetabled and staged appropriately or it is 'persuasive' in communicating the competency of the researcher and their skills. In keeping with the broad principles of qualitative research, Richards (2005: 74) places the researcher and understanding the research context at the heart of developing qualitative research design. She captures the interplay and interaction involved in this process: *Research design is created by the researcher, is moulded (rather than dictated) by the method, and is responsive to the context and the participants.* Predictably, building research design involves a series of decisions, many of which will be related implicitly or explicitly to the ontological stance and/or related to epistemology, as well as the theoretical framework. The methods selected will derive from such decisions and whether observational techniques are deemed appropriate, qualitative interviews are selected, or focus groups or group interviews are regarded as suitable.

The ordering and timing of methods and the justification for their order is an important planning principle which will enhance the credibility of the project. For example, whether focus groups are used at the onset in order to tap into group norms and beliefs and then followed up by face-to-face, individual interviews will depend on various factors, including the extent to which methods are conceived as complimentary or whether the research privileges one method of data collection over another. It may be that subjective accounts is the primary focus of the research, as opposed to accessing collective and group experiences. Connected to this will be decisions about group composition and whether focus groups are homogeneous (e.g. all male pupils in same year group), or heterogeneous (e.g. mixed sexed groups). This can impact on the potential to generate consensus and dissent, as well as silence some participants but not others.

Practicalities loom large in decision-making about research design. The feasibility of accessing research sites must be factored in to a tightly managed, commissioned piece of research. In education, access to schools can take time and familiarity with the temporal organization of school life, including exam timetables and busy points in the school year, is vital to a credible plan. Knowledge of this kind can be useful in negotiations with powerful gatekeepers, especially where there are a number of research projects vying for access to schools with limited capacity. Today competition between research projects is not unheard of, particularly where schools are over-researched.

Being realistic about what is doable is especially important for novice researchers because estimating how long various research tasks take is an experiential form of learning. Accessing and locating research participants, and getting focus group participants together at the same time and in the same place are labour-intensive and challenging activities. Consequently being too ambitious or, alternatively, being overly cautious regarding what is achievable in the time frame can be issues for researchers starting out. Those new to planning research frequently ask, 'How many interviews are enough?' but there is no magic bullet in terms of what is appropriate, because once again it is dependent on the intended purposes of the research, in addition to the theoretical and philosophical position undertaken (Edwards and Holland, 2013). Choices made in relation to methods, as well sample size, also have implications for the relative depth or breadth achieved by a study. While we know qualitative studies tend to be small-scale compared to most comparative studies (see Chapter 7), deciding whether to include a smaller number of in-depth, repeat interviews, as opposed to a greater number of one-off, single interviews, has implications for the kinds of experiences elicited. Using the example of a research focus on teacher career choices, follow-up interviews would allow the complexity of individual biographies and personal choices to be explored in depth at different time frames. Alternatively, a research design which included a larger number of one-off interviews with teachers at different stages of their career would enhance the study's comparative potential because a greater range of trajectories could be investigated.

Identifying the focus

A thorough groundwork in becoming familiar with the literature on the chosen topic is a predictable prerequisite for honing the focus of any research project. Student researchers tend to embark on this journey from a 'broad brush' position where the generic area of interest is identified but the specific focus remains somewhat ill-defined (Barbour, 2014). Identifying a topic is achieved through the process of 'progressively focusing' and this takes time. Some years ago, when asked about the focus of my Ph.D. research at the beginning of my studies, I recall somewhat naively responding that my area was childhood sexuality. Months later, after an extended period of reading, I identified a gap in the research literature, as well a tangible and achievable focus: an interview and observational study of early years professionals' views of sexuality in young children. I combined initial observations in nursery playrooms with follow-up one-to-one interviews with nursery staff. The staging of research was informed by ethical considerations given the sensitive nature of the topic and the need to build relationships with staff prior to interviews. The choice of interviews as the main method of data collection was made in order to capture nursery professionals' subjective understandings of sexual behaviour in young children. Accessing divergent and sometimes conflicting accounts was crucial due to the fact that the dominant conceptual framework evident in literature was one based on a clear-cut 'normal'/'abnormal' dichotomy which I aimed to question. Drawing on social constructionism, I analysed interview data by using a less rigid conceptual framework of a continuum of socially acceptable and unacceptable sexual behaviour. This flexible framework aligned more tightly with my theoretical position and stance, which enabled me to locate a range and variety of opinions about sexuality in very young children.

At the beginning of the research enterprise, a degree of uncertainty is inescapable and perhaps desirable. The elusiveness of a clear path at this early stage can be exacerbated by adopting a more open-ended and less structured approach such as ethnography or exploratory studies where the field is underdeveloped and little baseline information exists. At this point researchers need to be patient, be comfortable with 'not knowing' and immerse themselves in the literature. There are no shortcuts to this process. Branley (2004: 146) suggests practical tips for working through the early stage of the project. First, he suggests brainstorming; writing ideas down and sorting them can be effective in terms of clarifying thoughts at this embryonic stage. It can help assist analytical thinking and also act as an aide memoir for writing up at later stages. The habit of writing is crucial from the onset. Becoming familiar with the language of the chosen research field is also advised. Akin to strategies for the analysis of interview data, noting key terms and phrases that are commonly used in the supporting literature can help acclimatize the researcher to the field.

In the domain of education it is not unusual for research students to be 'insiders' in the sense that they are motivated by their experience as practitioners to investigate their own context and sometimes their own practice. It is not uncommon for students to conduct research in their place of work which raises some interesting ethical dilemmas and challenges. Invariably this involves 'wearing two hats' and negotiating contrasting roles and sets of values, one informed by professional training and principles, while the other is driven in large part by research evidence, theory and ethical values and principles (e.g. BERA, 2011). While inevitably there will be connections across these different knowledge bases, issues such as asking permission and securing informed consent, especially in relation to children and young people, require careful attention to ethical issues, including sensitivity towards existing power relations. Clearly, children and young people should be given opportunities to choose whether they wish to participate in research without pressure to do so, have access to enough information to make an informed decision and be aware of the fact that they can withdraw at any time without penalty. Such ethical standards are unlikely to translate seamlessly into the milieu of a busy school where relationships between teachers and children tend to be characterized by imbalances of power in most settings and circumstances. Brooks et al. (2014: 102) highlight the need for heightened awareness of ethical behaviour, especially if the research site is a place of work for the researcher: *teachers researching in their own schools need to ensure that their students or colleagues participate voluntarily.* Asking permission from children and colleagues as a high-status adult, such as a head teacher, requires skill and thoughtfulness and openness to nonverbal signals of young people.

Activity 4.2

Using the example of a researcher (i.e. a teacher or pupil) conducting a study in their own school, what issues might arise for the researcher who has high status within that institutional setting, in contrast to a researcher who has comparatively lower status (e.g. a pupil)?

Research questions and sampling

Becoming immersed in, and familiar with, the literature is the basic premise of formulating research questions. Accounts of their development however tend to be somewhat mysterious, a characterization which is rather unhelpful for a budding researcher. A basic question to ask is, 'What exactly do you hope to find out?' and the answer to this question can help generate initial questions. The most effective research questions tend to be straightforward, clearly articulated and unambiguous. In contrast, a surfeit of questions with a copious set of sub-questions can be risky in the sense that they can become a 'hostage to fortune' and may remain unanswered at the end of the project. Qualitative research design which is competently put together, carefully thought through and then well executed tends to produce multi-layered and complex findings. As a consequence keeping research questions simple and to the point can be advantageous. Agee (2009), one of the few researchers to devote a paper to research questions, highlights their dynamic and ongoing development:

> Good qualitative research questions are usually developed or refined in all stages of a reflexive and interactive inquiry journey.

(Agee, 2009: 432)

It is advisable, however, to strike a balance between open-endedness and responsiveness to issues arising over the course of the study, and the need for research questions to provide an overarching, guiding framework at the onset (Seale, 2004). Research questions, informed by the theoretical stance taken, frame the purpose of the study and can be likened to a 'coat hanger' on which the choice of research methods should hang comfortably. Given the interrelationship between theoretical framework, research questions and research design, it follows that they require revisiting at critical points in the study, for example, when developing schedules and topic guides, over the course of data analysis and write-up. Research questions may well be refined and adapted, particularly nearing the end of a study when it is possible to reflect on the research design, in conjunction with the findings with the benefit of hindsight.

In terms of sampling, research students can sometimes grapple with the idea that achieving representativeness is not, as a rule, the purpose of qualitative research. Developmental psychology as an important and influential way of understanding children, as well as a prominent discipline within Initial Teacher Education, may go some way to explaining this understanding of the purposes of qualitative research because it appears to be used as a defining comparator for understanding qualitative research design. There are, however, a range of 'non-probability sampling methods' (Bloor and Wood, 2006: 153) available to qualitative researchers and these commonly include purposive, snowball and theoretical sampling methods. Purposive sampling put simply has been described as 'the intentional selection of persons, settings, or documents thought to have something to contribute to the study' (Schwartz-Sheaf and Yanow, 2012: 87) while snowball sampling, as the term suggests, is where an initial contact with a person leads to another contact, which creates opportunities to link in with more extensive networks and willing participants.

Face-to-face interviewing and its variations

Qualitative interviewing has enjoyed a relatively long history across the interpretative research tradition (Denzin and Lincoln, 2005), and is a method widely used in a range of funded research programmes, either as a stand-alone technique, or as part of a multi-method approach. A wide variety of qualitative and interpretative informed studies adopt unstructured and semi-structured interviews. This reflects the importance of understanding the world view of participants through their eyes. Social constructionism, for example, as part of a theoretical framing for a study, would emphasize the importance of engaging with participants as a means of capturing and exploring their perceptions, beliefs and attitudes.

Face-to-face interviews, in particular, are a key method in qualitative research and they remain: *the dominant interview technique* (Opdenakker, 2006). They have been described as 'gold standard' and touchstone of qualitative research (Barbour, 2014), underlying the ongoing ascendency of the method. In keeping with core principles in the interpretivist tradition, knowledge is regarded as situated which underpins the qualitative researchers' understanding of the joint, co-production of meaning in the interview encounter. Who we are as people, our identity, whether we are 'insiders' or 'outsiders', are relevant because insider knowledge may help sidestep the building of rapport because good relationships are already in place. Our gender, age, race and sexuality are integral to how we engage with those we seek to understand. This is not only vital to how we interact with research participants but what is termed the 'positionality' of researchers shape what we see, how we are seen, and how we interpret what we see and hear in the field (Brooks et al., 2014). When I first started researching young children in nursery settings at that time I had my own preschool child and took for granted physical aspects of young children's behaviour such as a child sitting on my knee or putting their arms around me. Years later when carrying out research on gender and aggression in nursery playrooms (Brown, 2007), I was both surprised and charmed by children's behaviour, including being spontaneously kissed by young children. This demonstrated how my own awareness of young children and the assumptions I made about them was mediated by my gender and age, including my life stage.

One-to-one interviews are often invoked as a familiar and commonplace format in our present media culture. A high-profile example of 'doing an interview' is the combative, political style interview where interruption and pursuing questions with voracity are a feature of such encounters. This is the antipathy of what is understood as 'good' interview technique within the qualitative research tradition. More generally in the social sciences putting interviewees at ease and aiming to conduct the interview like a conversation are viewed as key to good interview technique (Lofland et al., 2006). As with acquiring numerous new skills, developing interview schedules is an aptitude that is built by experiential learning. It can also be enhanced by collaboration; by working as a member of a research team or, alternatively, sharing draft interview questions and the schedule with a trusted colleague.

Today the qualitative interview comes in many different guises. For instance, there is increasing interest in mobile interviews as a research tool and the walking interview has its origins in ethnography, although it is more focused and less opportunistic in approach (Edwards and Holland, 2013). In education, walking tours of school sites utilize the spatial context of the school in order to elicit the views of young people. Here young people have the opportunity to guide and lead the researcher around their school where they can be supported to tell their own story and identify significant places, artefacts on their own terms (see Mannion et al., 2015). This method aims to empower young people by facilitating control over the research encounter and encourage the expression of their thoughts and opinions which can be aided by the use of photographs or video recordings. The geography and material artefacts of the school can also serve as place-based trigger for spontaneous discussion. In a study of the way in which school design impacted on managing behaviour in schools (Brown, 2011), walking tours with pupils were revealing and I found out where pupils hid if they wanted to miss lessons (i.e. under stairwells off main corridors) and where teachers went to surreptitiously smoke in the school grounds (i.e. behind the bike sheds).

Other innovations have included interviews conducted by telephone, via the internet using Skype, facetime and email (La lacona et al., 2016). The ongoing development and potential of online communication open up new avenues of enquiry for researchers which transcend time and place. These methods sidestep the usual logistical challenges involved in arranging face-to-face interviews (La lacona et al., 2016). Moreover, they can also democratize the research process in the sense that they can help balance out power relations between the researcher and the researched because the discussion is mediated online. In terms of the future durability of qualitative interviewing, Edwards and Holland (2013: 94) reflect on the interview method and the fact that it must be responsive to contemporary developments and innovations. They conclude that it will need to adapt in order for qualitative interviews to be of continued relevance to young researchers.

Although regarded as a branch of qualitative interviewing, the purpose of focus groups diverges from that of the qualitative interview since focus group discussions are facilitated by a moderator whose role is to facilitate debate: *where the aim is to provide data (via the capture of group interaction) on group beliefs and group norms* (Bloor and Wood, 2006: 88). The argument made is that the demands of enabling focus group discussions is especially demanding and challenging requiring honed group work skills (Barbour, 2014). Wilson's (1997) earlier work in education summarizes the key components of this method comprehensively:

- a small group (4–12 people) who meet with a trained facilitator for up to 2 hours;
- discuss selected topic(s);
- in a non-threatening environment;
- explore participants' perceptions, attitudes, feelings, ideas;
- and encourage and utilize group interactions.

(Wilson, 1997: 211)

Gibbs (1997) observes that while focus groups are a type of group interview, there is a clear distinction between focus groups and groups interviews. While group interviewing, as the name suggests, involves interviewing a number of participants simultaneously in the same venue, focus groups aim to exploit the interaction generated within the group. Fern (1982) highlights the collective capacity of the method to harness group processes, *which attenuates the productivity of the group.* In their research with young people, Heary and Hennessy (2002) found that an advantage of this method was that it enabled them to explore shared and contradictory perspectives within the group context on a sensitive topic (i.e. sexuality). They found that the group context provided a supportive context for sharing experiences and promoting thoughtful discussions.

Representation and trustworthiness

Similar to the arguments made regarding well-executed research design which helps signal the competency of the researcher, parallel arguments are made about the trustworthiness of qualitative research findings. The idea that decision-making is transparent and fully explained, including strategies for the analysis of data, is key to this process (Barbour, 2014). With regard to the latter stage of analysis and write-up, here a developed sensibility towards the fair and balanced representation of the views of participants is important. In relation to this, Macfarlane (2009) raises the representational, as well as ethical, issues of concealment and exaggeration: *Determining how to analyse and represent 'findings' almost invariably involves a process of discrimination and selection* (MacFarlane, 2009: 99), adding that deciding what to include and what to exclude in the final write-up is a challenging decision for researchers. Clearly, 'trimming' information which contradicts, or presents alternative viewpoints to the general thrust of findings is unethical, as is exaggerating some findings at the expense of others. As Brook et al. (2014) observe, these outcomes are rarely the conscious intention of researchers. Some interviewees can be especially engaging and rewarding to interview. In such circumstances it is essential to be reflexive and alert to the potential influence of interactional dynamics produced in the interview encounter. Concealment, however, is a somewhat different notion in the sense it can be allied with researchers who hold a particular ideological or political position but their views remain implicit and hidden from those and the communities they research (MacFarlane, 2009). In the present risk-averse climate, it is likely that ethics committees in universities would look unfavourably on researchers withholding essential information given the fundamental ethical principle of securing informed consent from research participants.

With regard to some of the standard devices for gauging the trustworthiness of findings, triangulation is often raised as check, especially in the write-up in Ph.D. research in the field of education. Ironically, the term 'triangulation' originates from land surveying and its measurement which is somewhat out of kilter with the principles of qualitative research. Denzin argues that it is desirable to use methodological triangulation, 'Because each method reveals different aspects of empirical reality' (Denzin, 1978: 28). This may be workable if the study is well planned and tightly justified but if one method is weak or subsidiary to other methods, the benefits of triangulation would certainly be limited (Bloor and Wood, 2006). An alternative viewpoint is posited from an interpretative perspective some of which prefer the term 'intertextuality', suggesting that triangulation with its associations to the hard sciences should be abandoned (Schwartz-Sheaf and Yanow, 2012). Intertextuality, however, is used in a similar way to methodological triangulation because including a range of sources of information, including texts, interviews and observational data, as well as different kinds of reports and accounts, is advocated (Schwartz-Sheaf and Yanow, 2012: 88), although the underlying philosophical assumptions made and theoretical positioning differ markedly. From an interpretivist stance, contrasting and contradictory interpretations are to be expected and are viewed as integral to the epistemological stance taken, given the existence of a single 'truth' is rejected. Indeed this is regarded as a significant critique of realist identifiers of quality because it is at odds with a qualitative approach (O'Reilly and Kiyimba, 2015). A qualitative approach works with, rather than against, divergent positions and opinions that constitute social reality, at any given time.

Activity 4.3

A student carried out an ethnographically informed study in a primary school. The focus was inclusionary practice from different perspectives, that is, teachers, support assistants and children. School policies were also analysed. What might be the pros and cons of using 'triangulation' as opposed to 'intertextuality' for supporting the trustworthiness of findings in this particular project?

Conclusions

This chapter focused on critical points in the process of undertaking a qualitative approach and thinking through research design. Reference is made to the importance of theoretical positioning and its influence on research decisions as part of building research design.

Chapter key points

- Two main methods have been used here as exemplars of qualitative data collection techniques. Interviews were chosen as the accepted hallmark of qualitative research design, in addition to the focus group method because they are often used together in educational research, especially in health education, with teachers and children.
- The key argument made in this chapter was that well-thought-through and honed qualitative research design is the overarching framework and basis for a competently executed and ethically informed study.

Recommended reading

Bloor, M., & Wood, F. (2006). *Keywords in Qualitative Methods a Vocabulary of Research Concepts*. London: Sage.
This is a useful reference resource which identifies and explains key words and concepts in qualitative research design from the perspective of a medical sociologist.

Brooks, R., Te Riele, K., & Maguire, M. (2014). *Ethics and Research in Education*. London: Sage.
This is a comprehensive text for those working in education and carefully considers ethics of research from the onset of a project, through to the design stage, analysis of data and dissemination phases. Helpful illustrative examples are used throughout.

Schwartz-Shea, P., & Yanow, D. (2012). *Interpretative Research Design – Concepts and Processes*. London: Routledge.
An accessible and engaging text which sets out the key tenets of interpretative research design and the reasoning behind this position.

Advanced reading

O'Reilly, M., & Kiyimba, N. (2015). *Advanced Qualitative Research: A Guide to Using Theory*. London: Sage.
This text addresses the connections between theory and research design and offers advice and tips for using theory in qualitative research.

5

Theoretical Grounding in Case Study Research

Lorna Hamilton and Dimitra Tsakalou

Key points

- Case study as research genre.
- Studying a particularity.
- Conceptualizing the case and defining the case.
- Strength of multiple case studies and multiple sites.
- Need for rigorous and transparent research practices with ontological and epistemological positioning as part of this robust process.

Introduction

In this chapter, we are concentrating on case study research design and, in particular, the use of multiple case study use. Drawing on our own work on case study, we want to clarify how we have positioned ourselves theoretically and conceptually as we have begun to explore the lived world of our research participants.

Our focus on case study as a valuable genre in educational research reflects both our own strengths in that area and the increasing preponderance of case study use in research projects more generally within the field (Periera and Valance, 2006; Yazan, 2015). Case study is the study of the particularity and complexity of a single case or set of cases in order to understand its activity within significant circumstances and the interactions between its contexts (Stake, 1995). Additionally, a case study is a form of social science inquiry that investigates a complex phenomenon in-depth and within its real-life context (Seale, 2007; Young, 2008; Yin, 2014). However, one of the criticisms of such educational research is that the choice of case study can be made unthinkingly and mechanistically as a means of organizing a research project rather than doing so in a meaningful and rigorous way. Case study should be a meaningful choice of what is to be studied, requiring an understanding of similar cases but also the nature of the examined case alone (Stake, 1995).

Another criticism is that the single case study may provide rich individual contextualized material without a theoretical grounding or a hope of generalizability. In return, case study proponents would argue that the richness of the individual case may lead to powerful resonances for other institutions, courses, individuals etc. (Thomas, 2011; Hamilton and Corbett-Whittier, 2013). Additionally, the use of multiple case studies can lead to new conceptualizations of case study (Bartlett and Vavrus, 2017) through a critical engagement with issues of power within a sociocultural lens. Thus, case study research does not attempt to draw on a random sample but a meaningful choice of case exhibiting, for example, particular characteristics or, in the use of multiple case studies, showing contrasting or complementary characteristics.

Importantly, the quality of the genre can be supported by rigorous and transparent research processes. Yet the often a-theoretical nature of much-reported case study work, we would argue, undermines the claim to rigorous methods, transparency and quality by focusing on a mechanistic and technical accounting rather than ensuring sound underpinning of the research in coherent and consistent theoretical frames. In our work, we have focused on ensuring a strong theoretical underpinning for case study use but we have also found strength in the use of more than one case study allowing us to identify particular types of case study profile and the scope for strong comparisons and broader insights. In the next section, space is given to the sometimes-perplexing forms and purposes of case study and the need for careful interrogation of the choices on offer.

Conceptualizing the case

Key to adopting a case study approach is making critical judgements about the varied messages from diverse authors that may hold competing or sometimes contradictory information (Stake, 1995; Yin, 2003; Seal et al., 2007; Merriam, 1998; Hamilton and Corbett-Whittier, 2013; Punch and Oancea, 2014). Additionally, the authors may also reflect in their advice a particular outlook on ontology and epistemology that affects the suggestions made. An example of this is Robert Yin (2014), one of the early writers about case study research in 1983, who has developed highly respected contemporary texts with advice on case study. Interestingly, he reflects, at times, a post-positivist stance, we believe, especially when talking about bias and validity in case study use, but other authors may believe that he is mainly representing an interpretive or constructivist stance in other aspects of his work (Baxter and Jack, 2008). A post-positivist stance would entail looking for not the absolute truth, but instead a close approximation of 'truth' while someone taking an interpretivist stance might suggest that the world is socially constructed and so meaning is found in social interactions, beliefs and attitudes not in some abstract notion of truth. Thomas (2011) suggests that interpretive work supposes a deep understanding and immersion in the context of the subject under exploration. This may be true to some extent but the practicalities of research, especially doctoral research, mean that such an immersion may be aspirational rather than achievable.

In contrast to Yin (2003), Robert Stake (1995, 2000) talks of the art of case study, emphasizing the dynamics and complexity of a single case or small set of cases in order to understand its activity within significant circumstances and the interactions within and across its contexts (Stake, 1995).

When choosing your theoretical positioning, each author presents different ways of delineating the various kinds of case study you might choose to do. Yin (2003) suggests that there are three main types of case study – exploratory, descriptive and explanatory – reflecting the possible purposes of case study research. We would argue that for us, the most worthwhile case studies in education research are likely to draw on two or three of these during research – a purely descriptive case study would be tremendously limited in what it can say or offer to education research audiences.

Stake (2006) distinguishes among intrinsic, instrumental and multiple or collective case studies. Intrinsic case studies involve research into a particular situation for its own sake, notwithstanding outside concerns, while instrumental case studies explore the impact of both inside and outside variables and influences on one or more situations. An instrumental case study, then, is concerned with an issue, aspect or concern about the case rather than the case in its entirety. Stake (1995) also acknowledges multiple or collective case studies and further encourages us to think about the kind of case study being sought.

Hamilton and Corbett-Whittier (2013) expand on these ideas and present suggested ways of identifying and building multiple cases, while Merriam (1988) creates further subdivisions of case study underpinned by diverse disciplines. Determining the case or cases that a new researcher might wish to undertake, then, requires a careful perusal of the suggestions made by the varied authors mentioned and consideration given to the purpose of the case, the qualities of the case itself and an understanding of the potential permeable boundaries and contextual influences on the case or cases to be studied. A key part of this decision-making process will involve engagement with the ideas underpinning the researcher's theoretical positioning.

Activity 5.1

If you were to use Yin as your main reference in support of your chosen research approach – (Case study):
  a) Consider the differences there might be if taking a post-positivist or constructivist stance to inform decision-making.
  b) If you could adapt elements of Yin's work, combining with writing by Stake (1995) or Merriam (1988) or Hamilton and Corbett-Whittier (2013), how would you begin to build a coherent case definition and purpose?

Robert Stake views case study as an art, requiring thoughtful consideration of nuances and subtleties in thinking and design (Stake, 1995). He characterizes case study as providing a sophistication of understanding (Stake, 2006) rather than a transformation. This provides researchers with a much more complex engagement with the world he/she is engaged with. He highlights the different ways in which we should evaluate and value the ideas that can emerge from case study by removing it from the domain of quantitative positivist research measurements of validity and reliability and statistical generalizability. Lincoln and Guba (1985) engage with other more appropriate terms for evaluating qualitative case studies when they use the terms 'trustworthiness' and 'dependability' in place of 'validity' and 'reliability' (see also Hamilton and Corbett-Whittier, 2013 for ways to enhance trustworthiness and dependability). In doing so, the researcher moves away from positivist language and towards terms that reflect a more constructivist notion of value and quality.

Merriam (1988) highlights the diverse disciplines which can underpin case studies and also gives her own account of the various ways in which case study might be conceptualized (e.g. particularistic, descriptive or heuristic). Not to be outdone, Hamilton and Corbett-Whittier (2013) outline different forms that case study might take within education research (reflexive, longitudinal, cumulative, collective or collaborative) and acknowledge that each new researcher coming to case study needs to establish clearly the ideas which frame the study as well as the different ways in which case studies from diverse individuals may combine to create different kinds of multiple case studies.

So one of the most important decisions to be made is to do with the type of case study you wish to use, but in order for this to be a meaningful and robust decision, there needs to be both an understanding of the theoretical positioning being taken as well as the purpose and scope of the studies. This process of defining the nature and purpose of your case study is essential but just as important is the relationship between the case and the wider world and the influences and issues that may arise. One of the most popular definitions of a case involves viewing it as a 'bounded unit' but this can be used by some researchers to mean that the case is viewed as limited by boundaries despite acknowledgement of the positioning of the case within a real-life context.

In Dimitra's doctoral study, three secondary schools were examined as case studies as they were bounded units, each having its own functional regulations and approach towards inclusion, influencing and leading its decisions related to school structures, while also being affected by external influences such as the sociocultural context and international and national policies (Adelman et al., 1980: 49). From our perspective, the 'boundary' between the 'bounded unit' and the world is a permeable boundary allowing influences and issues to flow between the case and the world it inhabits. The permeable boundaries between the case and the contextual narratives of policy pressures, of community hopes and fears and of economic distress embed the case more deeply in the myriad influences and issues that may in turn affect perceptions and decisions within the case study school itself (see Figure 5.1).

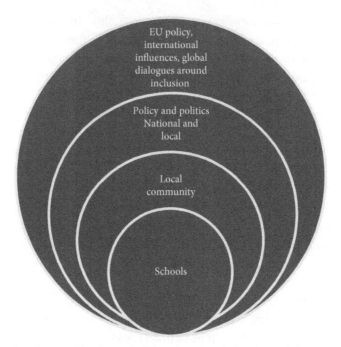

Figure 5.1 Permeable boundaries of case (school) and its contextual narratives, influences 'coming in' and 'going out' of school (taken from Tsakalou, 2014)

Use of multiple case studies

We do encourage the use of multiple case studies as a means of generating opportunities for robust comparison across cases, often in diverse contexts, for this can support a more strategic use of case study. For example, Dimitra was interested in the ways in which different kinds of schools might construct inclusive communities in light of a European and then national initiatives to introduce inclusive practices in state schools (Tsakalou, 2014). She chose schools with different characteristics (see Table 5.1) giving her the opportunity to create new insights through comparative case studies (CCSs) but also as a means of extending the possible ways in which such comparisons might allow for an extension of the 'fuzzy generalisations' espoused by Michael Bassey (1999). By this term, he describes the insights about educational action that arise from case study research and suggests that 'fuzzy generalisation' allows the researcher to replace the certainty of scientific generalization ('x in y circumstances results in z') by the uncertainty,

Table 5.1 Overview of three case study schools (adapted from Tsakalou, 2014)

School name and type – each case study school reflects distinct approaches to inclusion policy	Class(es)
Parthenon mainstream-inclusive Separate provision in integration units for students with Additional Support Needs but within the buildings of the mainstream school	Integration units (grade 7, 13–14 years old) Inclusive classroom/integration units (grade 9, 15–16 years old)
Acropolis Special school Segregated provision apart from mainstream schools but inclusive of a wide range of additional support needs young people	Special classroom (grades 7 and 9, 13–18 years old)
Caryatids Mainstream school with no specific provision for additional support needs	Mainstream classrooms (grades 7 and 9, 13–16 years old)

or fuzziness, of statements that contain qualifiers (Bassey, 1999). According to Bassey (1999), multiple case design should be preferred over single case design, primarily because it provides readers and researchers with the possibility of replication, while encouraging them to a new understanding of their own context and processes.

Example 5.1 (Tsakalou, 2014)

The strength of case study research is located in the collection of rich and in-depth data. Using multiple instrumental cases provided Dimitra's study with a deep understanding of the complexity of inclusive education in different types of schools that were also interrelated with sociopolitical and historical contexts (Stake, 2010). Thus, the use of a multiple case study design in this study contributed to achieving a richer experience and understanding of the phenomenon better than from consideration of just one single case (Merriam, 2001). In addition, according to Stake (1995) and Bassey (1999), the use of multiple cases encourages a new understanding of each context and processes. Hence, this current research created three different case studies to 'offer a means of investigating complex social units consisting of multiple variables of potential importance in understanding the phenomenon' (Merriam, 2001: 84). During this study, Dimitra gained insights into a specific educational context, examining inclusive education. Through this interpretive, instrumental approach, Dimitra also gained insight into the construction of inclusive communities, by examining the multiple realities and different conceptualizations, perceptions, decisions, practices and relationships of key school stakeholders (Pring, 2004; Silverman, 2010). As previously discussed, interpretive inquiry requires a particular approach to research questions, involving deep understanding and immersion in the context of the subject under examination (Thomas, 2011). It involves engagement with the perceptions and practices of participants in order to encourage reflection and to reach valid conclusions. It was used to enhance not only the quality of the research instruments but also my own reflexivity as a researcher.

Activity 5.2

Having chosen an issue or concern that you want to investigate within a case, identify the distinctive case profiles you might want to use and justify your choices.

Increasingly, researchers are being seen to build on multiple case studies (Periera and Valance, 2006; Stake, 2006) in order to further legitimize the value of case study as a means of deepening our understanding while at the same time supporting a broader range of contexts and profiles and thus challenging the criticism that case study may provide depth but is lacking in influence on any other case. The need for a rigorous accounting of research processes is usual in case study, but we also need to look to a deeper understanding and new conceptualizations of case study which draw on ontological and epistemological positioning as essential to the conduct of meaningful case studies (Hamilton and Corbett-Whittier, 2013).

Subjectivities

In research, there is a strong emphasis nowadays on the subjectivities of the researcher and the need to make these explicit as part of the transparency of the research process. As part of this reflexivity, it is also important to establish self-knowledge with regard to the ideas and principles which are informing researcher thinking. The stances that we take are such a significant part of research, informing key decisions about the research design including who participates and how we can understand them and their contexts. In doing this, we have been affected both by the research carried out by others in our field, but also by the various texts which discuss theoretical positioning. Having clarity over this aspect of our work helps to root it firmly in relation to particular views of knowledge and how that knowledge can be captured and understood. Yet, many people face problems at this stage as they find that many methods texts seem to use the same terminology in slightly different ways or can even contradict the clear understanding the researcher had thought he/she had reached earlier. Our advice would be to look at the range of ideas to ascertain the overlaps and inconsistencies and then determine which are appropriate for you, combining ideas at times from different perspectives, if it can be logically justified. Crotty (1998) and Stake (1995; 2006) are particularly helpful when trying to understand and build your theoretical stance. Stake (1995) provides a clear and robust framework of cross-case and multiple-case analysis, in order to develop cross-case 'assertions', made about the 'quintain' (inclusive education in our research), through an interpretive process so as to obtain evidence from case studies regarding the uniformity or inconsistencies that characterizes the final conclusions (Stake, 2006).

Our own work is placed firmly within the interpretivist paradigm. As the interpretivist paradigm asks us to explore and understand 'the subjective world of human experience as an insider', through the examination of conceptualizations, perceptions, practices, experiences and the relations of the school stakeholders. This places us within a paradigm which accepts the subjectivity of the research process and seeks to understand individual experiences in the world rather than focusing on the truth or near truth of positivist and post-positivist paradigms (see Chapter 3). Thus, we, as interpretive researchers, understand the particular meaning of the processes and experiences that constitute the knowledge to be gained from an inductive mode of inquiry, as to understand the subjective world within which people operate (Crotty, 1998). For the purposes of Dimitra's study, educational needs and inclusion were not perceived and understood as objects and universal truths, but rather as a deep social matter involving the interpretation of research participants, their historical and sociocultural context, and issues of power in Greek society (Larochelle et al., 1998; Burr, 2004). We use a small table to illustrate the different levels of thinking and decision-making which form part of our process.

Activity 5.3

Using these headings consider what you might put down as your own theoretical positions and think about how this might affect your methodology and methods.

A review of educational theorists provides what can be a bewildering array of theoretical positions as well as their post- and post-post versions (e.g. modernism, postmodernism and post-postmodernism). There is no one right answer and you may find yourself struggling with your own positioning and the question of where you 'fit'. Yet, you do not need to 'fit' in with a particular position; instead you can explore and determine your own place while also drawing on aspects of more than one position (see Table 5.2). For example, we both take a social constructionist perspective to our research but increasingly we have borrowed from critical theory and thus our work is concerned with social constructionism with a critical edge. This theoretical perspective focuses on the construction of social phenomena, acceptance of

Table 5.2 Possible paradigm positioning

Paradigm positioning	Interpretivist
Nature of the world	Socially constructed; influenced by critical theory
Conceptual frame Mid-level theory	Narrative identity theory
Methodology	Ethnography
Genre	Case study

Method
Multiple modes of data collection
  from diverse participants
	Group interviews, individual interviews,
	  shadowing and classroom observations
	Video
	Images/creation of images
	Photography

knowledge and reality as socially constructed and actively (re)produced by human beliefs, perspectives, actions and relationships (Parker, 1998; Lincoln and Guba, 2000; Reeves, 2009; Creswell, 2013). As noted by Crotty (1998: 42):

> [A]ll knowledge, and therefore all meaningful reality as such, is contingent upon human practices, being constructed in and out of interaction between human beings and their world, and developed and transmitted within an essentially social context.

In the social constructionist view, human beliefs are constructed through social interaction and exposure to sociocultural norms. They are also considered highly context-dependent, as no object can be adequately described in isolation from the conscious being experiencing it (Pring, 2004; Stake, 2006, 2010). Thus, from our constructionist perspective, meaning and truth cannot be described as simply objective or subjective. Critical theory emphasizes the need for action in order to bring about change or transformation and argues that research should always show an awareness of the power differentials that come into play. The importance of the latter theory's engagement with issues of critique and awareness of power imbalance have become increasingly significant as we delve into institutions (secondary schools) and the individuals who inhabit them and bring to life the interactions and interrelationships within them. Hence, a socially constructed reality is one that is seen as an ongoing, dynamic process, and inclusion emerges through a dynamic telling and retelling of school stakeholder narratives, based on lived experiences that are reproduced by means of acting on their interpretation and their knowledge of it, along with dialectic interaction with society at the time. For example, the nature of relationships both inside and outside Dimitra's case study schools – including the power, voice and agency of head teachers, teachers and parents – were found to be a key component in the construction of inclusive school communities. Educational policy making in Greece is characterized by unequal formal and informal power relationships (Liasidou, 2011); this inequality was found to impact both on decisions made about school structures, and the relationships developed within schools. More specifically, in this study, head teachers, as school leaders, held the greater share of power and authority within each case school surveyed. As there was an unequal distribution of authority from head teachers to both teachers and parents, or a flexibility to be taken according to each of the head teachers' will, in the school with the more inclusive structures, even as a special setting, the head teacher was found to have closer relations with authorities and an active involvement with the politics of education.

Additionally, collaboration between school stakeholders and communities – or the lack thereof – was found to have profound implications for school leadership and decision-making (Avissar, 2012). Indeed, the lack of shared ownership in decision-making and problem-solving processes was found to result from a failure on the part of all stakeholders to establish collaborative rapport. The contribution of teachers and parents in the construction of inclusive school communities was found to be particularly limited, as they were largely voiceless and powerless in decision-making and problem-solving processes. Although both groups of stakeholders believed in their power to change the educational system, their role was limited; indeed, they often expressed feeling sidelined, marginalized and unable to engage other stakeholders and authorities. New spaces for cooperation and partnership, as well as a renewed sense of agency, are therefore needed to resist dominant ideologies and traditional, authoritative systems of leadership in Greek secondary education.

On the other hand, if we were looking in particular at certain female- or male-dominated environments, we might explore feminism and masculinities to add an understanding of these specialist theories and how they might help us to use our critical social constructionism more meaningfully in these specific contexts.

Activity 5.4

Case study framing

In a study focusing on ways in which case study schools built or attempted to build inclusive communities, the following research questions were initially created. These reflect a simple social constructionist stance. How might you change or adapt these questions as a result of taking a social constructionist stance with a critical edge?

1. What are the key policies in relation to inclusive practices in education in Greece and what challenges/issues are there?
2. What is the nature of the perceptions of disability, special educational needs and the inclusive education policy process among the stakeholders involved (policy agents, head teachers, special/mainstream teachers, learning support teachers and parents)?
3. What are the key influences upon stakeholders' constructions of inclusion?

As stated above, we are going to concentrate here on a form of critical social constructionism in this chapter as the foundation for our research and will delve into how these theoretical positions have coloured the decisions being made about research design. However, later, we will also engage with a reconceptualization of multiple case study research design through a specific sociocultural lens as explored by Bartlett and Vavrus (2017).

For our most recent research, three case study schools were chosen, each typifying a particular form of organizational response to inclusion. Within each case, observations, interviews and documentary analysis played a key role in trying to understand the experiences and perceptions of key individuals' parents and teachers. Parents, it was thought, would reflect a more passive role as the government and teachers were thought to have the greater explicit power over organizations and decisions within the school and sometimes beyond. If we were to refine this work with the critical edge required by critical theory the nature of any power imbalance would need to be addressed and those most likely to be at the bottom of any power imbalance or sharing would be likely to be the young people themselves.

Consequently, we would have to revisit key participants and consider the importance of young people's voice in this process. Yet there are existing subtle power plays at work within groups as teachers may sometimes feel that they have little agency within the school. Dimitra noted:

> Another interesting statement made by Andrea (literature teacher) asserted that 'teachers do have a voice, but the people above them are deaf'. In other words, teachers remained excluded from the collective decision-making within school, while their perceptions and voices were not heard if they differed from those of the head teacher. (Tsakalou, 2014: 123)
>
> Teachers don't have the voice or the power to influence the education process. Their role is side-lined. I don't think that teachers are being heard, the same as parents. They have just voice and power in matters within school. Our voices are marginalised. (Jane, maths teacher)

Reflection point

What, if anything, could be done to bring about action with regard to the inequalities and power imbalances present in the case study schools? Does this create ethical issues for the researcher?

If we take this study which has used a critically insightful social constructionist stance and we add a conceptual framework (narrative identity theory), we can begin to use this mid-level theory to further refine the kind of data that will be most helpful in carrying out the research and it will situate participants in a particular position. The focus of the study then would be on the way in which narrative identity is used to create a new conceptualization of institutional identity. This is a way into understanding the different narratives which have helped to capture the complex nature of inclusion within the three institutions explored during the project.

In this theory, the individual is seen as having a complex and dynamic identity made up of a web of narratives. Specifically, this means that there is a weaving of stories told and retold by individuals, narrating past, present and future selves as part of a web of narratives. These narratives might include stories of family, culture, community and nation as well as bigger meta-narratives such as inclusion (Hamilton, 2015). Hence, this provides a web of interlocutions in which some strands or narratives hold greater importance at different times for each individual.

Applying narrative identity to case study schools, three narrative strands emerged through the narratives of school stakeholders, including:

1   *The conceptualizations of inclusion* of school members: head teachers, teachers and parents that influenced their decisions and approaches to school structures;
2   Their *decisions about the implementation of inclusive policy through school structures* linked to school purpose, strategies, access and teaching and learning provision;
3   and their understanding of *issues of Power, voice and agency* – present or absent – between school stakeholders along with the key relationships within and out – with schools such as local community, policy agents, policy makers and other schools.

Now, the multifaceted narratives of the case schools were captured through these strands and led to three different kinds of inclusion: surface, segregated and deep inclusion, as school narratives responded differently to three key strands.

This section has engaged with a particular research study and has highlighted shifting and evolving stances taken. Moving on from this very particular and individual accounting of theoretical positioning in relation to research we will look at work by Bartlett and Vavrus who have taken the idea of multiple case studies to generate a frame for CCS method.

Comparative case study (CCS)

Although the single case still provides rich insights and in-depth appreciation of an issue, increasingly we see researchers building multiple case studies in different ways (see Hamilton and Corbett-Whittier, 2013). When multiple case studies are involved, there is an even stronger imperative to ground the studies theoretically so that a sound cross-case comparison can be critically analysed. Bartlett and Vavrus (2017) take forward a strong reconceptualization of multiple case studies through the use of a critical CCS approach. The critical comparative case study approach embraces the existing notion of case comparisons but roots them very firmly in ontological and epistemological thinking and by doing so provides a highly interesting theory-based entity which helps to shape the possible participants, the kinds of data collection as well as the subtleties and nuances of power and inequity in the language used, whether in policy documents or interview transcripts. If we look firstly at the theoretical underpinnings for this approach, it can be seen that it acknowledges many existing aspects of case study – a strong awareness of the importance of context and comparison as part of a rich meaning-making activity – while also establishing a robust engagement with the many cultures and sub-cultures in which participants are embedded. They argue that it is necessary to engage with CCS, taking account of new ways of thinking in the social sciences more generally about spatiality, culture and policy within diverse contexts.

> They talk of policy as practice and suggest that in taking a sociocultural approach they understand policy as: a deeply political process of cultural production engaged in and shaped by social actors in disparate locations who assert incongruent amounts of influence over the design, implementation and evaluation of policy.

They advocate moving away from traditional case study notions of what they call static culture where meaning is sought within. Instead, they characterize meaning making as occurring across periods of time in diverse contexts and always within the influence of power and inequality and involving people beyond traditional notions of boundary. Likewise with the term 'context', Bartlett and Vavrus (2017) suggest that we rely too much on a restrictive, and again static, idea of context and they highlight the various influences of macro and meso levels of economic, social and political discourses. This echoes the earlier part of our chapter where the building of our ontological and epistemological positionings and conceptual framework helped us to engage critically with boundaries and influence, power imbalances and essentialist and non-essentialist cultural stories related to both current and historical aspects of now. It is then possible to generate your own theoretical and conceptual framing while acknowledging many of the ideas proposed by Bartlett and Vavrus (2017) but you might find that there is a very powerful reason for taking a very carefully and well-argued and conceptually robust model such as the CCS one as a formative foundation for case study work. Certainly, the authors present CCS as distinct from traditional approaches to case study and their work delves into reconceptualizing key ideas of culture, context and comparison. They argue that traditional case study views these ideas as static and that they do not acknowledge the myriad influences on them, thus denying the dynamic and nuanced aspects of each. This use of a rich, critical sociocultural lens which acknowledges power inequalities, power relations and social activities and interactions as fluid, dynamic and influenced by social and political and historical narratives leads them into looking beyond vertical comparison and towards vertical, horizontal and transversal axis (op cit see for an in-depth accounting of the ways that these three axes can and should be used in research and how looking across all three we can enhance CCS).

Conclusions

This chapter has explored the ways in which theoretical positioning helps to root a research project firmly within a strong but dynamic foundation, leading into a more coherent and robust research design and data analysis. The need for this kind of positioning becomes even more important when a researcher introduces multiple cases and attempts to ensure coherent design and analysis. We would argue that case study may be more successfully used to affect policy and practice when careful consideration is given to the theoretical lens being employed.

Chapter key points

- Each new project involves the researcher in redefining the nature and purpose of the case but it is important to revisit and critically engage with theoretical positions.
- Know your own placement within these diverse ideas and consider how different foundational positions might colour your decisions about case study.
- Ensure clear justification for your theoretical position and use it to reinforce the coherence of your research design.
- Visit and reflect on the ways of dealing with multiple case studies. An excellent example is the critical comparative case study approach outlined by Bartlett and Vavrus (2017). Its theoretical grounding is clearly established and illustrates effectively how to establish a sound theoretical base for case study work.

Recommended reading

Bartlett, L., & Vavrus, F. (2017). *Rethinking Case Study Research: A Comparative Approach*. London: Routledge.
A new text, this book establishes keen insights into comparative case study while engaging with a theoretical framing which adds to the quality of research design.

Bassey, M. (1999). *Case Study Research in Educational Settings*. Buckingham: Open University Press.
Bassey is particular helpful for exploring the nature of fuzzy generalization and its use in case study.

Crotty, M. (1998). *The Foundations of Social Research: Meaning and Perspective in the Research Process*. London: Sage.
A very accessible and thoughtful text that leads the researcher carefully through theoretical positioning.

Stake, R. E. (1995). *The Art of Case Study Research*. Thousand Oaks, CA: Sage.
Highly accessible and insightful read providing a good introduction to case study.

Advanced reading

Pring, R. (2004). *Philosophy of Educational Research*. London: Continuum.
Helpful reading for those wanting to delve more deeply into the philosophy of
   education.

Stake, R. E. (2006). *Multiple Case Study Analysis*. London: The Guilford Press.
A helpful text for those embarking on multiple case studies, especially as the
   analytical process can be particularly challenging.

Part III

Building Mixed-Methods Research Designs

Mixed-Methods Research: Achieving a Robust Design

Fiona O'Hanlon

Key points

- 'Mixed-methods research' is a broad term that can refer to the integration of qualitative and quantitative elements of research at several 'levels' (Biesta, 2010a: 99) – including the levels of data, method and research design.
- Mixed-methods research positions the researcher as an 'artful craftsperson' (Greene, 2007: 16) or as a 'connoisseur of methods' (Teddlie and Tashakkori, 2010: 8), who creates the most appropriate research design for the problem or issue in question.
- The novice researcher requires a knowledge of key aspects of debate and development within the field of mixed-methods research – the 'what, when, why and how' of mixed methods.

Introduction

Mixed-methods research, at its most simple, involves the collection, analysis and combined use of both quantitative and qualitative data to address a research problem within a single study or a series of studies. Miles and Huberman (1984: 15) defined quantitative data as that based on numbers, and qualitative data as that based on words, while others focus on other qualities of the data, for example, whether it is 'closed-ended' or 'open-ended' (Johnston and Turner, 2003: 299). Creswell (2015: 2) defines mixed-methods research as:

> an approach to research in the social, behavioural and health sciences in which the investigator gathers both quantitative (closed-ended) and qualitative (open-ended) data, integrates the two, and then draws interpretations based on the combined strengths of both sets of data to understand research problems.

Such a definition is a useful starting point, as it serves to illustrate two key points about mixed-methods research:

i. mixed-methods research requires at least one qualitative and one quantitative dataset.
ii. mixed-methods research involves the 'integration' or mixing of the qualitative and quantitative data.

Studies which involve the use of multiple qualitative *or* multiple quantitative datasets or approaches are therefore examples of 'multi-method', rather than 'mixed-methods' research (Teddlie and Tashakkori, 2003; Creswell, 2015).[1]

Mixed-methods and research design

Mixed-methods research may form part of other research designs, such as case-study design, quasi-experimental design, ethnography or action research (Coffey and Atkinson, 1996; Sandelowski, 1996; Reason and Bradbury, 2001; Luck et al., 2006), or may form part of a distinctly mixed-methods research design (Creswell and Plano Clark, 2011; Johnston and Christensen, 2014). The choice between a mixed-methods design and a mixed-methods approach embedded within another research design depends on the 'logic of enquiry' (Hedges, 2012) of the research – that is to say, the conceptual, theoretical and methodological framing of the study. Hedges (2012) notes that decisions about the logic of enquiry for a particular research problem will be shaped both by the discipline or 'intellectual traditions' in which the researcher is working and by the researcher's own conceptualization of the research problem, which is shaped by the researcher's experiences, values and beliefs.

---

[1]For more information on multi-method approaches, see Hesse-Biber and Johnson (2015).

Mixed-methods research – achieving a robust research design

This chapter aims to support your reflection on the logic of enquiry that will underpin your own mixed-methods research – whether you choose a 'mixed-methods design' or choose to use mixed methods within another research design. The chapter will first summarize key aspects of debate and development within the field – the 'what, why, when and how of mixed methods research' – and will then focus on key considerations and processes when planning a research design involving the collection and integration of both quantitative and qualitative data within education.

What is mixed-methods research?

In the introduction it has been stated that mixed-methods research, at its simplest, involves the collection, analysis and interpretation of both quantitative and qualitative data to investigate a particular phenomenon or research problem. This definition, which focuses on the use and integration of qualitative and qualitative data at a 'methods' level, emerged in what Tashakkori and Teddlie (1998: 15) would classify as the 'first stage' of the evolution of mixed research, from about the 1960s to 1980s. They note that wider discussions about the purposes, practices and possibilities of empirical research during this period – debates widely known as the 'paradigm wars' – facilitated such a movement from 'monomethod' to 'mixed-methods' research.

At their core, the 'paradigm wars' involved debates about the relationship between philosophy (epistemology, ontology) and practice (methodology, methods) within empirical research (for summary, see: Johnson and Onwuegbuzie, 2004). The debates were significant in the development of mixed-methods research, as they resulted in a move away from a purist paradigmatic approach – which argued there to be a suite of characteristics (from philosophy to method) associated with qualitative and with quantitative research, and for the two paradigms to be 'incompatible' due to incommensurable underlying beliefs about the nature of knowledge and of reality (Lincoln and Guba, 1985; Smith and Heshusius, 1986). Rather, there emerged a move towards consideration of how qualitative and quantitative methods could be used in a 'compatible' way to address research problems

(Reichardt and Cook, 1979; Bryman, 1988; Howe, 1988), with Reichardt and Rallis (1994: 85) calling for a 'new partnership' between 'qualitative and quantitative inquiries'.

The explosion of interest and work in the field of mixed-methods research in the attempt to explore the possibilities of pragmatically combining qualitative and quantitative approaches led to what Tashakkori and Teddlie (1998: 16) call the 'second stage' of the evolution of mixed research. Emerging around the 1990s, this involved 'moving away from the consideration of distinctions [between qualitative and qualitative approaches] in *method alone* to the consideration of distinctions in all phases of the research process' (1998: 16), for example, when framing the research problem or when engaged in study design. Early studies which mixed qualitative and quantitative elements at the methodological level were variously termed 'mixed model' studies (Tashakkori and Teddlie, 1998), 'methodological hybrids' (Bryman, 1988) or 'mixed-methodology design' (Patton, 1990; Creswell, 1995) to distinguish them from 'mixed-methods' studies that mixed only at the level of methods. Johnson and Onwuegbuzie (2004: 20) summarized the distinction when they noted there to be 'two major types of mixed methods research: mixed model (mixing qualitative and quantitative approaches within or across the stages of the research process) and mixed-method (the inclusion of a quantitative phase and a qualitative phase in an overall research study)'.

However – and significantly for our understanding of what 'mixed-methods' research is – such terminological distinctions have waned over time, with 'mixed-methods' research becoming an umbrella term for studies that integrate quantitative and qualitative elements at the level of data, method or more extensively, for example, in the research objective, methodology and/or worldview. This was acknowledged in the editorial to the first issue of the *Journal of Mixed Methods Research* in January 2007, when Tashakkori and Creswell noted that such a 'broad' definition of 'mixed-methods' research had been adopted for the journal 'as an effort to be as inclusive as possible' to those contributing to the field (2007: 4). Johnston et al. (2007: 118), following Greene (2006), note that what this means in practice is that the term 'methods' in 'mixed-methods research' should now also be interpreted 'broadly', encompassing consideration of the mixing of qualitative and quantitative elements at the level of methods, methodology and research design, and also encompassing 'related philosophical issues (e.g. ontology, epistemology, axiology)'. Such breadth is reflected in Johnston et al.'s 'general definition' of mixed-methods research, which emerged from analysis of definitions provided by twenty-one leading researchers in the field (2007: 119–20).

Why choose mixed-methods research?

Biesta (2012: 147) argues that mixed-methods research should be considered for a study if having both quantitative and qualitative data would provide a 'more accurate and adequate understanding' of the research problem in question than would have been possible with the use of quantitative or qualitative data alone. The criteria for the use of mixed methods here thus relate to their contribution to a *particular* research problem or research question(s) within a *specific* research context, a position supported by several other mixed-methods theorists (Tashakkori and Teddlie, 1998; Bryman, 2008; Symonds and Gorard, 2010; Creswell and Plano Clark, 2011; Hesse-Biber, 2015). Frameworks which outline the possible rationales for using mixed methods include those of Greene et al. (1989), who identified five purposes – triangulation, complementarity, development, expansion and initiation (Table 6.1), – and Bryman (2006), who identified sixteen.

Table 6.1 Purposes of using mixed-methods research (adapted from Greene et al., 1989)

Triangulation	Data derived from qualitative and quantitative methods are compared to test the consistency of findings produced. Aims to increase validity of findings by counteracting method or inquirer bias.
Complementarity	The complementary strengths of qualitative and quantitative methods (e.g. depth and breadth, inductive and deductive approaches) are used to clarify and illustrate results. Using both qualitative and quantitative approaches is believed to counteract 'weakness' or 'bias' in each method, and thus to increase the validity of study constructs and results.
Development	Use of one method to inform the use of the other method. For example, use of qualitative interviews to identify variables for inclusion into a quantitative survey, or use of a survey to identify participants for a qualitative follow-up study.
Expansion	Aims to expand the scope (depth or breadth) of the study through the use of both qualitative and quantitative data.
Initiation	Uses qualitative and quantitative methods as different lenses for examining a research problem – looking for contradictions, and the stimulation of new thinking.

Considering which rationale(s) underpin the choice of mixed methods for your study provides a *justification* for their use, which Bryman (2008) notes to be a crucial element of rigour when presenting mixed-methods research. Identifying the purposes of using mixed-methods approaches in your study also helps to inform decisions about the choice of research design (see pp.116–20).

What can be mixed, when and how?

It was noted earlier that mixed-methods research involves the combination of elements of qualitative and quantitative approaches - for example 'qualitative and quantitative viewpoints, data collection, analysis, inference techniques' (Johnson et al., 2007:123). However, Biesta (2012: 148) notes that such broad definitions do not make it sufficiently clear for the novice researcher 'what one is actually trying to mix and combine', and what types of mixing are possible. Biesta (2010a) explored this issue in detail, considering the possibilities for mixing qualitative and quantitative approaches at the levels of: (i) data, (ii) methods, (iii) design, (iv) epistemology, (v) ontology, (vi) purposes of research (e.g. to explain or to understand) and (vii) practical roles of research. Biesta (2010a, 2012) noted combining qualitative and quantitative approaches at the levels of data, methods and even research design to be relatively unproblematic. However, he challenged the notion that one can combine 'qualitative and quantitative viewpoints', that is to say, to mix at the levels of epistemology and ontology. Biesta (2010a: 102) notes:

> within the context of mixed methods research, the question is not *whether* it is possible to combine different epistemological assumptions or positions – this is obviously not possible. The question rather is *which* epistemological beliefs one wishes to use for the design and justification of one's research.

The mixed-methods researcher must thus identify a philosophical stance in relation to their research design, and must make decisions about when and how to mix qualitative and quantitative elements within their study. Key options regarding such philosophical positioning, and core considerations when combining qualitative and quantitative methods and data, will be outlined below.

Philosophical framing of mixed-methods studies

The literature on the philosophical underpinnings of mixed-methods research is vast and complex, and is often still entwined in the long-standing debates relating to paradigms – in which epistemological positions of positivism and interpretivism are respectively associated with quantitative and qualitative methodological approaches, methods and data types (Platt, 1986).[2] The philosophical framing of a mixed-methods study depends on a researcher's view of the relationship of epistemology and method (see Chapter 1), and on their position on whether it is the researcher's worldview, or the research design, that guides the philosophical assumptions underpinning a mixed-methods study. Creswell and Plano Clark (2011: 43) identify two main options in relation to framing mixed-methods research: (i) to use a single worldview or (ii) to draw on multiple worldviews. They argue that the choice of a single or multiple worldview can be guided either by researcher preference (selecting the approach that best fits with a researcher's epistemological, ontological and axiological positions) or by the research design. We will explore each of these options in turn.

Researcher stance: A single worldview

Within the mixed-methods literature, pragmatism and the transformative approach are the most frequently cited perspectives in discussions of 'single worldviews' that can underpin mixed-methods research.[3] The core components of these perspectives will be briefly outlined below. The philosophy of pragmatism is associated with a pluralistic ontological position (that is to say, reality is multiple and complex) and an epistemology which

---

[2]Niglas (2010) notes that, although the paradigmatic view advocated by Guba and Lincoln (2005) has now extended to five paradigms – positivism, post-positivism, critical theory, constructivism and participatory – there is still believed to be incommensurability between the epistemological and ontological assumptions underpinning those based on positivist epistemologies (positivism and post-positivism) and those based on interpretivist epistemologies (critical theory, constructivism, participatory).

[3]Realism is also emerging as a 'single worldview' philosophical stance for mixed-methods research (see Maxwell and Mittapalli, 2010; Hall, 2013a; Pawson and Tilley, 1997).

believes that building knowledge involves 'interactions' or 'transactions' with the environment (Dewey, 1929). Following Charles Sanders Pierce (1893), pragmatism advocates an anti-dualistic ontological stance of 'synechism' – that is to say, viewing the world in terms of continua, rather than binaries (Johnson and Gray, 2010), and following John Dewey (1929), emphasizes the importance of context in research, and the effectiveness of an intervention in solving, or furthering understanding of, a problem. In practice, a pragmatic approach eschews any paradigmatic divisions between qualitative and quantitative research and rather focuses on selecting the most appropriate methods from the 'quantitative-mixed-qualitative continuum' (Teddlie and Tashakkori, 2009: 28) for the planned research intervention to address the research question(s). The aim is to make justifiable conclusions, what Dewey would call 'warranted assertions', from the study in relation to the research environment. Mixed-methods methodologists who frame work within pragmatism include Tashakkori and Teddlie (1998, 2003), Johnson and Onwuegbuzie (2004), Morgan (2007), Denscombe (2008), Teddlie and Tashakkori (2009), Feilzer (2010) and Johnson and Gray (2010).[4] Some of these authors would argue mixed-methods research to be a 'third … research paradigm' (Johnston et al., 2007: 112), associated with pragmatism (see also Johnston and Onwuegbuzie, 2004; Denscombe, 2008). However, Biesta (2010a) outlines his views on the possibilities and limitations of pragmatism as 'the' philosophical framework for mixed-methods research. The 'transformative' perspective has also been suggested as a philosophical framework for mixed-methods research (Mertens et al., 2010, Mertens, 2012). Research conducted within this framework is focused on issues of social justice, and this axiological (values) dimension permeates the ontological, epistemological and methodological approaches in the study. A 'transformative' mixed-methods study typically starts with a qualitative approach to create a collaborative dialogue between the researchers and the community and is supplemented with quantitative approaches where this would take the social justice agenda forwards in the particular research context (Mertens, 2012).

---

[4]Johnson et al. (2007: 125) concord with the definition of pragmatism outlined above – what they would call the 'pragmatism of the middle' – but note there to be different versions of pragmatism to suit other mixed-methods researchers' philosophical stances: a 'pragmatism of the right' (Rescher, 2000; Putnam, 2002) for those who have a strong form of realism and a weak form of pluralism (broadly associated with positivism), and a 'pragmatism of the left' (Rorty in Brandom, 2000; Maxcy, 2003) for those whose position accords more closely with antirealism and strong pluralism (broadly associated with interpretivism).

Researcher stance: Multiple worldviews

This position involves a researcher drawing on *multiple* worldviews within a mixed-methods study, a stance associated with the work of Greene and Caracelli (1997, 2003), and developed by Greene (2007). This position is premised on the idea that 'differences between philosophical paradigms or logics of justification for social scientific inquiry not only exist but are important' (Greene and Caracelli, 1997: 8). The multiple worldview stance involves the mixed-methods researcher 'honouring' the philosophical assumptions 'regarding reality, knowledge, methodology and values' (Greene, 2007: 69) of each approach used in the study (e.g. interpretivism and post-positivism), and engaging with the evidence and insights produced by these different approaches in a dialogic or 'dialectical' manner in order to create 'enhanced understandings … perspectives and meanings' (2007: 8). Greene (2007) notes that a researcher's dialectical engagement with difference can occur at the levels of philosophy, theory, methods and values in mixed-methods research. She reflects that, within the dialectical approach, the researcher engages with:

> a plurality of philosophical paradigms, theoretical assumptions, methodological traditions, data gathering and analysis techniques, and personalized understandings and value commitments … patiently weaving and reweaving them into a meaningful pattern and a practically viable blueprint for generating better understanding of the social phenomenon being investigated. (Greene, 2007: 16–17)

Greene and Caracelli (1997: 10) note that the aim of mixing methods in the dialectical stance is to 'understand more fully by generating new insights', while the aim of mixing methods in the pragmatic stance is to 'understanding more fully by being situationally responsive and relevant'. Greene and Hall (2010) outline the implications of a researcher adopting a philosophical stance based on pragmatism, and one based on dialectics, to mixed-methods research in practice, while Mertens (2012) does so in relation to the transformative worldview.

Research design: Single or multiple worldviews

However, Creswell and Plano Clark (2011: 45) argue that the philosophical framing for mixed-methods research should 'relate to the type of mixed methods *design* used, rather than [to] a worldview based on how the researcher attempts to "know" the social world'. They argue that an approach based on a single worldview is appropriate for mixed-methods designs in which the qualitative and quantitative components are conducted concurrently (where they recommend pragmatism), for mixed-methods studies in which the transformative framework is employed (where they recommend a social justice approach), or in instances in which qualitative or quantitative data are employed to enhance a 'traditional' quantitative or qualitative research design (where they recommend using the worldview of the primary design). For example, an experimental quantitative study supplemented with a qualitative component may be framed within a post-positivist worldview, while a case study with a quantitative component may be framed within a constructivist worldview. Creswell and Plano Clark (2011) recommend the use of multiple philosophical positions in mixed-methods studies in which the quantitative and qualitative components are conducted sequentially – with different worldviews for each phase.

Reflecting upon the philosophical assumptions which underpin your mixed-methods research project is a key element of designing justifiable, rigorous mixed-methods research, as Hall (2013b: 15) notes that such philosophical assumptions inform what counts as 'credible' evidence in mixed-methods studies. Creswell and Plano Clark (2011: 38) also advise that researchers make their philosophical assumptions explicit in their mixed-methods project.

Research design for mixed-methods studies

The literature on research designs involving mixed methods is extensive, with Tashakkori and Teddlie (2010: 815) reflecting that 'design typology is perhaps the most explored area of mixed methods and at the same time the most confusing aspect of it'. Tashakkori and Teddlie (2003) noted that two key sources of such confusion are (i) the multiplicity of terms used to classify designs involving mixed methods and (ii) the different criteria by which various authors classify such designs. Natasi et al. (2010) provide a summary of the field, and draw a key distinction between 'the classification of mixed methods designs on the basis of the manner in which qualitative and quantitative *methods or data* are incorporated' and 'the classification of designs according to the *stage or stages* [of the research process] at which mixing occurs' (2010: 315, 317). In this section, the key options for mixing qualitative and quantitative elements at the methods and data levels will be outlined, as these are fundamental considerations for all research involving mixed methods (whether these form part of a mixed-methods design or are embedded within another research design). A consideration of options for mixing qualitative and quantitative elements at other stages of the research process will be presented in the final section, as part of a discussion about constructing robust and internally coherent mixed-methods research designs.

Creswell and Plano Clark (2007) identified three main dimensions for consideration when designing research involving mixed methods: (i) the *timing* of the implementation of quantitative and qualitative approaches, (ii) the relative *priority* of the quantitative and qualitative approaches within the study and (iii) the point(s) at which the quantitative and qualitative data will be *mixed* or integrated within the study.

(i) Timing

For 'basic' mixed-methods research – that is to say research involving only one quantitative and one qualitative phase – there are two key options with regard to the timing of the quantitative and qualitative data collection and analysis: concurrent or sequential.[5] Concurrent mixed-methods studies are those in which the qualitative and quantitative phases of data collection occur in parallel, broadly over the same time period (Teddlie and Tashakkori, 2009). Sequential mixed-methods studies, on the other hand, are those in which the researcher conducts one phase of data collection and analysis (e.g. quantitative) before conducting the second phase using the other approach (e.g. qualitative). Concurrent studies are typically used when the quantitative and qualitative approaches provide complementary information that will enable a more complete, or a more accurate, account of the phenomenon of interest. Sequential studies are typically used when the results of one method are required to inform the content or conduct of the research with the second method (see Creswell and Plano Clark, 2011: 85–86; Teddlie and Tashakkori, 2009: ch.7).

(ii) Priority

There are three possible options with regard to the relative priority of quantitative and qualitative elements within mixed-methods studies: equal

---

[5]Studies which contain more than two phases are called 'multiphase designs' (see Creswell and Plano Clark, 2011).

priority, quantitative priority (where qualitative methods have a supporting role) or qualitative priority (where quantitative methods have a supporting role). The mixed-methods literature has developed notation to reflect these key dimensions of timing and priority (Morse, 2003), with + representing a concurrent design and → representing a sequential design. Priority of elements is reflected in the use of upper or lower case letters, for example, QUAN → qual would represent a sequential study in which the quantitative element had priority, and in which the qualitative element played a supporting role. Square brackets are used to represent embedded designs - where one element has priority at the level of design, and the other element is embedded within this. For example, QUAN [qual] may represent an experimental study with an embedded qualitative component, while QUAL [quan] may represent an ethnography with an embedded quantitative component.

(iii) Stage(s) of mixing/integration

Finally, the researcher must decide when and how to mix or integrate the quantitative and qualitative data from their study. With regard to 'when' to integrate quantitative and qualitative data, Morse and Niehaus (2016: 56) argue that there are only two points in mixed-methods research that such integration can occur: (i) at the analysis stage, and (ii) at the stage of the discussion and interpretation of results. Morse and Niehaus (2016: 56) term the point of the combined use of the quantitative and qualitative datasets the 'point of interface', and note that the datasets are kept separate until this point.[6] In practice, Bazeley (2009) argues that *all* mixed-methods research involves integration of quantitative and qualitative data at the stage of discussion and inferences, noting that 'mixed methods research involves, as a minimum, integrating conclusions that are drawn from various [qualitative and quantitative] strands in the research'. In addition, *some* mixed-methods research also integrates quantitative and qualitative data at the analysis stage. With regard to 'how' to integrate qualitative and quantitative data, a suite of techniques exist for integrating qualitative and quantitative data at the analysis stage in mixed-methods research. The most frequently used of these are displayed in Table 6.2. Bazeley (2010) provides an overview of how these data analysis strategies can be conducted in practice, using data-analysis

---

[6]Thus, in mixed-methods studies that integrate data *only* at the inferential stage (discussion, conclusions), the quantitative data are analysed using quantitative methods and the qualitative data are analysed using qualitative methods (Greene, 2007).

Table 6.2 Mixed-methods data analysis strategies

Data analysis strategy	Description
Data transformation	This involves the transformation of qualitative data into quantitative data ('quantizing') or the transformation of quantitative data into qualitative data ('qualitizing') so that both can be analysed together. For example, quantitative data can be used to profile respondents, and this data can be converted to narrative form, and compared with in-depth interview data from the respondents.
Data consolidation	This involves merging qualitative and quantitative data to create *new quantitative or qualitative variables*. For example, Onwuegbuzie and Teddlie (2003) cite the creation of a new quantitative variable 'family attitudes to school ethos', constructed from data from a 5-point Likert scale questionnaire of students, and data from parental interviews that had been quantized using the same 5-point scale.
Typology development	This involves using the results from the analysis of one form of data to inform the analysis of the other form of data. The analysis of the first data type produces a set of substantive categories (i.e. a typology) which is then used to analyse the other data type. The typology could be categories of themes or categories of respondents, for example.
Data comparison	This involves the comparison of qualitative and quantitative data to identify patterns or meta-inferences. For example, matrices could be used to compare a theme identified in interview data (teacher confidence in teaching maths) by respondent group (1–5 years' experience, 6–10 years' experience, 11+ years' experience).

software such as NVivo and SPSS.[7] To integrate at the inferential stage, Johnson and Christensen (2014: 614) recommend data comparison, in which the analysed findings of the two datasets are compared, and data integration – in which the qualitative and quantitative findings are 'synthesized' (Creswell and Plano Clark, 2011: 67) or 'woven' (Greene, 2007: 17) into a coherent whole.[8] The decision on the point of integration of your

---

[7]For more detail on mixed-methods analysis, see Caracelli and Greene (1993), Onwuegbuzie and Teddlie (2003), Onwuegbuzie and Dickinson (2008).

[8]For further guidance on making inferences from mixed-methods studies, see Greene (2007), Chapter 9.

quantitative and qualitative data – whether at the stage of inferences only, or within analysis and inferences – relates to the purpose(s) of your research, and the types of evidence required to answer your research question(s). Woolley (2009: 7) notes that the researcher should aim to integrate the qualitative and quantitative data in a way that is 'mutually illuminating, thereby producing findings that are greater than the sum of the parts'.

The three dimensions of timing, priority and stage(s) of integration here outlined result in eight possible combinations which form the basis of the typology of four basic (two-phase) research designs involving mixed methods outlined in Table 6.3[9].

Table 6.3 Two-phase mixed-methods research designs

Timing	Priority	Mixing (of datasets)	Summary of the research design
Concurrent	Equal	Inferences only	QUAN + QUAL or QUAL + QUAN
		Analysis & inferences	
	Unequal	Inferences only	QUAN + qual or QUAL + quan
		Analysis & inferences	QUAN (qual) or QUAL (quan)
Sequential	Equal	Inferences only	QUAL → QUAN or
		Analysis & inferences	QUAN → QUAL
	Unequal	Inferences only	QUAN → qual or QUAL → quan
		Analysis & inferences	qual → QUAN or quan → QUAL

Examples of two frequently used types of mixed-methods studies in education (Ivankova and Kawamura, 2010) – the concurrent, equal status design and the sequential, qualitative dominant design – are outlined in the online materials that accompany this book.

The first example is a concurrent equal status study which integrates qualitative and quantitative elements at the stages of analysis and inferences, whilst the second example is a sequential, qualitative dominant design, which mixes datasets at the stage of inferences only (refer Examples 6.1 and 6.2 in online materials).

---

[9] Studies which contain more than two phases are called 'multiphase designs' (see Creswell and Plano Clark, 2011).

> ## Activity 6.1
>
> Consider both examples and reflect on how you could use or adapt the approaches taken for your own research

Designing mixed-methods research in education: key considerations

So far in this chapter, we have considered what mixed-methods research is, why you might like to use it and what can be mixed, when and how (in relation to methods and data). Throughout this discussion, we have noted that the suitability of the use of mixed methods, and of a particular research design, is assessed in relation to a *particular* research problem or research question(s) within a *specific* research context. In this final section, the steps involved in designing and conducting a mixed-methods research project will be outlined, using the three phases of research, as conceptualized by Tashakkori and Teddlie (2003), as the organizing principle. These three phases are: (i) the conceptualization phase, (ii) the experiential phase and (iii) the inferential phase. Within this, the different *stages* of research at which qualitative and quantitative elements can be mixed – which Natasi et al. (2010) noted to be an alternative way to classify mixed-methods research designs – will be outlined (see Table 6.4). However, the key focus will be on how to develop a coherent, robust and justifiable research design that fulfils the core quality criteria of mixed-methods research.[10]

Phase I: The conceptualization phase

The 'conceptualization phase' of research constitutes the thinking and processes involved in developing your research questions (Tashakkori and Teddlie, 2003). It involves three key stages of the empirical research process as identified by Natasi et al. (2010, Table 6.4): (i) conducting a literature review of existing theory, research, practice and policy, (ii)

---

[10] For an overview of the key quality criteria for mixed-methods research see O' Cathain, 2010.

Table 6.4 The mixed-methods research process: stages of potential integration of qualitative and quantitative strands[a]

Phase of research (Tashakkori & Teddlie, 2003)	Stages of the research process at which mixing of quantitative and qualitative strands can occur (Natasi et al. 2010)			
	Stage number	Quantitative Strand		Qualitative Strand
Conceptualisation Phase	1	Theory, Research, Practice/Policy	⟷	Theory, Research, Practice/Policy
	2	Worldview	⟷	Worldview
	3	Purpose/Question	⟷	Purpose/Question
Experiential Phase	4	Sampling	⟷	Sampling
	5	Data collection	⟷	Data collection
	6	Data analysis	⟷	Data analysis
Inferential Phase	7	Data inference	⟷	Data inference
	8	Inference quality	⟷	Inference quality
	9	Data representation	⟷	Data representation
	10	Application	⟷	Application

[a]Although presented in a linear fashion for the purposes of the diagram, in practice research design is an iterative process, and there would be interaction across the stages and phases (Ridenour and Newman, 2008; Natasi et al., 2010).

thinking about the worldview(s) that will be used to frame the research and (iii) specifying the research purpose and research questions. Several theorists have underlined the crucial importance of the first two stages within the conceptualization phase to the validity of mixed-methods research (Dellinger and Leech, 2007; O' Cathain, 2010; Collins et al., 2012; Hesse-Biber, 2015). These theorists focus on the importance of the researcher reflecting upon, and outlining, the philosophical stance that will frame their study, and the values, beliefs and experiences that have influenced their research interests. Greene (2008: 13) notes such a process of researcher reflection to encompass a consideration of ontology, epistemology and axiology (values and theoretical commitments), as well as a consideration of the influence of academic reading, previous disciplinary and methodological training, practical experience in the area of research interest and personal characteristics (e.g. socio-economic status).[11] Collins et al. (2012: 854) underline the importance of 'philosophical clarity' to evaluating the validity of mixed-methods research, while Dellinger and Leech (2007: 323) note the importance of knowledge of researchers' prior practical, theoretical and academic understanding of the phenomena under study to construct validity. Indeed, Preissle et al. (2015: 152) argue that such researcher reflexivity is an 'ethical practice in and of itself' within mixed-methods research as 'it specifies researchers' relationships with participants, and, as a corollary, to the data and the research.'

Other theorists have underlined the importance of the third stage of the conceptualization phase to the design of quality mixed-methods studies (Onwuegbuzie and Leech, 2006; Ridenour and Newman, 2008; Biesta, 2012). This stage involves the identification of the research purpose – defined as the 'primary intent, objectives and goals for the study' (Plano Clark and Badiee, 2010: 276) – and the specification of the research questions. For mixed-methods studies, Onwuegbuzie and Leech (2006) recommend that researchers also identify the purpose(s) for mixing qualitative and quantitative approaches [see Greene et al. (1989), Table 6.1] at this stage, as they note that both content and methodological objectives inform the development of appropriate mixed-methods research questions. Indeed, Creswell and Plano Clark (2011: 167) recommend the specification of separate content and method research questions for mixed-methods studies, with the methods research question 'directing and foreshadowing how and why the strands will be mixed' (see Activity 6.2, p.124).

---

[11]For guidance on options for the philosophical framing of mixed-methods studies, see pp. 113–16.

Activity 6.2: Developing your method research question

Identify the purpose(s) for using mixed methods in your study (see Table 6.1) and reflect on the proposed relationship between the quantitative and qualitative strands of your study with regard to priority, timing and mixing. Use this to formulate the method research question for your study.

- For example, an equal-status concurrent research study which aims for triangulation may pose the question, 'to what extent are the quantitative and qualitative results consistent with one another?'
- A sequential QUAN → qual study which aims for complementarity and expansion may ask, 'in what ways do the qualitative data help to illustrate and explain the quantitative results?'

Phase II: The experiential phase

The 'experiential phase' of research constitutes the thinking and processes involved in designing and conducting your research (Tashakkori and Teddlie, 2003). It involves three key stages of the mixed-methods research process as identified by Natasi et al. (2010, Table 6.4): (i) sampling, (ii) data collection and (iii) analysis. Mixed-methods theorists have underlined two key elements that a researcher should be mindful of when designing and conducting a mixed-methods study – design quality (Bryman, 2008; Teddlie and Tashakkori, 2009) and feasibility (Niglas, 2009; Creswell and Plano Clark, 2011; Johnson and Christensen, 2014). The issue of feasibility relates primarily to the time-intensive nature of conducting and analysing mixed-methods research. Thus, the scale and scope of your proposed study should be considered in relation to the time available, amending the research purpose, questions and design if necessary. With regard to design quality, Teddlie and Tashakkori (2009: 301) identified four criteria against which the design and conduct of mixed-methods research may be evaluated: (i) design suitability, (ii) design adequacy, (iii) within design consistency and (iv) analytic adequacy. These criteria respectively assess (i) the extent to which the research design is appropriate for the research questions, (ii) the quality of research conduct, (iii) the coherence of the research design and (iv) the extent to which the analytic procedures enable the research questions to be addressed. These criteria are necessarily broad due to the 'methodological eclecticism' (Tashakkori and Teddlie, 2010) inherent in mixed-methods research, which means that there are no 'typical' approaches in mixed research (Biesta, 2012: 149). Rather, it is up to the researcher to consider which sampling, data collection and analysis procedures are most suitable for the purpose, design and conceptual (philosophical and theoretical) considerations of their study (Bryman, 2008). It is this that results in a mixed-methods researcher being conceptualized as an 'artful craftsperson' (Greene, 2007: 16) or a 'connoisseur of methods' (Teddlie and Tashakkori, 2010: 8). However, key guidance is available. With regard to sampling, Creswell and Plano Clark (2011) advise consideration of (i) who will be included in the qualitative and quantitative samples, (ii) the size of the samples and (iii) how the participants will be recruited, with these considered in relation to the quality criteria for qualitative and quantitative research, and in relation to the purpose(s) of the mixed-methods study (see Table 6.1). For example, in a sequential QUAN → qual study which aims to use the qualitative data to expand on aspects of the quantitative findings, a smaller sample of the same participant group would typically be used. In relation to data collection, Greene (2008: 166) advises adhering to 'the quality criteria and procedures of the tradition in which the method is being implemented … for warranting the quality of method and the data obtained', an approach which is supported by Tashakkori and Teddlie (2008) and Morse and Niehaus (2016). Key mixed-methods analysis procedures were outlined in Table 6.2.

Phase III: The inferential phase

The 'inferential phase' of research involves developing theories or explanations from your research by means of the interpretation of data (Tashakkori and Teddlie, 2003). It relates to four stages of the mixed-methods research process identified by Natasi et al. (2010, Table 6.4): (i) data inference, (ii) inference quality, (iii) data representation and (iv) application. The first two stages relate to the processes of deriving conclusions from mixed-methods research (e.g. through data comparison or data integration [pp.119–20]), while the last two stages relate to the presentation of study results (in a thesis, academic paper or presentation), and their impact on theory, knowledge, policy or practice. Teddlie and Tashakkori (2009) argue 'interpretative rigour' to be the key aspect of quality when drawing inferences from a mixed-methods study. Interpretative rigour is defined as the 'degree to which credible interpretations have been made on the basis of obtained results' (2009: 303), and is evaluated against six criteria: (i) interpretative consistency, (ii) theoretical consistency, (iii) interpretative agreement, (iv) interpretative distinctiveness, (v) integrative efficiency and (vi) interpretative correspondence. The first four criteria pertain to all inferences you make from your research (whether from the qualitative data, quantitative data or from both) and respectively relate to the extent to which your interpretations are consistent with (i) the data, (ii) current theory and knowledge, (iii) what other researchers would be likely to interpret from the data and (iv) good researcher conduct (that is to say, that the inferences are plausible and defensible). The final two criteria relate to meta-inferences, defined by Teddlie and Tashakkori (2009: 152) as 'a conclusion generated through an integration of the inferences that have been obtained from the qualitative and quantitative strands of a mixed-methods study'. 'Integrative efficiency' considers the extent to which the qualitative and quantitative inferences have been effectively synthesized into a meta-narrative which makes 'meaningful conclusions', while 'interpretative correspondence' holistically considers the extent to which the inferences from the research enable the research questions to be answered, and the purpose(s) of using a mixed-methods research design (see Table 6.1) to be fulfilled. Self-assessment against these six criteria involves critical reflection on the ways in which your inferences have been derived from the data – a key aspect of ensuring that conclusions are valid or 'warranted' (Dewey, 1929) within the pragmatic stance – and also involves consideration of the study's contribution to knowledge, theory, policy or practice. Such reflection on the contribution of the study underpins the 'presentation' and 'application' stages of research.

Designing mixed-methods research in education: Achieving a rigorous, coherent design

The previous section has outlined the key considerations in designing and conducting mixed-methods educational research in practice. Within this, the importance of a strong 'inquiry logic' – that is to say, having 'coherence and connection' across all levels of your research project, between the conceptual and theoretical framing, research purposes and questions, research design and conduct, presentation and impact – has been emphasized (Greene, 2008: 9). The importance of rigour in mixed-methods research design and conduct has also been underlined, with the mixed-methods researcher

---

Activity 6.3: The 'armchair walkthrough' (Morse, 1999)

Take time to think through your proposed study from start to finish. Think about your research purpose – that is to say, the aims or objectives of your study – and what personal or academic factors prompted your interest in this topic. Reflect on your research questions, and your proposed philosophical, theoretical and methodological approach. Consider whether your proposed approach will enable you to collect relevant data from a sufficient number of respondents in an ethical manner, and if your plans for analysis and presentation of findings will enable you to effectively address your research questions and make a valuable contribution to knowledge, policy direction or practice. A pilot study may provide a useful opportunity to evaluate questions that arise from such an 'armchair walkthrough'.

---

required to ensure approaches to sampling, data collection, analysis and interpretation meet relevant qualitative, quantitative or mixed-methods quality criteria. Morse (1999, 2003) recommends that a researcher conduct an 'armchair walkthrough' when planning a mixed-methods study, in which the researcher thinks through all aspects of their proposed project, to ensure such coherence and rigour.

Conclusions

This chapter has provided an overview of mixed-methods research, and has outlined the key conceptual, theoretical and methodological considerations when designing mixed-methods research within education.

Chapter key points

- Considers key aspects of the 'pluralism and diversity at all levels of the research enterprise – from the more conceptual dimensions, to the more empirical ones' (Teddlie and Tashakkori, 2010: 9), which characterize mixed-methods research.
- Underlines the challenges and opportunities that such diversity offers the researcher during the research design process.
- Discusses key frameworks for research design, analysis and quality criteria for mixed-methods research.
- Provides the means to evaluate the suitability of mixed-methods approaches for early career researchers designing and conducting empirical research projects in education.

Recommended reading

Creswell, J. & Plano Clark, V. L. (2011). *Designing and Conducting Mixed Methods Research*, 2nd edn. Thousand Oaks, CA: Sage.
Creswell & Plano Clark provide practical advice on designing and conducting mixed-methods research. The book provides in-depth advice and examples in relation to six key mixed-methods designs: convergent parallel, explanatory sequential, exploratory sequential, embedded, transformative and multi-phase.

Greene, J. C. (2007). *Mixed Methods in Social Inquiry*. San Francisco, NJ: John Wiley & Sons.
An accessible book which covers all elements of mixed-methods research design and practice. Chapters 8 and 9 provide excellent overviews of mixed-methods data analysis and of quality in mixed-methods research.

Onwuegbuzie, A. J. & Leech, N. L. (2006). Linking Research Questions to Mixed Methods Data Analysis Procedures. *The Qualitative Report*, 11(3): 474–498.
A practical guide to developing and writing research questions for mixed-methods research, with advice on identifying mixed-methods data analysis procedures appropriate to your research questions and research design.

Advanced reading

Biesta, G. (2010). Pragmatism and the Philosophical Foundations of Mixed Methods Research, in A. Tashakkori & C. Teddlie (eds), *SAGE Handbook of Mixed Methods in Social and Behavioral Research*, 2nd edn, 95–117. Thousand Oaks, CA: Sage.
Biesta critically evaluates the contribution of pragmatism as a philosophical basis for mixed-methods research. The article also critically considers the extent to which it is possible to 'mix' quantitative and qualitative elements at seven different 'levels' of the research process.

Hesse-Biber, S. (2015). 'Mixed Methods Research: The "Thingness" Problem. *Qualitative Health Research*, 25(6): 775–788.
Hesse-Biber critically evaluates mixed-methods research from the perspectives of design, philosophy and practice.

Tashakkori, A. & Teddlie, C. (eds) (2010). *SAGE Handbook of Mixed Methods in Social and Behavioural Research*, 2nd edn. Thousand Oaks, CA: Sage.
A seminal edited volume, which encompasses conceptual, methodological and practical issues in mixed-methods research. Chapter 1 provides an overview of core characteristics of mixed-methods research, and also outlines key issues and challenges in contemporary mixed-methods research.

Web links

An Overview of Mixed Methods Research – Nora Jacobson, University of Wisconsin
http://videos.med.wisc.edu/videos/33600
An open-access lecture which provides an in-depth overview of the what, why and how of mixed-methods research.

William T. Grant Foundation Mixed Methods Resources
http://wtgrantmixedmethods.com
A collaboration with the University of California, Los Angeles. Provides mixed-methods resources, key readings (with an annotated bibliography) and links to other mixed-methods websites.

7

International and Comparative Research Design

Ellen Boeren

Key points

- Comparative education research is interested in learning through comparison, but can equally start from different ontological and epistemological preferences.
- Variable-oriented approaches to comparative research usually focus on large N studies interested in establishing an objective truth and generalizable results.
- Case-oriented approaches to comparative research usually focus on small N studies interested in understanding complexity and in-depth interpretations.
- Selection of countries in small N studies can be carried out through engagement with Most Similar Systems Designs and Most Different Systems Designs.
- Bereday's comparative method distinguishes between four analytical steps: (1) description, (2) interpretation, (3) juxtaposition and (4) comparison.

Introduction

This chapter introduces the reader to methodological approaches to comparative research in the field of education. It starts by introducing the main purposes of comparative education and draws upon core literature discussing major research streams and models as discussed within the international scholarly field, especially focusing on the different epistemological debates, linking back to the positioning of positivism and constructivism and/or interpretivism as discussed earlier in this book. Advice will be formulated on how to sample, collect and analyse data when adopting a comparative methodology, distinguishing between quantitative and qualitative comparative methodologies, both of which are being used in comparative educational research.

Comparative education research: Why is it important?

Comparing a range of educational aspects between countries, schools or students is often present in research. Comparative research is important as it gives both scholars and policy makers evidence of ideas and practices used in other countries with the aim to engage in a learning process on how to improve education practices and policies in the own context (see e.g. Phillips and Ochs, 2003; Raffe, 2011). Policy makers want their countries to do well on international education-related rankings and international organizations like the OECD (Organisation for Economic Cooperation and Development), UNESCO (United Nations Educational, Scientific and Cultural Organization) and the World Bank are behind several comparative research initiatives, the most well-known example being the large PISA (Programme for International Student Assessment) test organized every three years by the OECD. The field of comparative education also aims to increase knowledge on research-related techniques available to students and scholars undertaking comparative research, for example, to be better able to compare educational practices in different countries.

However, many postgraduate students and current academics have never received explicit training in how to compare different groups. Chapters on comparative methods are often absent from methodological textbooks.

As such, this chapter aims to expand insights on methodological aspects relevant to comparative education that are too often ignored or taken for granted.

Comparative versus international research

The idea of doing international and comparative research in the field of education is not new although earlier approaches were less systematic and mainly based on informal evidence gathered by those visiting other countries (see e.g. Bereday, 1964; Noah and Eckstein, 1969; Bray et al., 2014). While some encyclopaedic work in describing differences in educational systems across the world has been introduced around 1900, it was not until recently that the field of comparative research entered discussions on aspects like 'ontological beliefs' (della Porta, 2008: 202) and 'epistemological preferences' (della Porta, 2008: 198).

Before going into detail on how to design a comparative research project, it is important to explain that not all comparative education is automatically international in nature; for example, researchers who investigate a number of different schools in one town engage in a comparative inquiry, but do not undertake an international comparison. Comparative education has been defined as the 'theory and method of comparative inquiry', and is therefore strongly related to the research methodological side of the discussion; international education has been discussed in relation to 'domains of practice' and does often draw on comparative research (see Phillips and Schweisfurth, 2007: 10). As there is generally a strong focus within comparative education on comparing between countries, it could be argued the field is mostly international in nature. Therefore, examples exploring comparative methods in the remaining sections of this chapter will mainly focus on the comparison of countries.

However, it is important to understand that comparisons can thus occur at different levels beyond the level of the country such as cities, schools and classrooms. This idea of 'multilevel structures' has been discussed by a range of authors, for example, by Landman (2008) who writes about macro, meso and micro levels of analyses in comparative research, wherein the macro level mostly refers to the broader country level. In education research, the notion of different levels of interaction with each other has also been discussed by, for example, Bronfenbrenner (1979) using his ecological framework or Giddens's work on structure and agency approaches. In relation to education, one could argue that schools within countries might count as the meso level, and students or pupils within these schools as individuals at the micro level. A strong rationale for carrying out educational comparisons adopting a multilevel way of thinking has also been clearly present in a highly influential paper published by Bray and Thomas (1995) in the *Harvard Educational Review*. The authors proposed a cube at which it is possible to locate the specific angle of a comparative educational research project, as presented in Figure 7.1.

The cube's front side is important as the authors explain that comparative research often starts from comparison between two or more geographical locations at the same level, for example, countries, provinces, districts, and that the seven levels represent a nested structure, in which the lower level is part of the levels above.

At the upper side of the cube, the authors distinguish between non-locational demographic groups, including ethnicity, age, gender and religious groups between whom can be made a comparison as well, for

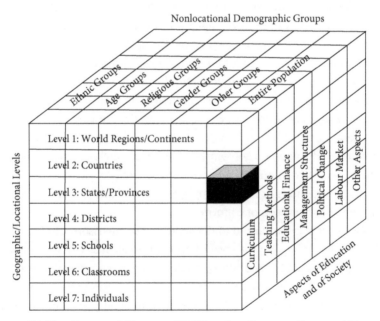

Figure 7.1 The Bray and Thomas (1995) cube. Source: Bray and Thomas (1995)

example, between boys and girls in the case of gender. The remaining side on the right mentions a number of aspects of education and society, more specifically referring to the topic of the comparative research.

While the cube by Bray and Thomas (1995) has been a good example that explains that comparative research in education can be conducted at different levels and does not automatically needs to be international in nature – for example, in case of comparing schools in a single country – the cube does not focus on the methodological issues of doing comparative research. Manzin and Areepattamannil (2014), conducting research on shadow education – a form of private tutoring in the shadow of daytime education, especially popular in South-East Asia – using the original cube, discussed the need to identify the theoretical underpinnings of comparative research, but also the researchers' ontological and epistemological preferences and their motivation on whether to use quantitative, qualitative or mixed-methods approaches. As in other empirical education research, it is equally important in comparative research to think through the research questions, the research design and analysis stages, being upfront about your stance on objective or multiple truths and the methodological approaches you thought were best suited to come to this position. Finally, Manzin and Areepattamannil (2014) mentioned the need for reflection on the possible impact comparative research can generate. This can be recommendations for policy and practice as well as suggestions for future research.

Designing a comparative education research project – where to start

Designing a new project – whether comparative or not – requires a lot of thinking about your ontological and epistemological position, leading to the research context, the topic or theme, the aims and objectives and the general and specific research questions the project strives to answer. Yet before these decisions can be taken, it is necessary to establish your own theoretical positioning. This is what della Porta (2008: 198, 202) labelled as thinking about your 'epistemological preferences' and your 'ontological beliefs'. At the same time, the project needs to be designed in such a way that appropriate resources are available to undertake the work and the researcher or research team needs to take ethical considerations into account. More general information about the role of research designs can be found within different chapters in this book. This chapter will explicitly focus on the epistemology of setting up a comparative project, which has been largely debated in the international literature, arguing whether all comparative research follows the same 'logic' or different 'logics' apply, specifically referring to the different stances being held by positivists versus interpretivists (della Porta, 2008). While it can be argued that all comparative researchers in the end are interested in finding out about differences and similarities between two or more countries (or districts, cities, schools, …), the way in which they aim to find these differences and similarities are not necessarily the same.

A helpful tool to check on the design steps to undertake when carrying out a comparative research project is the framework developed by Brannen et al. (2011), set up for researchers to reflect and report on international and comparative research projects they have undertaken themselves They distinguish twelve categories to reflect on when dealing with comparative research in the social sciences. These twelve categories are presented in Table 7.1. It is important to mention that it is not necessary to undertake the different steps you want in a chronological order. For example, the rationale for your research design naturally flows from your epistemological preferences and thinking about conceptual issues is likely starting earlier on in the project. However, the authors' work provides many insights that are helpful for comparative researchers and therefore worth consulting.

In focusing on the aims, objectives and research questions, Brannen et al. (2011) mention specific questions in relation to whether the aims of the project were to describe a phenomenon, to generate theories or to test a set of hypotheses. In order to reflect on these questions, it is advisable to

Table 7.1 Framework for international social research methods

1. Research context	7. Rationale for the research design
2. Research topic/theme	8. Rational for the research methods
3. Aims, objectives and research questions	9. Conceptual issues
4. Resources and governance	10. Data collection and analysis
5. Management and coordination	11. Interpretation and dissemination of findings
6. Professional and ethical standards	12. Lessons learned

Source: Brannen et al. (2011)

consult a theory on typologies of comparative research aims. Theisen and Adams (1990) constructed a classification of four different comparative research approaches, which have been labelled as 'descriptive', 'analytical', 'evaluative' and 'exploratory'. Firstly, descriptive comparative research does not do more than describe a specific educational phenomenon in different countries and might also explore the relationships between variables without engaging in furthering the understanding of why these relationships exist. Secondly, the analytical approach does dig more deeply into why we observe certain results and how we can interpret them. Thirdly, evaluative research approaches in comparative education are being used when it is important to find out whether specific programmes or policies are more efficient than others. This type of research is often relevant in policy-oriented research and aims to generate specific implications which can be used as guidelines for decision-making processes in policy or practice. Fourthly, exploratory research is recommended when the aim is to generate a new set of hypotheses which can afterwards be tested in new research. This might relate to both theoretical models and/or specific research methods.

Similar discussions on the different aims of comparative research have been offered by Landman (2008). Firstly, he discusses the comparison of countries as a means of describing contextual information and phenomena in these specific countries. As with Theisen and Adams's category of 'descriptive' comparative research, it can be labelled as 'research at a basic level', but as Landman rightly argues, providing a good description of the issues under study is an important starting point before moving on to a more analytical way of doing research, specifically searching for relations between variables instead of solely describing them. Landman also refers to the 'hypothesis-testing' type of research and seems most similar to what Theisen and Adams have called the analytical approach to comparative research in which there is more attention given to discovering relationships between variables and why that is the case. The testing of hypotheses is also seen as a good way to build and refine new theory. Landman also writes about comparative research as a tool for 'prediction' and this is very much in line with the evaluative approach as discussed by Theisen and Adams. Comparative research can engage in trying to find out how specific issues would unfold in the future based on evaluative approaches. However, one should always bear in mind that predictions and the formulation of recommendations for the future are not guaranteed to be fulfilled.

Activity 7.1

Based on the four types of comparative research as discussed by Thiesen and Adams, can you provide different examples for one of each and explore how these might affect the aim and research questions of a project.

Apart from situating your epistemological grounding and deciding on the aims of the comparative educational research project, it is also important to make sound methodological choices to be able to answer the initial research questions. As this chapter deals specifically with comparative research design, the remainder of the chapter will explicitly focus on sampling, the choice of methods and data analysis techniques.

Sampling and choice of methods in comparative research

One of the major questions to answer when designing a new comparative research project is 'how many countries should be included' and this is likely to be related to the researchers' epistemological preferences, as will become clear throughout this section. Generally, the literature distinguishes between (1) a large number of countries, (2) a limited number of countries or (3) one country (see Landman, 2008: 26; Lor, 2011). As stated above, comparisons made between schools in one single country are not automatically recognized as international education as there is no comparison being made at the country level. Lor (2011: 11) discusses how scholars in the past have disagreed on the comparative nature of single country studies. However, as Landman (2008) argues, single country projects that have the intention to discuss results outside the scope of the country of research can also be labelled as 'comparative' at the country level. Furthermore, researchers undertaking fieldwork in foreign countries are still likely to somehow interpret data from the lens of their own cultures, also labelled as 'ethnocentricity', leading to possible distortion in understanding the educational issues in a new context (see e.g. Phillips and Schweisfurth, 2007: 93).

Taking more than one country into account, it is important to underline that the number of countries being selected for participation in the comparative research project also tends to relate to whether the study is more likely going to draw on quantitative or qualitative methods. This difference has been labelled by Ragin (1987) as the 'variable-oriented' versus the 'case-oriented' approach. When many countries are involved, it will be more difficult to gather in-depth information about each individual, but there will be the opportunity to analyse how a set of variables differs in a wide range of countries. This approach of working with many countries and the search for generalizable patterns has been linked to Durkheim's research logic, focusing on the claim that 'science must favour generalizability over details' (della Porta, 2008: 203), thus leaning towards sociological positivism, in search for objective truth. A well-known example of a large quantitative comparative study in the field of education is OECD's PISA, which will be used as an example below.

When a limited number of countries are included, there is more space to do an in-depth analyses of each country and make comparisons between them using a more qualitative approach, linked to Weber's research logic of sociological interpretivism, aiming for complexity over generalization, striving towards higher levels of comprehension (della Porta, 2008: 203). In the sections below, more detailed discussions will be provided on doing comparative research with (1) many countries and with (2) a few countries, drawing on respectively variable- and case-oriented approaches.

Educational research comparing many countries

As stated above, researchers interested in understanding objective and generalizable truth are more likely to choose for quantifiable information obtained through representative samples. One of the most well-known examples of large-scale comparative research in education is the PISA test, developed by the OECD. Every three years, 15 year old pupils across the world are asked to fill in tests of which the results then get compared between countries. As so many countries are involved in this test, it would be impossible or at least be unrealistically time consuming to undertake an in-depth piece of qualitative research in so many countries and this is also not the initial aim of the project, which has been designed starting from the need to obtain objective and generalizable data on the skills attainment of fifteen-year-old pupils worldwide. These large N studies – the N referring to the number of countries – are much more likely to draw upon statistical methods to control for a range of correlations and multivariate testing including regression analyses (Landman, 2008).

The latest PISA results were announced in 2016 and were based on underlying analyses on test scores from fifteen-year-old students in seventy-two countries. Around 540,000 pupils participated in the test and they represent nearly 30 million fifteen-year-olds worldwide. Data analyses have been undertaken by analysts at the OECD, but datasets are also available to scholars who wish to undertake comparative educational research projects drawing on PISA data. Test scores are the major interest of PISA and most attention goes to comparing scores on literacy and numeracy across countries, but it would also be possible to analyse whether, for example, test scores for boys and girls correlate with each other or not and whether there is a 'logic' in relation to this in different countries (OECD, 2015). Do boys score higher than girls in all countries or can we identify a number of countries where this is not the case? If so, what type of countries are these? And how can these results be used to draw lesson on creating more gender equality in schools?

Despite the existence of large-scale comparative studies, it is important to note that their use generates a broad range of criticisms. Comparing between many countries raises the question about whether concepts are equally understood in different country contexts and thus have high levels of validity, whether common codebooks and questionnaires have been appropriately translated into country languages and whether the analyses pay enough attention to the underlying social, political and historical context (Landman, 2008). Holford and Mleczko (2011) found some interesting differences between how countries using a wider and more inclusive definition of adult education ended up with higher participation scores in adult learning activities, and whether this could potentially be related to the way in which the core item in the codebook had been translated. Jerrim (2016) has done some interesting analyses on PISA data to explore how PISA rankings can be influenced by whether students complete the test using paper and pencil or using computerized tools. Furthermore, not every educational researcher is equipped to work with large statistical data or has the time; for example, regression analyses tend to be time-intensive. Comparing between many countries does have the advantage that it is a good way to detect outliers or countries that do not follow certain trends. It can then be interesting to do more in-depth analyses in these countries, finding out why they are so different.

Educational research comparing a few countries

Working with a smaller number of countries has its advantages as well as disadvantages (Landman, 2008). It gives the researcher more room for in-depth analyses, but at the same time, it is important to provide a sound rationale for the selection of countries. Research based on a smaller number of countries is therefore more likely to fall into the case-oriented comparative strategy and will therefore provide more opportunities to generate in-depth information. Researchers interested in the complexity of educational aspects in certain countries, aiming to make interpretations of their situation in relation to the topic of their project, are thus more likely to select fewer countries, and favour details over generalization.

Selecting countries

Based on intuition, it feels problematic to compare countries that are too different from each other as it would be perceived as comparing 'apples to oranges'. However, tools are available to help compare countries based on their similarities and differences, and broadly speaking, a distinction can be made between the 'Most Similar Systems Design' (MSSD) and the 'Most Different System Design' (Ragin, 1987; Landman, 2008; Lor, 2011; Bray et al., 2014). The example used in this text comes from research in relation to analysing literacy levels in a number of countries and how this might relate to the presence of local public libraries. In the example of the MSSD, presented in Figure 7.2, a selection of countries has been made that are very similar in relation to a range of background characteristics.

Within this example, all countries are former British colonies with a medium level of GDP and multiple languages are being spoken in these countries. However, the project is interested in the presence of public libraries and the one country that has a low level of literacy among its population does not have availability of public libraries. As such, a conclusion is being made that a relationship between the presence of libraries and literacy levels exists, although it remains important to be cautious about causation, despite the tendency to call comparative smaller-N studies causal-analytical in nature (Ragin, 1987). Is it the lack of libraries that led to low levels of literacy or is it the low levels of literacy that have led to a lack of interest in establishing libraries?

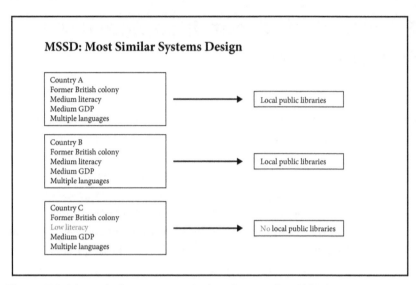

Figure 7.2 Most similar systems design. Source: Lor (2011)

Using a 'Most Different Systems Design', presented in Figure 7.3, does exactly the opposite. While the core variable of interest is the same – there are local public libraries in all three countries – it is also clear that the population in all these countries are characterized as having high levels of literacy. However, the background characteristics of the countries are very

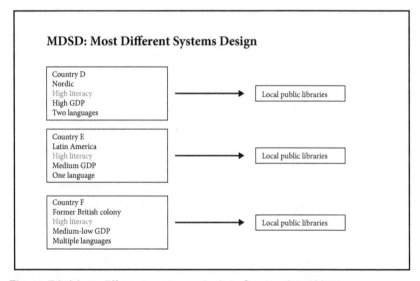

Figure 7.3 Most different systems design. Source: Lor (2011)

Activity 7.2

Look at the PISA test and explore whether countries with similar literacy and numeracy scores are those that you would expect to find together (e.g. Scandinavian countries, Mediterranean countries). Then discuss this in relation to MDSD/MSSD.

different. As there are public libraries available in all these countries, it is highly likely a relationship between the presence of libraries and high levels of literacy exists.

Manzon (2014: 98) also discusses the Most Similar and Most Different Systems Design, and based on work by Berg-Schlosser (2001), she further refers to Most Similar and Most Different Outcomes. In the example presented in Figure 7.2, the systems are similar, but the outcomes different. In the example of Figure 7.3, the systems are different, but the outcomes similar. Comparing a range of variables in-depth will then try to single out a factor explaining why this might be the case. In the example, reflections have been made on the role of the literacy level of a population in a country.

Case-oriented approaches with only a few countries are thus different from variable-oriented approaches as the focus is much more on an in-depth comparison of cases as a whole, both logically flowing from positivist versus interpretivist epistemological preferences. The drawback of case-oriented comparative research is that it is time-consuming, mainly because fieldwork is likely to be undertaken from scratch. Furthermore, it is also important to provide a good rationale about which countries to include in the research study, and to argue why they are most similar or most different from each other.

In thinking about selecting countries in the first place, I would like to refer to the notion of welfare typologies as they are useful to help making your selection in which specific countries you want to study in-depth. Especially in the developed world, nowadays, it is clear that some countries are more similar than others. Often, they are geographically close to each other, but they also share characteristics in levels of (in)equality of their population and the extent services are left to market forces or are centrally organized – think, for example, about the privatization and/or marketization of education in liberal countries. Terms used in the literature to explore these two problems are 'stratification' and 'decommodification'. As stated above, Esping-Andersen (1989) referred to social-democratic, conservative-corporatist and liberal countries, where social-democratic countries tend to have high levels of social services funded by the state and low levels of inequality; conservative-corporatist countries have good levels of state support as well, but often only for those in work and education systems tend to be stratified, leading to inequalities in society; in liberal countries, social services are often left over to the private market and there are therefore strong levels of inequality, for example, visible through the cost of higher education or the availability for well-off parents to send their children to private schools. Fenger (2007) investigated opportunities for extending the Esping-Andersen typology as a way to include Eastern European countries as well, especially important after the enlargement of the European Union when ten new countries were accepted as new members. In undertaking statistical analyses on datasets analysing country characteristics such as health expenditures, public spending on education, tax systems, gender issues in the labour market, unemployment rates and life expectancies, Fenger (2007) found six types of countries, including the three classic types from Esping-Andersen. He included the fourth 'former USSR-type' referring to the Baltic countries, Latvia, Lithuania and Estonia, and countries like Russia, Belarus and Ukraine. The fifth type was labelled as the 'post-communist European type' and included 'Bulgaria, Croatia, Czech Republic, Hungary, Poland and Slovakia' (Fenger, 2007: 24–25). Countries in this fifth type have similarities with those in the fourth type, but have generally adopted a bit quicker to transforming into capitalist societies. The sixth type represents Georgia, Romania and Moldova and has been labelled as the 'developing welfare states' type. Romania has now been included in the European country, but generally, these countries are still catching up with other countries to further mature towards states with high levels of welfare and stable economies. While most of this work on country typologies has been undertaken in Europe, including North America and Oceania, examples of similar work can be found relating to other regions in the world, for example, Franzoni (2008) who constructed a typology for Latin American countries and Park and Jung (2008) who applied insights from Esping-Andersen's work into the Asian context. In order to help you select the countries for inclusion in your research project, it is thus recommended to familiarize yourself with these country typologies. If you want to find out, for example, why a specific educational problem is present in Denmark, but not in Sweden or Finland, you could draw on a Most Similar Systems Design, finding an explanation for the different outcome. You could also be interested in a common problem that exists in a more varied range of countries (e.g. Spain, Sweden and Poland) and try to find out why, for example, all teachers experience stress, dependent of the country in which they teach, drawing on a Most Different Systems Design, trying to explain a similar problem.

Drawing on my own research interests, I want to give you an example of how I have dealt with the selection of countries in my own projects. Over the last decade, scholars have undertaken efforts to increase knowledge on lifelong learning typologies, undertaking similar exercises to those by Esping-Andersen (1989) and Fenger (2007), resulting in country groupings based on their educational characteristics. Discussions of such typologies can be found in Holford et al. (2008), Riddell et al. (2012) and Saar et al. (2013). Interestingly, this work on typologies has also been taken forward in designing new lifelong learning projects, for example, the Horizon 2020 project ENLIVEN 'Encouraging Lifelong Learning for an Inclusive & Vibrant Europe', in which I am currently involved, together with a range of other partners in Europe. To represent a wide range of countries, a selection of European countries had to be made. We did not want a project with countries that follow similar systems, but rather different systems that have problems with generating higher participation in lifelong learning among the most disadvantaged adults in societies. As a result, we included England and Scotland representing the liberal type, Austria and Belgium (Flanders) representing the conservative-corporatist type, Italy and Spain as Mediterranean countries – sometimes distinguished as a separate type – Estonia as a former USSR type country and Bulgaria and Slovakia as 'post-communist Europe' type countries. The project also has an Australian partner doing parallel work to the European team. It is thus clear from this example that countries have not been randomly selected, but are present in the project for a specific purpose, which is to further understand common lifelong learning problems in a range of distinct European societies. While some parts of the project use variable-oriented approaches, usually drawing on datasets that include all countries of the European Union and therefore using all these countries, the project consists of several work packages in which a case-oriented approach is being used. As Landman (2008) discusses in his book, case-oriented approaches differ from variable-oriented approaches as the approach is much more 'intensive' and in-depth than exploring a range of trends based on data from a large number of countries. The case-oriented approach leaves less room for making broad generalizations as within the variable-oriented approach, but provides the researcher with a much more in-depth understanding of both the differences and similarities between countries.

Activity 7.3

Starting from your own research interest, set up samples of three different countries, one in which you use a Most Similar Systems Design and one in which you use a Most Different Systems Design. Explain the choices you made.

Analysing data

In relation to analysing data, different techniques are being used for variable-oriented quantitative research and case-oriented qualitative research. For analysing quantitative data, it is recommended to consult the Chapter 2 section on quantitative data analysis. This will provide you with insights on how to compare countries based on both categorical and scale variables. For example, comparing the gender distribution in a sample across countries can be done through cross-tabs; comparing PISA literacy and numeracy score between two countries can be undertaken using a t-test.

In relation to qualitative data, core texts on comparative education, such as the one by Bray et al., make explicit reference to the comparative method as constructed by Bereday in his 1964 contribution 'Comparative Method in Education'. He argues that in the more in-depth qualitative comparative research projects, four distinct steps have to be undertaken in the data analysis phase of the study. Firstly, a description of all data against agreed parameters – set out by the research team – needs to be provided for each of the countries. Secondly, data for each country need to be interpreted against the social, economic, historical and political context of the country with the aim to better understand why specific findings might have come out of the data, paying attention to the need to further contextualize the research topic and the locations in which it is interested. Thirdly, countries need to be put next to each other in order to check the comparability of the data – which is also called 'juxtaposition'. Fourthly, data are then effectively compared with the aim to generate new hypotheses and to formulate the conclusions of the study. Bereday's four-step model is represented in Figure 7.4,

I. DESCRIPTION

Pedagogical Data Only

II. INTERPRETATION

Evaluation of Pedagogical Data

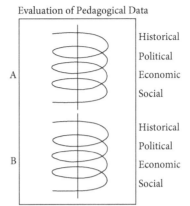

III. JUXTAPOSITION

Establishing Similarities and Differences

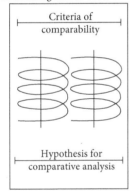

IV. COMPARISON

Simultaneous Comparison

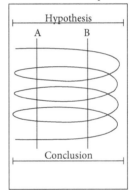

Figure 7.4 Bereday's comparative method. Source: Bereday (1964: 28)

visually demonstrating the stages of (1) description, (2) interpretation, (3) juxtaposition and (4) comparison.

Conclusions

Comparative research in education has often been undertaken; however, its methodological approaches have so far received less attention in research methods texts. This chapter has demonstrated that researchers in comparative education start from their own understanding of truth and their epistemological preferences and that this is linked to the types of research they will undertake, likely drawing on large-scale quantitative or smaller-scale qualitative research, representing more positivistic versus interpretivist research logics.

Chapter key points

- Most comparative research published in the field of education tends to be international in nature and comparative between two or more countries, although the comparisons of different schools in a single city can also be labelled as 'comparative education research'.
- This chapter made a distinction between comparisons among many countries and comparisons between a few countries, and the likelihood that large N studies are using variable-oriented approaches, drawing on statistical methods, with the aim to find the objective and generalizable truth, while small N studies are more likely to draw upon case-oriented approaches, focusing more on in-depth understanding of countries as a whole, providing in-depth interpretations of educational problems.
- In comparing a few countries, this chapter has provided insight to the reader that selections can be made either based on their similarities or differences and their relation to either similar or different outcome variables.

Recommended reading

Bray, M., Adamson, B., & Mason, M. (2014). *Comparative Education Research: Approaches and Methods*. London: Springer.

This book is a recent comprehensive book, specifically focusing on comparative research in the field of education. Written by specialist at the UNESCO centre for Comparative Education at the University of Hong Kong, this book focuses on the theoretical and historical underpinnings of comparative education, but also provides detailed information on research methods.

Landman, T. (2008). *Issues and Methods in Comparative Politics: An Introduction.* London: Routledge.
Landman is a political scientist whose work is highly relevant to everyone interested in carrying out comparative research in the social sciences. His work provides an excellent explanation of the differences between large and small N studies, drawing on variable- and case-oriented approaches.

Phillips, D. & Schweisfurth, M. (2007). *Comparative and International Education: An Introduction to Theory, Method and Practice.* London: Continuum.
This book provides a comprehensive overview on the field of comparative education. It includes sections on comparative methodology, but also discusses wider themes in comparative education such as the importance of policy borrowing.

Ragin, C. (1987). *The Comparative Method. Moving Beyond Qualitative and Quantitative Strategies.* Berkeley, Los Angeles: University of California Press.
Ragin's book is a core text that provides an in-depth explanation of the differences between qualitative and quantitative research strategies in comparative research. It is therefore a good source for everyone wanting to know more about variable- and case-oriented approaches in comparative social science.

Advanced reading

della Porta, D. (2008). Comparative Analysis: Case-oriented versus Variable-oriented Research, in D. della Porta & M. Keating (eds), *Approaches and Methodologies in the Social Sciences: A Pluralist Perspective*, 198–222. Cambridge: Cambridge University Press.
This text is a book chapter that provides a good summary on the differences between case- and variable-oriented approaches and helps readers to further understand this in relation to ontology and epistemology.

Noah, H. & Eckstein, M. (1969). *Toward a Science of Comparative Education.* New York: Macmillan.
This is an older text that provides good insight into the history of comparative education and has been frequently cited by, for example, Bray. This is thus recommended reading for those who want to go back to the original sources.

Theisen, G. & Adams, D. (1990). Comparative Education Research, in R. Thomas (ed.), *International Comparative Education*, 277–300. Oxford: Pergamon Press.
This book chapter will help the reader to further understand the different types of comparative research, including descriptive, analytical, evaluative and predictive comparative education research.

Web links

http://www.oecd.org/pisa/
The OECD's PISA website is a great resource for everyone who wants to explore how big international organizations deal with setting up a large-scale comparative education project. The website also provides details on the results of the project.

http://www.tandfonline.com/toc/cced20/current
Comparative Education is one of the leading journals in the field of comparative and international education that publishes the output of high-quality research, drawing on both quantitative and qualitative methodologies. This journal is a great source for everyone who wants to consult examples of comparative research in the field of education.

Part IV

Other Possibilities for Shaping Research Design

8

Collaborative Ethnography: What Is It and How Can You Start Doing It?

Luke Eric Lassiter

Key points

- Collaborative ethnography is seen here as a participatory approach that involves researchers and research participants or consultants in a common field-based project of co-research, analysis, interpretation and textual production.
- What collaborative ethnography is not, and what it is.
- Different kinds and approaches.
- How different ethnographers have applied the approach.
- Suggestions for starting such collaborative projects.

Introduction

In many academic circles collaborative research often invokes images of researchers working together in some sort of joint effort, one that, in its ideal sense, involves assumptions about sharing responsibility and engaging in dialogue, idea exchange and reciprocation. In many fields, this image of collaboration – on which this idea of collaborative research rests – is taken for granted as a necessary condition for getting work done. Those involved in documentary research, for example, are quick to point out the necessity of involving various experts – writers, videographers, sound engineers, editors, producers and the like – who all must more or less work together to complete a complicated task of making, say, a documentary film. In other fields – in many lab sciences, for example – collaborative research often summons a kind of collaboration in which colleagues from the same or different disciplines may (again, ideally) work on different parts of a common project, which then may yield co-authored journal articles, books or other collaboratively produced academic products.

This notion of collaborative research is not the topic of this chapter. Well, it *is*, to a certain extent – but not entirely. In other academic circles, particularly in field-based disciplines (i.e. those in which fieldwork approaches dominate) like anthropology, folklore or ethnomusiciology, 'collaborative research' has come to denote very specific meanings that are different from how it is often used by, for instance, documentary researchers or lab scientists. These meanings may certainly include the involvement of multi-expert or multidisciplinary teams. But collaborative research in fields like social or cultural anthropology more often implies a very specific approach to research that engages researchers (often academically situated) and so-called research participants (often situated in local communities, where academic researchers may do field research) in common collaborative research projects in which academics and local research participants may engage a variety of participatory approaches in which they share responsibility for research design, research implementation, write-up or dissemination. Beyond sharing control of research and its results, however, such approaches ideally emphasize the dynamic intersections of academically and community-based dialogues about the topic or topics under study – and thus may shift the agendas of research from those traditionally more academically based and controlled to those more collaboratively based and controlled with members of local communities. This also means, of course, that these processes may yield other results – such as collaborative or community-based action to solve (not just research) a local problem – which, in turn, may move a project well beyond research for its own sake.

Such participatory approaches are well known and go by a number of different names, including Participatory Action Research, collaborative inquiry or community-university research – to name just a few. These various types of collaborative research are not the same, however; indeed, they each have their own sets of assumptions, emphases and outcomes. I focus here on one of these kinds of collaborative research: collaborative ethnography, which assumes and emphasizes the centrality of collaboration in ethnographic research in particular *and* how that collaboration can frame the activities of research design, research implementation and, importantly, the final product (whatever form it may take, but most often as text). Defined in an ideal sense, collaborative ethnography, '*deliberately* and *explicitly* emphasizes collaboration at every point in the ethnographic process, without veiling it – from project conceptualization, to fieldwork, and, especially through its writing process' (Lassiter, 2005: 16). Given this, though, collaborative ethnography can imply a wide range of approaches or kinds, which I briefly review below via a comparative framework. I then offer some suggestions for initiating these kinds of projects.

Kinds of collaborative ethnography (some case study comparisons)

Doing collaborative ethnography often implies a diverse set of collaborative research practices that wrestle with concepts of collaboration, dialogue and reciprocation; foreground difference and power; and theorize collaboration. Approaches to collaborative ethnography range widely from involving key research participants as readers and co-editors (which may proceed via one-on-one discussion, but may also include the use of focus groups, community forums and even more formally organized editorial boards who respond to and edit the text as it develops), to incorporating contributions from research participants, to creating teams of both academic and community-based research participants to collaboratively research and write 'cowritten texts' (see Lassiter, 2005: 138–54).

One of the most common ways that collaborative ethnography has been done in the past and is still done today involves research participants or 'consultants' (a term that, in the context of collaborative ethnography, replaces the older 'informant' label) as readers, editors or contributors of ethnographic texts as they develop. This conscious decision shifts the process of collaboration inherent in fieldwork (as is required for doing participant observation or interviews) into the process of interpretation and writing. In this sense, 'the field' is not just a place to collect 'data'. In this approach 'the field' is also the place to re-engage consultants in the processes of analysis and interpretation. For example: when I wrote my dissertation – and then my first book – on an indigenous community, the Kiowas of southwestern Oklahoma, and their song traditions, I shared each chapter with a group of Kiowa consultants who read, made editorial suggestions and offered other comments on my interpretations of their song traditions (see Lassiter, 1995). I would then incorporate their editorial suggestions and integrate their comments, which often shifted my own interpretations – as well as how I presented them – as they developed. I did this several times with each chapter in both the dissertation and then the book manuscript, and with each reading and editing – as in any process when engaging other readers – the text changed, and, I think, for the better.

I should note that this is a bit different from so-called member or participant checking – common in many qualitative research approaches – in which researchers ask research participants to check the verity of, for example, interview transcripts or research findings. The process of involving consultants as readers and editors in the process of ethnographic writing encourages a further step, one that involves dialogic participation in ethnographic representation as it unfolds. As Kiowa consultants reviewed the text in its various iterations, for example, in some cases they suggested additions that I had not considered before; in more than a few instances, they asked that I take material out. Sometimes I made those changes without discussion; other times, when I felt strongly about it, I countered with my own position about why we should keep or discard a particular point. Sometimes I was persuasive; sometimes my Kiowa collaborators were more so. Of course, I experienced the same requests for additions and subtractions from – and sometimes engaged in similar negotiations about the text with – my dissertation committee when writing the dissertation, and from the Content Editor when rewriting the manuscript for publication as a book. Just like my dissertation committee members and the book's editor – and me – Kiowa consultants also had key investments in the ethnographic text as it materialized: it was, after all, about *them* and something they cared deeply about, Kiowa song. Taking this investment seriously, and making it a central part of the ethnographic writing process, is thus a critical part of doing this kind of collaborative ethnography.

In traditionally framed ethnography, critics might point to the limitations of involving research participants in the final ethnographic analysis. But in this kind of collaborative ethnography, the goal is to expand dialogue across boundaries between academic researchers and the communities in which they study. In his book *Abalone Tales* – which is about the significance of abalone to California Native peoples – Les Field (2008: 6) notes that this kind of 'collaboration makes possible research that would not otherwise be so', creating more nuanced and better results. As Native collaborators read and responded to Field's developing ideas and texts, for instance, several offered their own written accounts to supplement Field's analysis about the role of abalone in their lives. Field incorporated these accounts into the text as contributions authored by his Native collaborators, which, in the end, deepened the collaboration and enhanced the dialogic meanings of abalone as represented.

In a similar vein, some approaches to collaborative ethnography organize sections of books (chapters, for example) written by research participants. In her book *The Pull of the Earth*, Laurie Thorp (2006) writes about the role of an elementary school garden and how the garden helped to cultivate community, encourage learning and enhance curricula. Throughout, she explains how children learn and internalize lessons about the environment, stewardship, nutrition and sustenance. But one of the chapters, written by the children involved in her study, locates the children's experience with and meaning of the garden within their own lives. The shift of voice, tone and style from Thorp to that of the children is dramatic but effective. The result is an expansion and deepening of dialogue across lines of age, education and experience.

Thorp points out that her plans for the work did not begin this way. 'What began as a typical qualitative research design', she writes, with 'purposive sample, interview protocol, content analysis, and case study write-up – quickly evolved into an emergent, participatory, and performative learning community' (Thorp 2006: 118). Thorp raises an important point about the emergent qualities of collaborative ethnographic research. Because collaborative ethnography must work at the nexus of a particular and evolving set of co-commitments, relationships and dialogues that surround a particular idea or topic, its approaches must be flexible, creative and dynamic. It requires an openness to developing research design in ways that are emergent and invite commentary and discussion. This can be a challenge, of course, especially when any given context for doing ethnography may be very different from any other context.

Take, for example, an ethnography that I read as a graduate student, which inspired me to think more deeply about the range of possibilities for doing collaborative ethnography in diverse settings. The book was by ethnomusicologist Steven Feld, who writes about the Kaluli, who live in the forested highlands of Papua New Guinea, in the book *Sound and Sentiment*

(1990). With great precision and care, Feld elaborates how Kaluli song comes into being through a complex relationship between the symbolism of the forest and Kaluli expressive culture. Kaluli notions of song, however, do not easily translate into notions of Western music. Song, in fact, is fleeting and only occasionally springs forth along a continuum of speech, poetics and deep sentiment associated with death and rebirth that, once surfaced, materializes in the form of a Muni bird. It is not enough for Kaluli song to 'sound' like the birds of the forest; it must *become* those birds in form. Just how that happens is a difficult relationship to summarize in sentences and paragraphs (as I am struggling to do here). But as detailed and eloquent as Feld's description is, he, too, openly confronts this difficulty of relaying across linguistic and cultural boundaries the complexities of thought that make song what it is for many Kaluli people. In the second edition of the book, he thus explains how he went about a process of 'dialogic editing' to invite commentary from Kaluli consultants to help give texture and depth to the account after the book was published. Feld's Kaluli collaborators did not speak or read English, so Feld translated sections of the already published book, and then discussed those translations with his Kaluli friends and teachers. Feld names the process 'dialogic editing', which for Feld (1990: 244) 'refers to the impact of Kaluli voices on what I tell you about them in my voice; how their take on my take on them requires a reframing and a refocusing of my account'. Their discussions led to several points of reframing and refocusing, and help to hone for the reader how the Kaluli understand their song.

The kind of 'dialogic editing' undertaken by Feld – in which ethnographers seek commentary about an already finished monograph or book *after the fact*, as it were – a response that might be included in a book's second edition or a follow-up article – is less common today, especially as collaborative ethnographers now seek to integrate consultant response and commentary *up front*, as a part of a project's design, research, and writing process as the book unfolds in the first place. (Computer and online technologies, of course, also allow for more emphasis on using collaborative approaches much earlier in the process: see e.g. King 2010.) Importantly, though, this example points to the diversity of ways in which the impulses for doing more collaboratively based projects can inspire deeper and more nuanced understandings across boundaries, linguistic, cultural or otherwise. Too, these earlier experiments, coupled with ongoing experiments like that of Field's and Thorp's, have added to the broad range of possibilities for doing collaborative ethnography today, which also include iterations that involve consultants even more intimately in the process as collaborative research and writing: as teams, to which I now turn.

For many years, the most common form of 'teamed' collaborative ethnography was done as a two-person team made up of an ethnographer and a single 'informant' or 'consultant'. This goes way back, actually, and, at least in North American anthropology, to the late nineteenth and early twentieth century. Back then, ethnographers and Native consultants sometimes co-created ethnographic texts about language, song or other indigenous traditions. In many instances, the two were both from more or less educated backgrounds, with the indigenous consultant bi-lingual and conversant in writing English (i.e. in the case of most North American ethnology). In other cases, the researcher worked in ways similar to Feld with the Kaluli, translating and discussing with a key informant or consultant the ethnographic text as it developed in the context of ongoing discussion. These experiments served as inspiration for later ethnographers and their indigenous collaborators as many together co-wrote, for instance, collaborative autobiographies of the indigenous consultant as a two-person team. These kinds of collaborative projects are still very common today in fields like North American Native American studies (see Lassiter, 2005: 26–47 for more detail on these early and later developments). My second book on Kiowa song, for instance – a book on Native Christian church hymns, titled *The Jesus Road* (Lassiter et al., 2002) – took inspiration from this approach; but its inclusion of another researcher into the mix (an historian) makes it more like other forms of teamed collaborative ethnography that I describe next.

These older, mostly two-person, co-authored works have commonalities with two other forms of teamed collaborative ethnography that add more people – either researchers or research participants – into the process of co-researching, co-interpreting and co-writing an ethnographic text. One of these is a kind of collaborative ethnography in which a single ethnographer works with a select group of two or more consultants to construct a collaboratively inscribed account about a particular topic. An oft-cited, now classic case study is *Holy Women, Wholly Women*, a book about women working in several different US Protestant churches, written by folklorist Elaine Lawless (1993) along with a small group of ten women ministers. In a form of collaborative research that she calls 'reciprocal ethnography', Lawless presents her findings and interpretations about women in parish ministry, which includes her academic-based discussion about religion, sexuality and gender. But the book also includes numerous biographical sketches written by the ministers themselves, stories that both compliment and provide contrast to Lawless's ethnographic account throughout. Though Lawless and each of the research participants wrote their own accounts, they still worked as a team from its initial stages, and produced a collaborative project with diverse voices and perspectives about what it means to be a woman and a minister in US protestant churches.

The other form of teamed collaborative ethnographies pulls together multiple researchers (perhaps from different disciplines) and multiple research participants (perhaps from various parts of a given community) in a common collaborative ethnographic project. This is perhaps the most idealized image of 'collaborative ethnography'. But, as should be obvious by now, it is certainly not representative of the broad range of possibilities for doing collaborative ethnography. In any case, I've done several of these projects, and I consider them to be the most rewarding, but also the most challenging. My favourite, and one about which I've written the most, is the 'Other Side of Middletown' project (see Lassiter et al., 2004; but see Lassiter, 2012 for a more recent analysis of lessons learned). This project brought together a group of faculty and students with members of a local African American community (in Muncie, Indiana, the site of the famous 'Middletown' studies) to research and write about black experience there. Over seventy-five people in all were involved in the project, all of whom participated at varying levels. At its core was a smaller group that included interdisciplinary faculty (with expertise in anthropology, folklore and history), students from a broad range of disciplines (including English, history, journalism, anthropology, theatre, communication studies, among many others), and a core group of community advisors from various parts of the community (which included businessmen and women, local politicians, homemakers, professionals, church leaders and the like). Much of our process is outlined in the book *The Other Side of Middletown* (Lassiter et al., 2004) (and described in an accompanying documentary, 'Middletown Redux'); suffice it to say that we used a broad range of approaches. Students conducted most of the research and wrote the bulk of the book. But as they wrote their chapters, they continually engaged community consultants (people they had interviewed, for example) for reader and editorial response, as well as for incorporating consultant-written contributions. Community consultants also reviewed the chapters in focus groups and in larger community forums in the more involved work of collaboratively interpreting the study's results. And finally, our group of community advisors, students and faculty served as an editorial board of sorts, as a group making final editorial decisions as we moved the book from its various drafts to its final publication.

The Other Side of Middletown project was more complex in its scale than any other collaborative project I had ever done up to that point and have done since. Its scale and depth was made possible primarily by an exceptionally unique and unusual programme at Ball State University (where I taught at the time), the Virginia Ball Center for Creative Inquiry, which funded the project and compelled it to unfold in the way that it did. Faculty and students, for example, were required to have no other commitments – academic or otherwise – during the research period; the project enjoyed a generous budget, a dedicated project space, separate from campus, housed in an old mansion with a full-time support staff; core community advisors were compensated for their time; community forums and other meetings were regularly sponsored with meals paid for by the programme; and each student had access to the very latest field recorders, laptop computers and other cutting-edge technology – to name just a few things (more about this unusual programme is described, in part, in Trimmer, 2006). I mention all of this because while I have done other teamed collaborative research projects, no others have materialized at this scale. It is, to be sure, uncharacteristic of most US universities to invest in these kinds of community-university collaborative research projects. The vast majority of teamed projects of this type can be thus more modest affairs, and often take much longer than the year or so it took us to research and write this book from its earliest planning stages to its final publication with a trade press (see Crow, 2017 for a fuller discussion of how such community-based projects compare).

Examples more typical of team approaches to collaborative ethnography are, fortunately, increasingly more common. Many of these also materialize in the context of community-university research and writing partnerships similar to the Other Side of Middletown project, which may often engage undergraduate students as researchers and writers as a part of the larger collaborative research programme (see e.g. Hyatt, 2012). Other community-university collaborative research projects involve students at multiple levels, and even integrate these approaches into overall programmes of study (which, in turn, may generate other modes and types of collaborative research) (see e.g. Hart et al., 2007; Rabinow et al., 2008). An exemplary example that comes to mind is the collaborative ethnography *Thinking Outside the Girl Box* (Spatig and Amerikaner 2014), a project facilitated by Linda Spatig, who, along with her daughter and co-author/editor Layne Amerikaner, weaves together a complex and multifaceted collaborative ethnography about the rise and subsequent demise of a young women's youth development programme in one of the poorest regions in the United States, the Appalachian Mountains. The successes of this youth organization, the Girls Resiliency Program (GRP) – to provide young women with pathways out of poverty and a range of other challenges facing young women there – are remarkable. But so, too, is how the programme began to decline at a time when it was perhaps needed most. This collaborative ethnography is especially unusual because it engages a group consisting of several of Spatig's graduate students (working on their doctorates in education, who are also following the girls' academic lives), organizational leaders, local community activists, and the young women themselves in a reflective evaluation of what went wrong and how those lessons might inform better understandings of youth development and education in rural Appalachia and beyond. The problem is not just one in which Spatig and her graduate students are interested, of course; it is also one of great interest to the organizational leaders, community activists, and the young women themselves. The book thus unfolds as a dynamic, multi-level and multi-relevant conversation that not only includes methods like collaborative reading and editing, consultant contributions and teamed research and writing (all of which the young women were involved in); but also offers some of the very best of what collaborative ethnography can offer as it absorbs both academics and local community participants in deep conversation about something that matters to everyone involved.

Critically important to this book's success – and indeed, to all collaborative ethnography – is a kind of accessible writing that travels well across boundaries often separating academic and community discourse (see Lassiter, 2005: 117–32). But, it should be said, this kind of collaborative ethnography is not just limited to community-university research partnerships, or only initiated by academic scholars. It also surfaces in other kinds of partnerships, such as within not-for-profit organizations working in contexts of community-based research. An exemplary example in this regard is the Neighborhood Story Project (NSP) in New Orleans, 'a collaborative ethnography and publishing organization' that works with a variety of organizations from public schools to museums 'to create books and other printed material' that advance the organization's mission: 'our stories told by us'. The NSP's collaborative efforts are meant 'to help people be the authors of their own stories in ways that will create relevant literature' (Neighborhood Story Project 2017). Though the organization collaborates with the University of New Orleans to publish many of its works, the NSP initiates their projects within its own space at a house in a New Orleans neighbourhood, where various community members pitch and negotiate diverse projects for joint research and writing. The result is a multimedia medley of collaborative ethnographic projects ranging from books to posters to films (see e.g. their website in the suggested web links below; see Haviland, 2017: 70–81 for more on the NSP and its approach as it relates to larger theories and methods of collaborative ethnography).

Steps towards a collaborative ethnography: Suggested activities for starting projects

So what to do with all of this? Large teamed collaborative ethnographies (in the vein of well-resourced ones like the Other Side of Middletown project) are just not possible for most of us most of the time. Nor can most spend a year or more in a community researching things like song traditions or material culture. But we can nonetheless integrate various ideas, theories and methods of collaborative ethnography in our work should we choose to, even if in modest ways.

For example: In my current position, I am jointly appointed in a college of liberal arts and a school of education. In the former case, I direct a small graduate humanities programme (that, like most academic units of its kind, struggles within very limited streams of funding), and work with a multidisciplinary group of students working towards their master's degree in the humanities. In the latter, I teach courses in research methods and work with a variety of educators researching and writing their doctoral theses in education. In both cases, the vast majority of students already have full-time jobs, are not funded (having neither scholarships nor graduate assistant positions), and have very limited resources for doing research, much less collaborative ethnography of the kinds I described in the last section. To be practical (and so students can finish their degrees in a timely fashion), I suggest to those interested in collaborative ethnography that they first become thoroughly familiar with the collaborative ethnographic literature, its history and its various kinds, and then, second, seek ways to integrate collaborative theory and methods into, for example, a single thesis chapter, into their approach to doing and writing up interviews, or – in cases, for instance, when committee chairs have other agendas and interests – even using the thesis, per Feld, to engage in 'dialogic editing' with consultants 'after the fact'. None of these adaptations are completely ideal, of course, but the goal is to be open to the possibilities of dialogue and collaborative exchange that are available in the specific context of a given research and writing project.

To help encourage collaborative research and writing in research, I often engage students in a variety of exercises. Many of these are outlined in detail in a recent book I co-authored with Elizabeth Campbell, titled Doing Ethnography Today (Campbell and Lassiter, 2015). In what follows, I briefly summarize some key points of some of these exercises, which here focus, in particular, on steps for getting started with collaborative ethnographic projects. I do, though, recommend that interested readers refer to this work in its entirety to get a fuller sense of the variety of exercises in which to engage and begin work on collaborative method and theory.

Activity 8.1

Personal assessment: Are you ready for collaborative research? A critically important aspect of deciding to do collaborative research of any kind is recognizing how your own experiences and interests shape your agendas and positions on any given topic. Some students find it helpful to write a personal statement, a position paper of sorts, that lines out how backgrounds like culture, ethnicity, class, gender, religion or other experiences have affected how they see and understand the world, as well as what things they care about. Discussing these openly with other students almost always helps more. In any case, assessing these positions can help to elaborate how experiences and backgrounds have yielded the particular interests (research and otherwise) one has, why they are important to her or him, and how these particular backgrounds and experiences might lead to certain kinds of collaborative research and not others. The purpose of this exercise is not to account for bias (so that it can be hidden from consultants or potential readers); its purpose is rather to prepare you for working collaboratively through inter-subjective frameworks in which you will regularly need to openly and explicitly clarify your position as you learn about others'. It is, of course, overly presumptuous to assume that a specific member of a collaborative group can be the 'objective one' and all others are not, or that any particular 'researcher' can go without disclosing their own positions as they work on any particular issue. Moreover, working within modes of collaborative research means that all parties must recognize up front that all bring backgrounds and experiences – as well as expertise – to the table. Negotiating methodological processes – and ideas, interpretations, outcomes and so forth – requires an openness to the voicing of various experiences and backgrounds via inter-subjective dialogue and exchange, not via more traditional modes of research that presumptuously separate 'objective' academic researchers from 'subjective' research participants (which, of course, is more about power than about yielding genuine dialogic understandings). Positioning research like this can make some academics feel vulnerable, and not everyone is cut out (or is willing) to do this kind of research, so it's important that you figure this out at the outset

Activity 8.2

Choosing groups: Towards creating collaborative research projects. The best place to begin with doing collaborative ethnography (especially for the first time) is with relationships you already have – and with common interests had with others – that are well-established in contexts that are already rich for building another layer of relationship around collaborative research. While I have done several projects that emerged entirely from my personal research interests (in which I then sought out collaborators), what I consider to be the best collaborative projects – for example, my work on Kiowa song or on Middletown or many of the projects I am now undertaking with non-profit groups, faculty and students in West Virginia – have emerged out of already existing relationships born of prior relationships or projects. This is true for many others doing collaborative ethnography today as well. Several of my own students, for example, working in non-profit organizations or schools, have turned to already existing relationships with parents, teachers, students and others to establish 'interest groups' who might have a bent towards working collaboratively to generate new knowledge or to figure out a solution to a particular problem in which everyone shares an interest (and who, of course, may have very different takes on that issue or problem).

With this in mind, students of collaborative ethnography may find it helpful to do another, separate assessment – this one on already established relationships with others (friends, co-workers, neighbours and so forth) – which maps out different groups in which they are already members and, importantly, groups embedded in ongoing conversations that have produced common desires to know something or address a problem. One of my doctoral students in education, for example, has a relative who once taught in a coal camp school that had long been torn down for the development of a highway. He had heard the stories since he was a child, but didn't have any research interest in the school until one of his professors, who attended the school as a boy, began talking to him about the school. By way of several conversations with the professor – and via further conversation with and encouragement from his relatives – the student eventually decided to do his doctoral dissertation on the history of the school through the framework of collaboratively produced oral histories that include his former professor, his relatives and many others he has met since the project's origination. Opportunities like this are all around us – identifying them, and knowing which ones are ripe for collaborative ethnography, of course, is the key. So, too, is recognizing that we might not be the only ones with research interests – such as the professor who originally planted the seed for my student to do an oral history of the school.

Activity 8.3

Starting collaborative ethnographic projects. Once you have identified your own agendas and positions, discovered what might be of interest for study within already existing groups of which you are a member, what next? In many of the projects I have done, I've begun with informal surveys of potential research participants to informally narrow focus. I also find it immensely productive to gather that small 'interest group' (mentioned earlier) for an informal meeting or a potluck meal. (Facilitating that meeting in a community space [like a community centre or in someone's home] is preferable to hosting it in an academic space [like a classroom], especially when hosting in the latter context may prompt participants to make assumptions about the trappings of conventional academic divides between 'researchers' and 'subjects'.) Common interests, in general terms, may be already established, so in the context of such a meeting (or several, if needed), all participants can, as a group, talk about the project, their various agendas and what they want to find out and accomplish.

Importantly, these meetings can provide the context to begin negotiating an agreed-upon set of collaboratively derived research questions. This process can take time, of course, and may call for several meetings before the project actually begins. In addition to asking yourselves What do we want to know? or What do we want to accomplish? or What questions do we, as a group, think are the most important to address? you will also need to begin talking about which collaborative methods and approaches will best serve the project, how they will be carried out and who will do them. Sometimes those approaches and methods apply only to the academic researcher, who wants to work within a collaborative framework; sometimes the group as a whole, of course, may plan to conduct the research and writing as a teamed collaborative ethnography.

These meetings can also be the occasion to involve conversations that begin to document and outline sets of agreed-upon commitments to one another that will serve as a kind of 'ethical code' unique to the project. For example: when we did the Other Side of Middletown, Hurley Goodall (a local black activist and politician), Elizabeth Campbell (who, at the time, worked in a local museum), Michelle Natasya Johnson (a graduate research assistant) and I facilitated several meetings (all in the basement fellowship hall of a local black church) with African American community leaders and others who would be involved with the project. During these meetings, several project participants voiced their concerns about being a part of 'another' academic study in which results were neither published nor made widely accessible. These initial conversations led to a series of deeper conversations that eventually yielded an agreed-upon ethical guideline for the project, in which we promised each other that, among other things, we would, to the best of our abilities, see the project through to its wider dissemination in an accessibly written book. This code (which included seven 'commitments' in all) was written down, copied and distributed among all participants involved in the project (see Lassiter et al., 2004: 20–21).

For project participants who work in academe, university and disciplinary guidelines for doing ethical research – discipline-specific ethical codes or university-based Institutional Review Boards (IRBs) – can also enter the conversation during this stage. As we were developing our ethical guidelines for the Other Side of Middletown project, for instance, students and faculty (from a variety of disciplinary backgrounds) introduced ethical expectations from their own disciplines (e.g. remaining true to historical accuracy) that the larger group agreed to integrate into our context-specific set of ethical commitments. In that project and in many others, I often have students review and compare a variety of ethical guidelines from different disciplines (such as oral history, anthropology or folklore) to get a sense of the various guiding principles of research that can be, in turn, openly discussed with the larger collaborative ethnographic research team, and then integrated into projects as they begin and evolve. The same can be said of more formal guidelines from university-specific IRBs, which can have their own sets of expectations and regulations (see Campbell and Lassiter, 2015: 39–34 for more on this issue, in particular). While such guidelines and collaborative commitments of all sorts may place certain limits on what any given project might accomplish, one should also recognize that being open to this emergent research process can also mean engaging in a much broader and diverse array of possibilities for knowing or doing something than if one were going at it alone.

Conclusions

Collaborative ethnography in field-based disciplines has very specific meanings that differ from how forms of collaborative research are often understood in other disciplines (e.g. in lab sciences where collaboration among other colleagues is common). Collaborative ethnography refers to a kind of research that often involves academic-based researchers and research participants in common collaborative research projects that emphasize and integrate collaboration into the research process and, importantly, into the process of interpretation, writing and dissemination.

Chapter key points

- Collaborative ethnography engages diverse approaches for both research and writing, with different collaborative ethnographies emphasizing different processes and results.
- Approaches range from single ethnographers involving research participants as readers and editors of, or contributors to, ethnographic texts as they develop, to the formation of large, teamed collaborative projects, initiated by either academic-based or community-based researchers.
- Whether large or small, several principles are always at work: among the most important of these concerns how well such work travels (via, for example, accessible writing) across boundaries often separating academic and community discourse.
- Much of this chapter compares already published collaborative ethnographies, so it focuses in the main on the various approaches and practices for doing collaborative ethnography after a project has been initiated.
- The last section elaborates in more depth steps towards beginning collaborative ethnographic research projects in the first place.
- Several things are important to keep in mind when initiating a collaborative project, including one's willingness to engage in the kind of inter-subjective relationship-building that can produce collaborative research; how to go about choosing groups with whom to work; and how to initially determine a project's collaboratively derived goals, research questions, ethical guidelines and the like.
- In the end, the key to doing collaborative ethnography well is being open to the emergent research processes that characterize both the limitations and possibilities of collaborative research.

Recommended reading

Campbell, E., & Lassiter, L. E. (2015). *Doing Ethnography Today: Theories, Methods, Exercises*. London: Wiley Blackwell.

Field, L. W. (2008). *Abalone Tales: Collaborative Explorations of Sovereignty and Identity in Native California*.

Hyatt, S. B. (ed.) (2012). *The Neighborhood of Saturdays: Memories of a Multi-Ethnic Community on Indianapolis's South Side*. Indianapolis, IN: Dog Ear Publishers.

Lassiter, L. E. (1995). *The Power of Kiowa Song*. Tucson: University of Arizona Press.

Lassiter, L. E. (2005). *The Chicago Guide to Collaborative Ethnography*. Chicago: University of Chicago Press.

Lassiter, L. E., Ellis, C., & Kotay, R. (2002). *The Jesus Road: Kiowas, Christianity, and Indian Hymns*. Lincoln: University of Nebraska Press.

Lassiter, L. E., Goodall, H., Campbell, E., & Johnson, M. N. (eds) (2004). *The Other Side of Middletown: Exploring Muncie's African American Community*. Walnut Creek, CA: AltaMira Press.

Lawless, E. (1993). *Holy Women, Wholly Women: Sharing Ministries through Life Stories and Reciprocal Ethnography*. Philadelphia: University of Pennsylvania Press.

Neighborhood Story Project. (2017). Neighborhood Story Project – Our Stories Told by Us. Https://www.neighborhoodstoryproject.org, accessed 26 February 2017. An exemplary programme organizing projects around collaborative ethnography.

Spatig, L. & Amerikaner, L. (2014). *Thinking Outside the Girl Box: Teaming Up with Resilient Youth in Appalachia*. Athens: Ohio University Press.

Thorp, L. (2006). *The Pull of the Earth: Participatory Ethnography in the School Garden*. Walnut Creek, CA: AltaMira Press.

Advanced reading

Crow, G. (2017). *What Are Community Studies?* London: Bloomsbury Academic.

Feld, S. (1990). *Sound and Sentiment: Birds, Weeping, Poetics, and Song in Kaluli Expression*, 2nd ed. Philadelphia: University of Pennsylvania Press.

Hart, A., Maddison, E., & Wolff, D. (eds) (2007). *Community-University Partnerships in Practice*. Leicester: National Institute of Adult Continuing Education.

Haviland, M. (2017). *Side by Side? Community Art and the Challenge of Co-Creativity*. New York: Routledge.

King, M. (2010). Documenting Traditions and the Ethnographic Double Bind. *Collaborative Anthropologies*, 3: 37–68.

Lassiter, L. E. (2012). 'To Fill in the Missing Piece of the Middletown Puzzle': Lessons from Re-Studying Middletown. *Sociological Review*, 60: 421–437.

Rabinow, P. & Marcus, G. E., with Faubion, J. D. and Rees, T. (2008). *Designs for an Anthropology of the Contemporary*. Durham: Duke University Press.

Trimmer, J. F. (2006). Teaching and learning outside and inside the box. *Peer Review*, 8(2): 20–22.

Web links

Collaborative Anthropologies
http://coll-anth.anth.ubc.ca/
Currently based at the University of British Columbia, a journal on the theories and methods of collaborative research in anthropology, especially as it relates to collaborative ethnography.

Imagine – Connecting Communities through Research
http://www.imaginecommunity.org.uk
An Economic and Social Research Council Connected Communities UK wide project emphasizing several different modes of collaborative research (including collaborative ethnography) in the context of community university research partnerships.

Neighborhood Story Project
https://www.neighborhoodstoryproject.org
A New Orleans neighbourhood-based programme emphasizing collaborative ethnography.

9

Participatory Action Research with Young People

Christina McMellon and Mary Mitchell

Key points

- Participatory Action Research is an approach rather than a prescriptive process. Each research project is different but each is located within a clear epistemological understanding of the world and is underpinned by a set of guiding principles and values.
- Participatory Action Research opens up spaces for young people to identify things that are important to them and to conduct research that focuses upon action and practical solutions.
- Participatory Action Research requires researchers to reflect critically upon their practice in order to challenge power imbalances and ensure that young people's participation is meaningful.
- Young people participate in Participatory Action Research projects for many reasons. Participatory Action Research offers young people the opportunity to: build positive relationships; have fun; and develop skills and confidence.
- In addition to traditional research outcomes, Participatory Action Research has the potential to impact positively on organizations and individuals.

Introduction

Participatory Action Research (PAR) is an *approach* that has the potential to challenge and disrupt long-held assumptions about research, institutions and social/cultural norms. Historically used in communities and practice settings, PAR is a methodology that is increasingly used in academia. Rather than positioning academic researchers as the sole experts in producing knowledge, PAR places the people affected by the issue and their desire for change at the centre of the research process; this is both a strength of the approach and a challenge for more traditional academic researchers.

This chapter explores the opportunities and challenges of using PAR and the ideas and values underpinning this approach. PAR has been conducted with people in all types of communities and, although the case study examined in the chapter focuses upon work with young people, many of the opportunities and challenges discussed clearly transfer to other contexts. Young Edinburgh Action (YEA) is a project which uses PAR to support young people's meaningful participation in local authority decision-making. Throughout this chapter, the authors use their experiences of working with the project to provide examples and illustrations of the day-to-day realities of undertaking PAR.[1] We begin with a discussion of the principles and assumptions that underpin PAR before giving a brief description of Young Edinburgh Action and the ways that it makes use of PAR to further its twin aims of improving services for young people in Edinburgh and providing learning and development opportunities for the young people involved. The chapter finishes with an exploration of practice issues that have arisen while collaborating with young people involved in PAR.

Conceptualizing Participation Action Research

Lincoln and Guba (1985) make a distinction between positivist research, which is about identifying objectively true and generalizable knowledge, and

---

[1] At the time of writing, both of the authors are employed by City of Edinburgh Council to support Young Edinburgh Action; Mary developed YEA's current model and operates mostly at a strategic level, while Christina works directly to support young people to undertake PAR. We are also both associate researchers with the Centre for Research on Families and Relationships, based at University of Edinburgh.

post-positivist research, which emphasizes knowledge of particular instances in specific contexts. Heron and Reason (1997) suggest that there is a third possible research paradigm that locates the discovery/creation of knowledge in experience, and views experience as an encounter with other humans or with the world. According to this view, therefore, research 'is concerned with the development of living knowledge' that is grounded in our subjective relational experiences (Reason and Bradbury, 2001: 2). Individuals are 'epistemologically privileged' (Balen et al., 2006: 31) in relation to their own subjective experiences but can work together towards mutual understandings that may point to possible objective universals. This epistemological importance of subjective experience supports a political commitment to sharing the stories of those whose opinions are often silenced and whose experiences are often hidden in the public sphere (Heron, 1996a and b). Such epistemological and political beliefs require us to develop ways of doing research that genuinely involve participants and value their participation as individuals who bring experience, skills and time to the research process.

PAR can be located within this participatory research paradigm developed by Heron and Reason (1997). PAR is, however, difficult to define largely since the focus on collaboration means that each project is different. The research questions, methods used and analysis emerge over time in discussion and interaction between the co-researchers rather than follow a plan set at the outset. The emergent nature of the practice means that at the beginning of the project the group often have very little idea where it will end up.

Often PAR is described as a 'process' of research which implies a rather linear and static set of stages with an end result. The types of activities conducted as part of PAR are, however, difficult to standardize: activities are context specific and fluid; relationships and ideas materialize; methods and activities may change and develop (Mackenzie et al., 2012). We would argue that PAR is not a fixed process with defined stages; rather it is a 'research practice' that is made up of a dynamic interaction between: *inquiry; participation; action and reflection*. PAR occurs through recurring co-reflective cycles of these key elements. In reality, PAR is likely to be more successful where participants have not faithfully followed a set of steps, but rather where they have a 'strong and authentic sense of development and evolution in their *practices*, their *understandings* of their practices, and the *situations* in which they practice' (Kemmis and McTaggart, 2005: 277).

A strength of the PAR approach is that it has the flexibility to generate information based on the needs, ambitions, interests and desires of all those involved, yet those involved do not need to participate in the same way or at the same intensity. Unintended (and intended) knowledge can be produced, and change can occur, at any time in the PAR project for individuals, communities and/or organizations. At the centre of any PAR is a group of people who care about an issue and are committed to taking action in order to gather empirical evidence and to use that evidence to effect change. Unlike traditional positivist research that aims for value-free research, PAR sees research as a value-led process of people together examining, learning about and changing their worlds. PAR is not a purely intellectual exercise but remains focused upon its potential impacts. As expressed by Guzman and colleagues:

> The researcher is a committed participant and learner in the process of research, i.e. a militant rather than a detached observer. (2017: 24)

As an approach to research PAR uses a set of practice principles for identifying, designing, conducting, analysing and acting on a piece of research.

Reflection point 9.1:
Why might you choose to use PAR over traditional research methods? What might be the benefits and challenges of using PAR?

Collaboration: All those involved in PAR are recognized as having valuable skills, ideas and knowledge to contribute to the project. PAR challenges long-held traditions about the types of research and knowledge that are valid and have value. PAR emphasizes the validity of different people's experiences and perspectives. Therefore, where more traditional research posits the academic researcher as the expert with the knowledge required to design and undertake a research project, PAR is committed to the principle that the research design and implementation is enriched by the unique ideas, abilities and experience that all participants bring.

Reflection point 9.2:
How is a collaborative approach different to a traditional research approach? How would you enable collaboration if you were a researcher using PAR?

Reflection: PAR trusts people to ask questions about their lives that need to be asked and credits them with the ability to work together to find answers and solutions. Spaces for individual and group reflection are built into all elements of the approach. Consequently, the questions, the findings and the solutions are likely to be different to those that would be identified by the researcher using a more traditional methodology because they are grounded in the realities and lived experiences of those involved. This adds value to the research as it ensures the knowledge constructed is more relevant to the lives of the people affected by the topic.

Reflection point 9.3:
Reflective questions are open-ended and begin with, for example, what, how or why. Identify key questions that could be useful to encourage reflection by individuals and groups involved in PAR.
   How would you enable space for reflection when using PAR?

Acknowledging and challenging power within research relationships: PAR explicitly and continually challenges the traditional power dynamic between academic researcher and research participant by positioning all those involved as active agents in all elements of the research project. By recognizing people's expertise in their own lives, PAR is able to access data and knowledge that may be inaccessible to a more 'objective' researcher. In this way, PAR breaks down assumed hierarchies between academic, professional and personal knowledge. PAR can be challenging to academic researchers because it requires us to relinquish our control over the research process and its outcomes.

Reflection point 9.4:
What hierarchies are assumed within traditional research paradigms and how do these impact the balance of power between the researcher and the research participants?
   How do you feel about the idea of 'giving up' the traditional researcher role?

Action: People do PAR because they want things to change. Change is at the centre of PAR and the research is inextricably linked to action. The research experience not only identifies what is required to change but change occurs through the research itself. Those who wish to maintain the status quo rarely support PAR because it almost always finds that the status quo is not good enough.

Reflection point 9.5:
If you were using PAR what would help you remain action-focused?
   How would you recognize when action and change were occurring?

There is a tendency among many academics to view PAR as 'fluffy', something that benefits the people involved but does not produce *valid* research or *real* impact. Throughout this chapter, we argue that PAR is not only politically important, because it allows us to challenge existing power imbalances, but that it is also epistemologically and methodologically important because it offers opportunities to access new knowledge that can effect real change (Cammarota and Romero, 2011; Mackenzie et al., 2012). This can only happen, however, if we, as researchers, commit to engaging reflectively in an approach to research that is far more than a set of methods to get people involved. PAR requires us to become aware of, and challenge, the implicit assumptions that we and other people hold about knowledge and about young people. PAR is not always comfortable and it isn't always successful but we argue that it is important.

Essentials

We have argued that reflection is a key skill in PAR. Some examples of activities we have used to assist reflection are:

Critical thinking: Personally or as a group reflecting critically upon what is occurring at any moment in time: how could things be improved? What is working well?

Research Journal: Asking each of the individuals involved in the research to record their thoughts and emotions regarding the research in a journal. This activity enables a personal reflection on circumstances and opens up creative and critical thinking about the research throughout the time of the project.

Group reflection: These are group activities which enable a quick reflection of what members of the group are thinking and feeling.

Example 1: 'A round' – each person is asked in turn to answer a particular question and then listen, without interrupting, to others in the group. Examples of questions might include: 'What is something that has gone well with the research?' or 'How are you feeling about this research right now?'

Example 2: 'Taking the energy in the room' – get an expression of group members' energy levels by asking everyone to raise or lower their hand in relation to how they feel.

> **Reflection point 9.6:**
> *Name three additional reflective activities which could be useful in PAR.*

Participatory Action Research with children and young people

The predominant emphasis of research involving children and young people since the start of the twentieth century has been that they are most often the 'objects' of research. However, there has more recently been an interest in children and young people as the 'subjects' of research, perceiving them as having something relevant to contribute to the research process (Tisdall et al., 2009). Kirby (1999) makes a distinction between a practical approach to research for the purpose of service improvement and academic approaches where the involvement of children and young people can make the research more rigorous. The benefit of involving children and young people in research has been hypothesized by a number of scholars suggesting that specific organization/s require information to improve their services (Tisdall et al., 2009; Davis et al., 2015) and that children and young people can also personally benefit from the experience (Bell, 2011). However, even research models that acknowledge young people as active contributors to research generally still position young people as research participants with the aims of meeting the needs of academic research. PAR in contrast, seeks to acknowledge and challenge such power imbalances, positioning young people as co-researchers and constructors of knowledge who have their own agendas and desired outcomes. These differing agendas are made explicit within the PAR approach, and are negotiated throughout the life of the project and recognized as adding value to the research.

Children and young people traditionally face an extra power dynamic when participating in research: not only are they viewed as non-researchers but they are also non-adults. PAR, however, fits clearly into the wider literature charting the new sociology of childhood, which makes explicit the conceptualizations of childhood that have traditionally underpinned research about children and argues for the recognition of children's agency and capabilities (Prout and James, 1997; Christensen and James, 2008).

PAR with children and young people is underpinned by a belief in the capacity of children and young people to meaningfully participate in all elements of PAR alongside adults. This includes setting the research topic and research questions, designing and implementing the methodology, analysing data, dissemination and impact. Young people *can* be involved during each of these elements but however, might not *want* to be. There is a need to ensure flexibility within PAR based on the needs, ambitions and desires of those involved; not everyone needs to be involved at the same level or in the same ways.

Through enabling children and young people to identify research issues that are relevant to their lives, PAR focuses upon the investigation and resolution of real life issues and problems. It is for this reason we argue that PAR is particularly useful for integrating research into practice and service improvement, and informing change and action in the longer term. Finally, as Mackenzie et al. (2012: 13) remind us, PAR needs to be widely inclusive of the diversity of experience and capacities among participants of the research to assist engagement in the practice and ownership of the findings.

Just as PAR requires academics to relinquish control to groups of people with lived experience of the research issue, so it requires adults to relinquish control to children and young people. Children and young people are capable of asking and answering questions; adults need to trust and value the questions that they ask and the answers that they provide. From a PAR perspective, children and young people are seen as valuable members of communities who have equal rights and capabilities to participate in taking action to effect change regarding issues that they care about.

This does not mean, however, that adults are not needed in the research process; PAR with children and young people is a collaborative process where all parties (adults and children) contribute valuable experiences, ideas and/ or skills. There is a need to create a space where all collaborators' knowledge, experience and views are equally respected in order for meaningful PAR to take place. This requires all collaborators, but particularly the adults involved, to remain aware of and challenge the existing structural constraints (be they cultural, institutional or academic) that seek to invalidate children and young people's ability to construct useful knowledge and effect change.

Thinking about spaces for participation moves us away from the idea of participation as set processes and activities, instead inviting professionals to open up opportunities for young people to define and develop their own ideas (Percy-Smith, 2010). This can be challenging because it requires us to reassess the professional's ideas about the types of participation that are appropriate and acceptable (Gallacher and Gallagher, 2008; People's Knowledge Editorial Collective, 2017). It is, of course, important that these spaces feel 'safe'; that all young people who want to be involved in the research feel able to share their experiences and trust that their ideas will be valued. We argue, however, that it is also important that these spaces are 'brave'; we should not shy away from controversial topics about which young people feel passionate, even when these topics might make adults feel uncomfortable. Concurrently, we argue that adults should feel confident to challenge young people and explain when they disagree with them, or why a particular topic makes them feel uncomfortable. Equally young people should feel brave and safe to challenge and disagree with each other and professionals. That all opinions and thoughts are valued, acknowledged and welcome links back to the principles underpinning the practice of PAR. Embracing the possibility for disagreement is, however, often difficult in practice and staff need to remain aware of how they interact with young people and contribute to the research, through reflective conversations with each other and with young people.

Essentials

Children and young people are capable of asking and answering questions but they do not always have the skills and confidence to do so. In YEA we use a variety of participatory activities which build trust between individuals and allow people to explore and exchange sometimes challenging ideas safely. Some examples of activities we have used to create safe and brave spaces for dialogue include:

- Use of printed images on a particular theme, for example images related to women's rights and feminism. Spread the pictures on a table/floor and ask individuals to pick images that they relate to and share the feelings and thoughts that the images raise.
- 'Agree, disagree, don't know': this activity requires a number of controversial statements (not questions) prepared beforehand which cover a range of issues relevant to the group. Place signs saying 'agree' and 'disagree' at opposite ends of the room. Ask the group to stand and then read one of the statements. Members of the group are encouraged to move to the place between the two signs that most reflects their reaction to the statement. Ask group members in different positions to volunteer to share their reasons for where they are standing.
- Using quotes from famous people: print a number of quotations on separate pieces of paper. Ask the group to pick one quote which resonates with them and then discuss why different group members like different quotations.

Reflection point 9.7:
If you were conducting PAR how would you enable participants to express their views, ask questions and identify research topics?

The case study: Young Edinburgh Action (YEA)

This section briefly explains YEA and its use of PAR. YEA is an innovative approach to implementing the City of Edinburgh Council's (CEC) Young People's Participation Strategy. This section briefly explains YEA and its use of PAR. YEA enables young people to set an agenda for action and supports young people to undertake research and make recommendations on topics they feel strongly about.

As one of the largest local government areas in Scotland, the CEC is a main provider of services for local people. In 2012, CEC elected members agreed that a new approach was required to ensure young people's active citizenship and input in the improvement of young people's services in Edinburgh, moving towards an approach based on inquiry, dialogue and spaces for meaningful participation. YEA believes young people's participation is important because it leads to: improvements in services for young people; and learning and development for the young people involved (McMellon and Mitchell 2016).

YEA has a cyclical process (see figure 9.1) which engages young people in the implementation of the Edinburgh Young People's Participation Strategy:

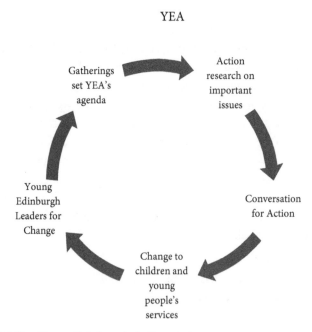

Figure 9.1 The Young Edinburgh Action cycle

Youth gatherings

Gatherings, which take place annually, are events for young people across Edinburgh that are planned and facilitated by young people who have completed a leadership training programme with YEA. Gatherings ensure that young people set the agenda and focus for YEA. By the end of each Gathering, young people have chosen the priority topics that YEA will focus on for the next year.

Reflection point 9.8:
This example utilizes an event to identify the research topics to be addressed. Are there other ways, if you were conducting PAR, that these decisions could be made?

Action research groups

Action research groups are at the heart of YEA's approach and enable a core group of young people to explore and present the views of a wider group of young people in Edinburgh. An action research group is established for each of the topics chosen at the Gathering. The group is open to any young people who are interested in the topic and is usually made up of between six and fifteen young people.

The way that the group operates is flexible, depending upon the topic and the participants, but with the support of YEA staff each action research group will:

- *Think* about the topic and what it means for young people in Edinburgh.
- *Investigate* the current situation around this topic and find out the views of other young people in Edinburgh.
- *Create* a resource (e.g. a poster, a video, a piece of drama or art, a song or a blog) to share what the group learns.
- *Make recommendations* to the people who make decisions about this topic.

Examples of topics undertaken so far in these groups include: bullying, mental health support in schools, poverty and inequality, sex education and gender inequality, support for LGBTI+ community in schools and skills you need to live your life.

Reflection point 9.9:
YEA recruit voluntary participants from across Edinburgh using social media, youth work networks, distributing information to schools and word of mouth. If you were conducting PAR how would you recruit participants and how would you ensure that these were the most appropriate people to take part? What are the ethical considerations?

Conversation for Action

From the beginning of the action research process the groups discuss the impact that they hope to have. The Conversation for Action is an important interface, where young people and adult decision-makers invited by the young people come together to discuss the topic and develop an action plan. A Conversation for Action is convened at the end of each action research process. Young people set the agenda for the conversation and the senior worker in YEA chairs the meeting.

Young people present their learning, ideas and recommendations in order to facilitate meaningful dialogue with relevant policy makers and senior officers. The minutes of the meeting take the form of a list of action points assigned to specific adults and young people. Follow up meetings ensure that professionals and young people are held accountable for completing their agreed actions.

Reflection point 9.10:
YEA utilize Conversations for Action as a form of knowledge exchange and decision-making. We consider this a vital element of the PAR impact. If you were undertaking PAR, how would your group share information in order to have an impact on the research topic? Who will they share information with?

An example: 'Alex and Charlie'

Young people at the 2015 YEA Gathering decided on the issue of gender inequality as an important issue for young people in Edinburgh. A small group of approximately ten young people met to discuss the issue and to identify and clarify the research questions that they wanted to pursue. The research group decided to run a day-long event of inquiry activities to explore and reflect on the issues of gender inequality with their peers. About sixty young people came along to the event and took part in a variety of activities and discussions about different aspects of gender, all of which were recorded. The group then analysed the evidence gathered from the inquiry and identified that two key themes emerged strongly from their data. Firstly, the vital importance of challenging gender stereotypes and secondly, that this needs to happen when children are very young to counteract the strong messages about gender that young children get from the media, wider society and their own families.

Learning from previous action research projects carried out by YEA, the group decided that, rather than simply telling decision-makers that they should be challenging gender stereotypes with young children, they wanted to offer a tool that would enable this to happen. After much thought and discussion, they made the decision to write and design a storybook challenging gender stereotypes for four to six-year-olds.

The group worked with a graphic designer for six months, using the data from their event to inform a first draft of the story. They then ran a focus group with early years professionals to get feedback on their work, which they incorporated into the book.

A prototype of the book, called 'Alex and Charlie (see Figure 9.2)', was presented to adult decision-makers at the YEA Conversation for Action along with a proposal that the book should be published and distributed to all primary and nursery schools in Edinburgh. The attendees were impressed by the group's work and the meeting resulted in the CEC underwriting the production and publication of the storybook. Members of the research group piloted the book with children in primary schools and incorporated their feedback into the final version. A teaching pack with activities to accompany the book that can be used in the classroom was also designed by young people with additional input from teachers, and the book was launched in April 2017.

Figure 9.2 Alex and Charlie (HT)

Reflection point 9.11:
In this example young people chose to organize an event to get data for the inquiry. If you were conducting PAR what other ways could you undertake research regarding the topic?

Participatory Action Research with young people: Practice issues

The research context

No social research happens in a vacuum, rather, the context within which the research is situated impacts upon the research. While an important part of the PAR is seeking to make visible and to challenge inequalities of power and influence, it also has to exist and function within these limitations. Policies, legislation, resources, organizational structures, procedures and attitudes, individual limitations, communities and cultural attitudes all impact on the research we do, why we do it and what we can achieve with it. In practice this can be frustrating. Restrictions and challenges that we have faced in our work include:

- YEA exists in the context of a local authority structure but not all of the topics that young people think are important are wholly within the remit of the local authority For example, 'Votes at 16' was identified at a YEA Gathering as one of the top topics, but the right to vote in elections is a legislative issue which can only be addressed at the Scottish Government and Westminster levels.

Reflection point 9.12:
In the example above, the group acknowledged that the original focus needed to change in response to the changing context and group interests.
If you were undertaking PAR, how would you enable the group to reflect on the relevance of the research question and whether the research has the potential to create the desired impact?

- Change often happens slowly within local authorities. In order to have the best chance of having an impact, research needs to follow bureaucratic processes and involve multiple people. However, young people get involved because they want change and the slowness of movement can cause frustration. Young people may move onto other interests before recommendations can be fully achieved.

Reflection point 9.13:
YEA keeps in touch with past participants, updating them on the progress of PAR projects. If you were undertaking PAR, what might be the challenges of time and action? And how would you manage those challenges?

- Not all adults think that young people should be involved in decision-making about topics that affect them. Many adults have reservations about young people's ability to be involved in certain decision-making processes and question the appropriateness of sharing power in these processes with young people.

Reflection point 9.14:
YEA takes time to meet adults separately to discuss the involvement of children and young people. How would you manage adult attitudes to participants' involvement in your PAR?

- Where people (adults and young people) hold strong views about a topic, they can find it difficult to hear different, potentially challenging, points of view. See earlier Top tips: PAR with young people.
- Most of the adults involved with YEA are paid for their time while most of the young people are not. This creates inequalities relating to different people's motivations and abilities for participating in the research.

Reflection point 9.15:
YEA acknowledges young people's involvement in a number of ways, for example: public awards, publicity and promotion on Facebook, fun events and training opportunities. How would participants be rewarded or acknowledged for their time and work in your PAR? What are the ethical considerations of rewarding participants?

- People (adults and young people) have multiple claims upon their attention and some parts of the PAR are more engaging than others. Keeping young people and professionals motivated and focused on the research throughout the process can be challenging.

Reflection point 9.16:
YEA PAR groups meet regularly and are flexible with attendance, recognizing the time commitments of all those involved. If you were undertaking PAR, how would you enable participants to be involved while sticking to your timescale and maintaining flexibility regarding attendance?

Example: YEA's 'Votes at 16' Action Research Group

In the aftermath of the Scottish Referendum, in which sixteen- to eighteen-year-olds had been able to vote, and with the prospect of the upcoming Westminster elections where sixteen- to eighteen-year-olds would return to not being eligible to vote, the most popular topic chosen by young people at the 2015 Gathering was 'Votes at 16'.

'Votes at 16' was immediately a challenging topic for YEA because the local authority does not decide whether or not sixteen-year-olds get to vote. Then, after the Gathering and following the Smith Commission's devolution of decision-making about voting age to the Scottish Government, a bill was passed to give sixteen-and seventeen-year-olds the right to vote in Scottish and local government elections in Scotland.

At the first meeting of the group of young people who were interested in participating in the action research group on this topic, we discussed whether we wanted to pursue the topic since it seemed like the ultimate aim had already come into being. However, the group felt strongly that, firstly, the topic was still important since sixteen-and seventeen-year-olds would still not be able to vote in Westminster elections and, secondly, that they felt that young people did not have all the information that they needed in order to make informed decisions about voting.

The group designed and circulated an online survey to see what other young people thought about the topic. They then analysed the results of the survey and made a light-hearted short film to share the findings and their thoughts about the topic. The action research group's recommendations, based on the survey findings, were:

- That sixteen–eighteen-year-olds should have the vote in all elections including Westminster elections and local council elections.
- That political education in schools should be improved to ensure that all young people could make fully informed choices about voting.

Despite there being an increased interest in the topic publically and a drive from the Scottish Government to have citizenship as a recognized area for the secondary education curriculum, Mary found it difficult to identify key decision-makers in the local authority who had any influence in this area. The topic crossed over various employees' remits but did not fit totally with any one officer's role within the council. This, and a general malaise regarding the importance of involving young people in curriculum development, delayed the group's conversation with decision-makers. The Conversation for Action finally happened significantly after the research had been completed and the group had lost momentum. The meeting focused upon political education for young people, and unfortunately the conversation became dominated by adults. Unsurprisingly, the young people (who were all sitting at one end of the long table) quickly disengaged. Although an action plan was agreed, many of the actions identified were not achieved.

Learning from this example related to context

- Some action research topics work better than others; in the particular context of YEA topics that work best are those about which the local authority has clear capacity and remit to take action.
- Context changes and PAR needs to reflect and respond iteratively to these demands. Although we did discuss the policy changes related to sixteen- and seventeen-year-olds getting the vote, with hindsight we believe that we could have been clearer about the ways in which the scope and aims of the research were changing throughout the life of the group.
- Having the right people around the table for the Conversation for Action is vitally important. One value that young people's action research brings to the table is that it can bypass existing politics and enable an open discussion about the topic. However, when the topic isn't entirely clear and people are not clear what is being asked of them and how this fits into existing remits and initiatives, it is easy to get mired in challenges rather than look for solutions.
- Simple practical things can be done in meetings to challenge structural inequalities and to enable young people to feel engaged. During a debrief with the young people involved, we decided together that at subsequent Conversations for Action we would ensure that young people were integrated into the meeting space rather than sitting together at one end. Young people asked if, for subsequent meetings, they could meet with the chairperson beforehand in order to explain what they wanted to get from the meeting. We also determined to make better use of an ice-breaker activity to make everyone feel comfortable, and a clear agenda to keep the conversation on topic.

Essentials

The group and group members are an important resource to help find solutions to challenges experienced in PAR.

Solutions don't need to be complicated; they can be simple like, for example, changing seating arrangements in meetings or meeting the chair prior to the meeting.

Roles: Academic/researcher/facilitator/ adult/child?

In most traditional positivist research there is a clear distinction between the 'researcher' and the 'researched'. The researcher has a clear role as an expert who creates the research questions, designs, implements and writes up the research design. In action research, however, the boundary between researcher and research participants is less clear. Young people are simultaneously co-researchers and research participants; adults are simultaneously co-researchers and facilitators.

PAR often blurs the boundaries between different roles and the (for want of a better name) 'lead researcher' role becomes one that includes elements of facilitation, training and advocacy. The primary role of the adults involved, therefore, becomes one of setting up a research space which values different perspectives, experiences and skills. There can, however, be a tension between a desire to 'share experiences' and a desire to 'do research'. The adult facilitator has to find a way to allow both of these to happen, keeping the focus upon the research process while simultaneously providing space for the group to explore their own stories.

Just as the young people bring their own ideas, skills, opinions and experiences to the group, so do the adults. In YEA, we consider it not only important that we, as staff, are aware of these different roles but also that we explicitly raise and discuss them with the groups of young people with whom we work.

Reflection point 9.17:
How would you describe PAR to a group of participants?

In groups we find ourselves moving between the roles of lead researcher (pushing the group to stay focused on the wider research aims) youth worker (managing group dynamics and supporting everyone to participate) and group member (mindfully sharing our own ideas and opinions). This can be confusing since the groups are fluid and often veer off on unexpected tangents. There is no clear structure and there are not set times when different roles are required. We, therefore, discuss with young people about the different roles that we all play and, when we notice we have moved into a different role or a different agenda, we try to be explicit and transparent about the role that we are playing and why.

An example of this is that, when developing research questions with an action research group, a member of staff might talk about 'putting my researcher hat on' in order to share their experience about what makes a good research question, but then might mime taking that hat off and 'putting my council hat on' in order to talk about what research aims might have more chance of success within the local authority limitations. As youth workers, we might encourage group members to share their personal experiences of a topic but would jokingly put our researcher hats back on if the group ran the risk of becoming a 'talking shop' that was moving away from its action research remit.

Reflection point 9.18:
How would you identify and discuss roles and power differences in PAR with a group of participants?

Web of impact

Changes can occur during PAR for the individual young people working on the research, the wider organization commissioning the research, and the broader population of young people can be affected. We argue that impact happens at any point in the research and in multiple and interconnecting ways; outcomes are not experienced in a purely linear format the end of a clear research process.

Benefits for individual young people

Young people express that they have benefited in different ways from their involvement in PAR. To begin, young people have said that they like PAR because it makes a difference, when things change it feels good and they like seeing results of their work. Secondly, they enjoy getting to know other people, hearing different experiences and stories. Thirdly, young people learn new skills and have new experiences which are good for their CV. Finally, young people recognize that being involved in PAR fulfils their right to be involved in decisions that affect them.

Benefits for organizations

The organizations involved in PAR also benefit from the research practice in a number of ways. An important impact for CEC is that the work has improved services for young people in the city. CEC has been able to understand the nuances of different issues from young people's perspectives, accessing knowledge and information that was not previously available. PAR has also assisted CEC to fulfil its legal and policy obligations to involve young people in partnership working in a way that is meaningful rather than tokenistic. The range of different issues identified and researched has supported increased partnership working between the council and other organizations including NHS Lothian, schools and voluntary youth organizations. Our interactions with young people have made us reflect on our practice and question the way things have been done historically which has, in turn, affected the overall culture and practice of engagement within the organization.

Benefits for the wider community of young people

The wider community of young people in Edinburgh have also benefited from PAR as they can see that the council and its partners are committed to listening to young people and are responsive to their concerns, ideas and experiences.

YEA has also resulted in real improvements to the support and services that CEC provides for young people. A discussion on the substantive changes in services made as a result of PAR with young people can be found in McMellon and Mitchell (2016).

Reflection point 9.19:
What impact do you hope your PAR will have? How would you capture impact for all stakeholders?

Conclusions

Participatory Action Research is located within a participatory research paradigm that situates the creation knowledge in interaction between people and supports a political commitment to sharing the stories of those whose opinions are often absent (Heron, 1996a). PAR, therefore, requires researchers to develop ways of doing research that genuinely involve participants and value their participation as individuals who bring experience, skills and time to the research process.

'To end with a quotation from a young person who has worked with YEA: Young people are passionate about making a difference for the better and YEA and action research help to facilitate these changes.' (YEA participant aged 15)

Chapter key points

- Participatory Action Research with children and young people has a number of strengths, particularly in its capacity to engage a diverse range of individuals in exploring real life issues and problems.
- Research interventions are based on priorities set by children and young people themselves, thus providing helpful information to the local authority and partners about how service users experience problems and how these might be resolved.
- Where young people identify topics and are engaged in all aspects of research design and implementation, then the recommendations and practical solutions emerging from the research respond to the needs of those directly affected.
- The experience of PAR importantly also supports the capacity and personal development of participants themselves. Young people who have been involved in Young Edinburgh Action action research groups are passionate about the topics that they work on and express their pride in the outcomes of the research. However, they also emphasize the importance of the skills that they learn, the friends that they make, the fun that they have and the confidence that they develop from being involved in the project.

Recommended reading

Bell, M. (2011). *Promoting Children's Rights in Social Work and Social Care: A Guide to Participatory Practice*. London: Jessica Kingsley Publishers.
A book which discusses participation of children and young people in social work care from a rights perspective. It is useful to understand the benefits of positive work for the individual or service.

Cammarota, J. & Romero, A. (2011). Participatory Action Research for High School Students: Transforming Policy, Practice, and the Personal with Social Justice Education. *Educational Policy*, 25: 488–506.

Christensen, P. & James, A. (2008). Researching Children and Childhood: Cultures and Communities, in P. Christensen & A. James (eds), *Research with Children*. London: Routledge.

Davis, J., Ravenscroft, J. & Bizas, N. (2015). Transition, Inclusion and Partnership: Child, Parent and Professional Led Approaches in a European Research Project. *Child Care in Practice*, 21: 3–49.

Gallacher, L. A. & Gallagher M. (2008). Methodological Immaturity in Childhood Research?: Thinking through 'Participatory Methods'. *Childhood*, 15: 499–516.
Really useful book considering power relations between adults and young people.

Kemmis, S. & McTaggart, R. (2005). Participatory Action Research: Communicative Action and the Public Sphere, in N. Denzin & Y. Lincoln (eds), *Handbook of Qualitative Research* (3rd edn), 559–604. Thousand Oaks, CA.
A good introduction to PAR.

Kirby, P. (1999). *Involving Young Researchers*. Joseph Rowntree Foundation.

Advanced reading

Mackenzie, J., Tan, P.-L., Hoverman, S. et al. (2012). The Value and Limitations of Participatory Action Research Methodology. *Journal of Hydrology*, 474: 11–21.
While this journal article is not specific to young people, it is useful to assist in understanding the values and challenges of PAR as a methodology.

McMellon, C. & Mitchell, M. (2016). Reinvigorating Young People's Participation in Edinburgh. *CRFR Briefing Paper* 85. https://www.era. lib.ed.ac.uk/bitstream/handle/1842/16875/CRFR%20briefing%2085. pdf?sequence=1&isAllowed=y.

Percy-Smith, B. (2010). Councils, Consultations and Community: Rethinking the Spaces for Children and Young People's Participation. *Children's Geographies*, 8: 107–122.
A helpful journal article discussing the different conceptualizations of young people's participation. It has been a fundamental influence in the development of YEA model.

Prout, A. & James, A. (1997). A New Paradigm for the Sociology of Childhood: Provenance, Promise and Problems, in A. James & A. Prout (eds), *Constructing and Reconstructing Childhood: Contemporary Issues in the Sociological Study of Childhood.*
A seminal text on the new Sociology of Childhood.

Scottish Parliament (2015). Children and Young People (Scotland) Act 2014. Scotland: Scottish Government.

Tisdall, E. K. M., Davis, J. M., & Gallagher, M. (2009). *Researching with Children and Young People: Research Design, Methods, and Analysis.* Los Angeles; London: Sage.
A practical book which investigates the research design, methods and analysis of research with children and young people. It contains many helpful activities and ideas we which have used in practice.

United Nations (1989). Convention on the Rights of the Child, retrieved 2 June 2017 from http://www.ohchr.org/EN/ProfessionalInterest/Pages/CRC.aspx.

10

Speculative Method as an Approach to Researching Emerging Educational Issues and Technologies

Jen Ross

Key points

- Speculative method offers a way to investigate possible futures.
- It works against complexity reduction and a flawed 'what works' agenda.
- Issues around emerging technologies can be particularly well suited to a speculative approach.
- Four key aspects of enacting speculative method are the question, object, audience and analysis.

Introduction

'Speculative method' is a term that describes research approaches that explore and *create* possible futures under conditions of complexity and uncertainty. Art and design disciplines have developed a number of these approaches, for example, 'design fictions' and 'cultural probes' (Hales, 2013; Sanders and Stappers, 2014). Increasingly, social scientists have been examining the potential for thinking speculatively about method to help address the kinds of questions less amenable to more conventional approaches to research – indeed, to 'shift from seeing research as answering a research question to seeing it as the opportunity for asking more inventive questions' (Wilkie et al., 2015: 80).

Epistemologically, speculative method treats the world as 'ongoing', which means that research taking this approach does more than investigate the issue at hand – it explicitly takes a role in creating it. In other words, speculative approaches go beyond 'ascertaining' or 'predicting'; they involve themselves in 'configuring what comes next' (Lury and Wakeford, 2012: 6). They move researchers away from viewing the world as a static or stable entity, and encourage the understanding that method is always part of the problem it addresses – this will be discussed in the case studies below. These methods:

> enable research to follow forked directions, to trace processes that are in disequilibrium or uncertain, to acknowledge and refract complex combinations of human and non-human agencies, supporting an investigation of what matters and how in ways that are open, without assuming a single fixed relation between epistemology and ontology. (Lury and Wakeford, 2012: 4)

For researchers aiming to understand emerging ideas or technologies, this ability to work with uncertainty is a key benefit of such an approach. It requires, however, a willingness to take risks with the design and implementation of a research project – moving away from approaches which are well-established with clear protocols. In practical terms, inventive method tends to be designed around an experimental or fictional object (like a potential future technology), or around an object or process that can be used to shed unusual or new light on a topic or question. These objects are not deployed in the research in order to be tested as new products, but are 'objects to think with' (Turkle, 1997). Sometimes they are objects in an unconventional or mainly conceptual sense: in Lury and Wakeford's collection, 'devices' of inventive method include the tape recorder, the list, and the photo-image. This chapter takes a more straightforward, applied approach to speculative method, showing how these approaches can be useful in educational research, and most specifically research on digital and technological issues in education. First, I want to outline some trends in current educational technology research that make a valuable space for speculative method – most particularly an unhelpful tendency towards what Gough (2012) describes as 'complexity reduction' (see the next section for more on this).

A critique of educational technology research

A great deal of research around educational technology focuses on testing existing practices and tools with a view to understanding what is effective in terms of meeting particular educational goals. This can be important work, although it very often overemphasizes the idea of 'what works' and does not pay enough attention to the complexities and contradictions inherent in evidence-based practice (Biesta, 2010b). Educational technology is often treated as a domain in which considerations of efficiency and enhancement are paramount, and assumptions can go unchallenged (Bayne, 2014) – including the pervasive assumption that learning and teaching can be broken down into constituent parts and analysed to identify 'what works' and replicate this in digital environments (Selwyn, 2012).

Educational researchers are under pressure to produce findings which can inform what is currently called 'evidence-based practice'; and the 'evidence' that counts is increasingly limited in nature. For example, in the United Kingdom, randomized controlled trials, where research participants are randomly allocated to either a baseline 'control' group or one or more 'intervention' groups, have been recommended by the Department for Education in England (Goldacre and Plant, 2013) as the 'gold standard' for educational research (see Chapter 1 for more on the difficulties of this approach). An influential concept for research around technology and education is 'design-based research', which is an applied research methodology where interventions are iteratively designed and tested in real educational settings, with a view to ensuring that design principles and theoretical constructs are established and advanced (Anderson and Shattuck, 2012). Design-based research proponents claim that its value is primarily in its ability to use generalizable principles to have direct impacts on practice.

As a result of these emphases in educational and digital education research, a whole range of methodological approaches developed and adapted by educational researchers gain less traction, as they are dismissed as being insufficiently scientific, or difficult to translate into practice (Biesta, 2010b). This dismissal of research approaches might be seen as little more than an unfortunate consequence of shifts in the field, but there are also problems with 'evidence-based practice' itself which need to be addressed in order to understand the role that speculative method might play. Walker (2011) hints at these when he points out that design-based research achieves some of its reputation for utility at the expense of meaningful engagement with epistemological issues (pp. 53–54). The educational philosopher Gert Biesta has discussed these issues in detail in relation to claims of generalizability in educational research. He identifies three areas of 'deficit' in evidence-based practice – in knowledge, efficacy and application – and argues that these deficits should lead us to a much more critical position in relation to evidence (Biesta, 2010b). To summarize, the nature of these deficits come about because of the constantly changing nature of the social world, the way the world changes as a result of our experiments and the non-linear nature of cause and effect in a system like education. So, Biesta claims that research cannot tell us what to do, only provide possible understandings of the problem. Research can help us with 'intelligent selection of possible lines of action' (2007: 16), but only if we remember that:

> what counts as 'effective' crucially depends on judgments about what is educationally desirable. … The focus on 'what works' makes it difficult if not impossible to ask the questions of what it should work for and who should have a say in determining the latter. (Biesta, 2007: 5)

Most research approaches involve what Gough (2012) calls 'complexity reduction'. Complexity refers to characteristics of processes and activities that are 'open, recursive, organic, nonlinear and emergent' (p. 42) – qualities of the social and natural world that are poorly served by explanations that are 'mechanistic and reductive' (p. 42). Gough refers to the tendency of research to 'deliberately reduce the complexity of the objects of their inquiries and/ or the data they produce', and urges us to view complexity reduction as a political tactic:

> acknowledging complexity should dispose us to ask questions about how complexity reduction is achieved and, perhaps more importantly, who is reducing complexity for whom and in whose interests. (p. 47)

Educational research methods, if not approached critically, can easily become 'animated by the desire for certainty, willing to sacrifice complexity and diversity for "harder" evidence and the global tournament of standards'

(MacLure, 2006: 730). A mistaken belief that *any* research method will deliver simple answers or clear guides for action in education leads us to underestimate the value of multiple kinds of research, and research questions, to help us engage with problems intelligently. It also leads to what McArthur (2012) calls 'bad mess', where – 'seeking to force the inherently messy into a respectable tidy form can result in something that distorts, hides or falsifies the actual social world' (421). When our understanding of what is legitimate research is limited to just a few methodological approaches, research questions and hypotheses can only be framed in particular, limited ways – leaving many topics unexplored and unexplorable and many questions unanswered – some questions like these are set out in the case study examples to follow.

To sum up, I am not trying to persuade you that speculative method is the only appropriate approach to digital education research, or that it is an easy way to navigate problems and questions in this complex area of practice. However, I do want you to consider for a moment the types of questions that can – and perhaps cannot – be explored through the methods you have experienced in your research journeys so far. We are going to move on now to think about emerging technologies and the practices and pedagogies around them, to suggest how speculative method might help try to open up some new kinds of questions, ones that are not so amenable to being answered by more traditional methodological approaches.

Why speculative method for research into technology and education?

There is an area of digital education for which speculative method is particularly appropriate, and this is usefully described as the sphere of 'emerging technologies'. Veletsianos (2010) describes these as 'not yet fully understood' and 'not yet fully researched, or researched in a mature way' (p. 15). Such technologies, and the practices and pedagogies associated with them, are always part of the landscape of education, though the specifics change as things move from 'emerging' to 'established' (or 'failed' or 'defunct', as the case may be).

How do we research such technologies, practices and pedagogies? In other words, what sorts of questions are appropriate to ask about emerging technologies, and how can they be answered? At present, we are limited in this endeavour by educational research methods that are designed to explore and explain what *is*, not what *could be*. Taking a critical approach to technological change in education requires imaginative resources and the ability to engage with 'not-yetness' (Ross and Collier, 2016) – including treating complexity, uncertainty and risk as *necessary* to digital education. These imaginative resources come from engaging in 'inventive problem-making' (Michael, 2012), and this is exactly what speculative method supports us to do. It is aimed at envisioning or crafting futures or conditions which may not yet currently exist, to provoke new ways of thinking and to bring particular ideas or issues into focus. It may tend to blur boundaries between research, design and teaching, and therefore to provoke questions about how best to understand it *as* method, and about the nature of the researcher's responsibilities when adopting such approaches. So there is a requirement in all of this (as in all research) for reflexivity, criticality and careful attention to the kinds of 'truth claims' being made.

All educational researchers need ways of engaging with the epistemological and ontological debates in the field. However, digital education researchers, educators and technologists within education communities have to be especially ready to engage productively with varied approaches. Digital education research, positioned at an intersection of social sciences, design, and a variety of technical disciplines, works with ideas and methods from fields including cultural studies, informatics and design, as well as from more traditional educational research disciplines such as psychology and sociology, and such a variety of influences and sources of knowledge inevitably will lead to the kinds of tensions that the question of 'what works' cannot respond to. Trying to understand and shape emerging technologies and the discourses around them means accepting volatility and not-yetness because, as Selwyn (2012) puts it:

> There is rarely (if ever) any pre-determined outcome to the development and implementation of technologies in education – despite all the rhetoric to the contrary. Instead technologies are subjected continually to complex interactions and negotiations with the social, economic, political and cultural contexts into which they are situated. (pp. 214–15)

The other reason why speculative method is so useful for researching emerging technologies in education is that the field is strongly influenced by visions of the future put forward by a range of stakeholders, including political, corporate and media interests. There is a clear orientation in digital education towards 'the next big thing', and no shortage of evangelists with a whole range of agendas who seek to define matters of interest and concern for the field (Selwyn, 2016) – sometimes without reference to issues like social justice that many educational researchers find important. For this reason, as I have written elsewhere, 'maintaining a creatively critical stance towards digital futures for education involves navigating multiple and often competing visions without succumbing to cynicism, a narrowing of perspective, or a turn away from not-yetness' (Ross, 2017: 218). Speculative method gives us one way to develop our creativity and criticality in relation to the future of education and educational technology. We can see speculative method as a response (not the only one) to the question John Law asks in the first chapter in his book titled *After Method* (2004): 'How might we catch some of the realities we are currently missing?' (p. 2).

Case study examples

The two examples that follow were research projects undertaken in the Centre for Research in Digital Education at the University of Edinburgh. They explored very different contexts and questions: the teacherbot project aimed to shed new light on the question of automation and how it might affect teaching; the artcasting project looked to bring new ideas to bear on the difficulty of evaluating visitor engagement with art.

Teacherbot

The Teacherbot project[1] explored how the nature of teaching might change in light of increasing moves towards automation of parts of the teacher function. With the emergence and rapid rise of Massive Open Online Courses (MOOCs) in the years between 2012 and 2015, considerable attention was paid to how extremely large groups of students (in the tens or sometimes even hundreds of thousands) could be 'taught'. Many of the proposed responses to these challenges came in the form of automation of some kind – including automated marking of multiple choice questions and even essays (Balfour, 2013). This period also saw the large-scale emergence of learning analytics, which are algorithmic methods for tracking and

---

[1]http://www.de.ed.ac.uk/project/teacherbot-interventions-automated-teaching.

evaluating student activity in online learning environments, with the ultimate goal of predicting performance and personalizing automated engagement and feedback. Questions and concerns about the role of the human teacher, and scepticism about possible directions of travel for teaching in the context of massiveness and analytics, followed suit (Bayne and Ross, 2013).

The teacherbot project team created an automated Twitter agent, or 'bot', to participate in the third instance of the E-learning and Digital Cultures MOOC (EDCMOOC), a five-week open course aimed at educators and learning technologists and exploring the significance of digital cultures on digital education practice. In this run of the course, about 12,000 people were enrolled, and the teacherbot could respond to tweets sent to the Twitter hashtag #edcmooc. Its responses were triggered by keywords or phrases appearing in tweets related to the course. The bot responded to these with statements, questions or provocations written by the EDCMOOC teachers and based on course content and frequently asked questions or common topics from previous instances of the course. Teacherbot's responses could be written in advance, or added as the course progressed, through the dashboard created for the project. MOOC participants were informed of the nature of the bot and invited to engage with it and provide feedback on it – and many participants did so (Bayne, 2015), helping the project team understand teacherbot as a point of shared experience for the group, an 'assemblage' of human and non-human teachers, and a provocative method for generating new insights into:

> ways of theorising and practising digital education and automated teaching which are driven neither by technical-rational efficiency models, nor by equally instrumentally focused social models which assume a position of humanistic opposition to, or appropriation of, digital technology. (Bayne, 2015: 460)

Teacherbot's interventions produced a new set of relations within the course which provoked new questions and perspectives for both participants and teachers as researchers, including very important and timely questions about the value of teaching within algorithmic cultures (Bayne, 2015).

The project team involved educational researchers, software engineers, and design and computational specialists – indicative of the kinds of interdisciplinary partnerships speculative method can benefit from. As an example of speculative method, teacherbot was both playful and provocative, and it intervened in a key moment of debate about automation to produce entirely new insights from the data generated by and with the bot, and the responses made by participants in the MOOC.

Artcasting

The Artcasting project[2] was a research collaboration between educational and design informatics researchers, developers, designers and art galleries, to develop new ways of understanding how cultural heritage organizations can evaluate visitors' engagement with art. The project's methodology was centred around the development of an Artcasting app and dashboard which was piloted during two exhibitions of the ARTIST ROOMS On Tour exhibition in 2015–2016. ARTIST ROOMS is a collection of more than 1,600 works of international contemporary art, jointly owned and managed by Tate & National Galleries of Scotland, and shared throughout the United Kingdom in a programme of exhibitions organized in collaboration with local associate galleries.

The Artcasting app invited visitors to digitally relocate artworks they encountered in the exhibitions to other places and times, along with short narratives – so each artcast consisted of an artwork, a location and time, and a description of the reason for the choice. A digital map allowed visitors to explore other artcasts, and see the trajectories of travel from the gallery to the new location. Visitors who had the app on their own devices could also encounter artcasts by receiving notifications if they physically went to the location of an artcast. Artcasts, individually and in aggregated form, were used to challenge the galleries and researchers to develop new approaches to evaluating visitor engagement.

The Artcasting concept was developed to investigate the potential for *mobilities theory* to shape our understanding of evaluation and engagement. Mobilities theory offers an understanding of social phenomena in the context of networks and flows, rather than fixed or bounded locations (Sheller and Urry, 2016). Artcasting, with its focus on mobilities, challenged dominant approaches that separate engagement from evaluation (Belfiore and Bennett, 2010) by simultaneously encouraging visitors to make connections and reflect on what they experienced, and capturing those connections for sharing, analysis and evaluation. It aimed to both reframe and reconfigure evaluation.

Artcasting as a speculative method aimed to fulfil different purposes, with complex relationships to audience as a result:

> to engage visitors in the gallery; to inform galleries about that engagement; and to extend the gallery experience to others no longer (or never) present.

---

[2]http://www.de.ed.ac.uk/project/artcasting.

> The audiences of existing visitors, gallery educators and staff, and potential future users who might encounter artcasts were not necessarily aligned in terms of their needs and expectations, and the value proposition for Artcasting was therefore multifaceted. This served to highlight in a very immediate way tensions around evaluation itself – whose values predominate? Whose needs would be foregrounded, and which audience would Artcasting address itself to? (Ross et al., 2017)

In other words, Artcasting helped to create the problem-space it engaged with.

How to do speculative method

I hope I have been able to persuade you of the value of speculative method as a way to research emerging ideas and perspectives, including those around digital education and teaching and learning with technology. If so, you may now be wondering 'what next?' – and this section attempts to answer that question. I should stress that there are many ways to enact speculative or inventive method – and some are explicitly theoretical in nature. I am going to focus here on more applied approaches, and specifically those that are can be used to think about the future of education and educational technology. These can be described as 'designerly' ways of doing research, which 'involve creative acts of making' (Sanders and Stappers, 2014), with the roles of designer, researcher, respondent and participant all important to the process. These are not methods that can be implemented by following a straightforward recipe; they have to be designed in relationship to the question they are seeking to illuminate or the topic they seek to develop new questions around. This is not as different from other ways of approaching research as it might seem, as Crotty (1998) points out:

> [Perhaps it] sounds as if we create a methodology for ourselves – as if the focus of our research leads us to devise our own way of proceeding that allows us to achieve our purposes. That, as it happens, is precisely the case. In a very real sense, every piece of research is unique and calls for a unique methodology. We, as the researcher, have to develop it. ... Even if we tread [a] track of innovation and invention, our engagement with the various methodologies in use will have played a crucial educative role. (pp. 13–14)

However, there are some ingredients which are likely to be significant:

A speculative question. What will it mean to teach or learn with an automated process like a 'bot' (see teacherbot case study, above)? How could mobilities approaches affect arts evaluation (see artcasting case study, above)? What learning does learning analytics not capture (Knox, 2014)? How can communities be stimulated to reimagine or reframe their understanding of energy demand reduction (Wilkie et al., 2015)? These examples of questions that have been addressed through speculative method have in common a flexible orientation to a situation which is either on the horizon or missing from current thinking around a topic or practice. Speculative questions may often focus on the future, but a focus on the future is never only about the future – it is also about articulating what is currently valued by particular people or communities or in particular settings, and what may be absent or unspoken in privileging those values.

An 'object to think with'. The researcher developing a speculative method must create something with which participants or respondents can engage – an 'object to think with'. This could be a scenario or set of scenarios, a technology like an app, a design prototype, a narrative or a combination of these. The object should be designed to provoke responses that will illuminate the topic of the research, to help construct the horizons or become aware of the absences that the questions of the research are aimed at addressing. A pragmatic consideration is whether the project will require specialist skills to accomplish it, and how the researcher might access the resources they will need. For example, if you want to create an engaging video narrative as part of a design fiction, do you have the technical and creative skills to make this? The two case study examples above were both created in collaboration with technical partners who were able to code the prototype teacherbot and artcasting platforms – this is possible with larger, funded projects, but for masters or doctoral research, other approaches might be necessary. There are DIY methods for creating, for example, Twitter bots that you might be able to adapt.[3] Taking the making requirements of your method into consideration early on will help you ensure you can address your question.

An audience to engage with. It is possible – as in the case of Knox's speculative experiment around a tweeting book (Knox, 2014) – to make the object itself the focus of the research, without a strong focus on participant

---

[3]For example: Cheap Bots Done Quick (http://cheapbotsdonequick.com) which helps create Twitter bots.

response and reaction. More commonly, however, the object, which might in its own right take considerable time to design and create, is put into a context in which it can be used, or can serve as a provocation, irritation or invitation. This context might be online, offline or a combination of the two. The speculative object and its design, along with the responses to it, form the data from this method, so the identities and expectations of participants or respondents need to be carefully considered, along with the ethics of the approach to the object. For example, with teacherbot, the research team were clear about who we would engage with – the participants on EDCMOOC – but needed to plan in detail how the bot would be introduced to and engage with the participants – would we identify the teacherbot as a bot, or not (we did)?

A way to capture and analyse design decisions and responses to the object. In some cases the responses to the speculative object can be integrated into the object itself – as in the case of an app that gathers data, or a twitter stream involving a bot. In other cases, responses need to be captured for analysis via other approaches – for example, making a video or audio recording of a workshop; asking participants to keep a written or photo diary of their interactions with the object; or conducting interviews or surveys. Analysis of speculative method should analyse both the object and the responses it generates. Decisions about how the object has been designed should be captured so that the object and the considerations informing it can be

---

Activity 10.1

Think of a point of debate or discussion about the future in your own area – ideally one that seems to include a lot of unspoken assumptions that would benefit from more explicit exploration. Consider what options are being offered within the existing terms of this debate, and see if you can formulate a question that, by being explored, could fill in a gap in the discussion. Design a scenario or prototype of a tool to help foreground this question, and decide who you could work with to explore it, and how it could be used with participants and data collected. Once you are happy with your speculative design proposal, think about how this could interact with other methods and approaches you are planning for your project. Is there space for a speculative method in your research?

understood and shared. It may be helpful to consider the speculative object as both an instrument and an outcome, and keep notes about the design process accordingly.

Conclusions

Speculative method can be a powerful approach to generating and examining new perspectives and questions, and to helping understand and shape complex topics, especially those that deal with the future. It can complement other methods, or can (as in the case of Artcasting and Teacherbot) form the basis of a research project. As with other interpretive approaches, questions of validity must be addressed on terms specific to the philosophical underpinnings of the work:

> Interpretive social science, unlike positivism, argues that method can't guarantee validity and that any 'finding' is simply an interpretation which rests on other interpretations. (St Pierre, 2015: 75)

Chapter key points

- Speculative method is a powerful means of dealing with complexity and future thinking.
- The prospect of guarantee is obviously well beyond the scope or purpose of speculative method, which is about designing and engaging possibilities.
- Tracy's (2010) 'big tent' criteria for quality in qualitative research may be helpful to researchers as they look to frame conclusions and further questions generated through speculative data – '(a) worthy topic, (b) rich rigour, (c) sincerity, (d) credibility, (e) resonance, (f) significant contribution, (g) ethics, and (h) meaningful coherence' (p. 839).
- But each of these criteria will need to be approached critically to ensure that the generative qualities of the speculation are foregrounded and valued in analysis and reports of findings.

Recommended reading

Biesta, G. (2007). Why 'What Works' Won't Work: Evidence-Based Practice and the Democratic Deficit in Educational Research. *Educational Theory*, 57(1): 1–22.

Biesta is a key educational philosopher exploring the concept of evidence-based practice. This article (and the follow-up article noted in the advanced reading below) sets out the philosophical case for being critical of simplistic ideas about how research and practice should interact.

Gough, N. (2010). Can We Escape the Program? Inventing Possible~Impossible Futures in/for Australian Educational Research. *The Australian Educational Researcher*, 37(4): 9–42.

Debates about education futures have a significant history, and Gough's article uses complexity theory to reflect on these debates as they took place in the 1980s. He highlights key principles for conducting research on curriculum futures, and connects these with the concept of 'emergence'.

Lury, C. & Wakeford, N. (2012). *Inventive Methods: The Happening of the Social.* London: Routledge.

This edited collection introduced the use of 'inventive method' in the social sciences, and each chapter is focused on one such method. The introductory chapter is particular helpful in gaining a good understanding of how social scientists might approach inventive or speculative method.

Ross, J. (2016). Speculative Method in Digital Education Research. *Learning, Media and Technology*, 0(0): 1–16.

This article offers more on the conceptual underpinnings of speculative method and its connections to digital education and educational futures.

Wilkie, A., Michael, M. & Plummer-Fernandez, M. (2014). Speculative Method and Twitter: Bots, Energy and Three Conceptual Characters. *The Sociological Review*, 1–23.

This is a concrete example of speculative method in action, describing and analysing a project about energy futures conducted by sociologists, using Twitter bots.

Advanced reading

Biesta, G. J. J. (2010). Why 'What Works' Still Won't Work: From Evidence-Based Education to Value-Based Education. *Studies in Philosophy and Education*, 29(5): 491–503.

Following on from Biesta's earlier article (see suggested reading), this article sets out three key deficits in 'evidence-based education' and proposes a more critical values-based approach.

Gough, N. (2012). Complexity, Complexity Reduction, and 'Methodological Borrowing' in Educational Inquiry. *Complicity: An International Journal of Complexity and Education*, 9(1).
Gough introduces complexity theory and its role in education research, critiquing models of education that assume 'linear thinking, control and predictability'. He offers cautionary tales of using methodological approaches from other disciplines without sufficient attention to complexity.

Lather, P. (2006). Paradigm Proliferation as a Good Thing to Think with: Teaching Research in Education as a Wild Profusion. *International Journal of Qualitative Studies in Education*, 19(1): 35–57.
This article argues against experimental design as the 'gold standard' in educational research, and suggests that researchers in educational fields need to be well-versed in 'paradigm proliferation' in order to 'locate themselves in the tensions that characterize fields of knowledge'.

Law, J. (2004). *After Method: Mess in Social Science Research*. Psychology Press.
A key text in the field of social science methods, Law's book encourages engagement with messy realities through methodological multiplicity and inventiveness.

Michael, M. (2012). 'What Are We Busy Doing?' Engaging the Idiot. *Science, Technology & Human Values*, 37(5): 528–554.
Michael looks at public engagement and knowledge exchange in research through a lens of speculative method and speculative design.

Web links

Near Future Laboratory
http://nearfuturelaboratory.com
Examples of design fictions, from an influential team of designers.

Speculation and Speculative Research
http://www.gold.ac.uk/unit-of-play/research/speculation/
The website of a research group at Goldsmiths, University of London.

11

Evaluating Technologies for Children's Learning: The Challenges, and Steps to Address Them

Andrew Manches

Key points

- Current research approaches to evaluating learning for children's technology are problematic.
- Consider how technology itself may be integral to our definitions of knowledge and learning.
- Consider how many complex contextual factors shape interaction with technology.

Introduction

From doors and driers to maps and magazines, the world around children is increasingly getting digital, with more products being specifically designed for children. In trying to appeal to adults (purchasers of children's technologies), these technologies often make claims about their benefits, in particular their benefits for learning, such as their ability to provide immediate feedback, or simply to help engage children. Many 'learning technologies' explicitly target formal education, leading to a number of initiatives trying to integrate these resources into schools (e.g. John and Wheeler, 2012). Unfortunately, while the transformatory impact of technology is evident across other sectors, the impact in education is less clear. For example, a recent OECD report (Peña-López, 2015) suggests that the heavy investment in school computers and classroom technology has not resulted in increases in pupils' performance (although this report has since been criticized (e.g. Berry, 2015)).

Claims about the learning benefits of technologies also extend to those marketed at parents, and increasingly to younger children. In fact, according to a 2012 report by the Joan Ganz Cooney Centre (2012), 58 per cent of educational apps were categorized for toddlers/preschools. More recently we have seen more hands-on digital technologies for children (e.g. Figure 11.1). These also tend to promote their educational benefits, indeed, retailers such as Amazon have created a new market label: STEM (Science, Technology, Engineering, and Mathematics) toys with this pretext (i.e. they support learning in STEM areas). Yet, again there is limited evidence that such technologies really do benefit children's learning, despite their claims.

Therefore, given the appeal of 'learning technology' in both home and school contexts, we are justified in asking: do technologies designed and promoted for children's learning actually support children's learning? This translates to more focused evaluation questions, typically adopting the form: does [name of technology] support learning?

This chapter emphasizes that epistemic questions such as those above are deeply problematic. First, it is not always clear how we are defining the technology. Devices come with many applications. Applications come with many activities. But perhaps, more significantly, such questions required others to be addressed first: what do we mean by 'supporting learning', or any variations, e.g. improve results, beneficial effects. And even if we agree on what we mean by 'learning', what do we consider as rigorous evidence or be certain in the knowledge that it has been 'supported/ improved/ increased/ enhanced/ enriched' etc. Of course, questions about what constitutes 'evidence of learning' is pertinent across the field of educational research. However, this chapter proposes that there are unique implications when evaluating technology: both in how technology is repeatedly presented as a having a contextually independent effect on learning, and also in its ontological relationship to what we mean by 'learning'.

The contribution of this chapter is to problematize the goal of evaluating 'learning technologies' and the role of ontology and epistemology in the methodological process. The chapter aims to help the reader critically reflect

Figure 11.1 Technologies designed to support learning (Image credits: Douglas Robertson Photography, http://www.douglasinscotland.pwp.blueyonder.co.uk/)

upon core methodological challenges by drawing attention to two key issues: (1) the complexity of the context in which technologies are used and (2) the challenge of defining 'learning' relative to technology. This chapter does not advocate specific methods, as the value of each method will ultimately depend upon the questions being asked. Instead, the chapter proposes a methodological approach that recognizes the two key issues discussed.

Why evaluate?

How we evaluate children's technologies will inevitably reflect what we intend to achieve (as well as more pragmatic factors such as time/budget). Often the intention may be quite pragmatic: to inform a decision to acquire or use a particular technology. For example, parents may want to evaluate a particular app before sharing with their child, or a teacher may want to be informed about the value of a new technology such as 3D printers before integrating them into the classroom. Similarly, evaluation may be desired to develop guidance for others, from a head teacher developing a school-wide strategy to a government developing national policy. In previous work, for example, my colleagues and I have evaluated the evidence for a wide range of technologies in order to inform non-departmental public bodies (Manches et al., 2010) and independent foundations (Luckin et al., 2012). In such reports, the need to provide an overarching picture of technologies for learning limits the ability to provide a more nuanced account of any particular example (although case studies are sometimes provided).

In contrast, the intention to evaluate may be driven by the research goal of increasing our knowledge of *how* a particular technology, or group of technologies, influences learning. Such work can inform theory which can then be drawn upon to guide individuals towards the most effective way to integrate particular technologies in their context. Some researchers adopt this approach to design technologies; they test and build theory through iterative developments of a particular design, hence the term 'design-based' research (Anderson and Shattuck, 2012).

In reality, 'informed decision' or 'theory-driven' approaches to evaluation are less easy to separate: understanding how a particular technology influences learning can help inform decisions of whether to adopt the technology. Nevertheless, the key message is that we cannot consider how to evaluate technology independently of why we are evaluating. Understanding how a technology influences learning may be interesting but cumbersome to interpret for a practitioner wishing to make a quick purchase decision. Indeed, it is no surprise that many online evaluations offer simple scale ratings (e.g. Common Sense Media's app reviews), such as a score of 1 to 5 for terms including 'educational value'. In contrast, research, particularly doctoral research, will seek to provide a more substantial in-depth understanding of how technology influences learning. For example, in my own doctorate (Manches, 2010), I evaluated the potential of tangible technology (digitally augmented objects) for early learning by examining how physically manipulating objects (e.g. wooden cubes) influences children's strategies when solving number problems. My research compared how children solved problems using physical materials compared to specifically chosen other materials such as squares on paper, or squares children could manipulate on a touch-screen tablet.

Limitations of current evaluation work

A quick search on the internet demonstrates the wide, possibly overwhelming, amount of research published on different learning technologies. As a crude example, at the time of writing, searching 'virtual reality' and 'education' reveals over 389,000 hits on Google Scholar, although only a selection of these will be empirical studies evaluating particular designs. Unfortunately, despite the wealth of empirical evaluations, most focus on qualities other than learning. As an indication of this, a key text in this field: 'Evaluating Children's Interactive Products' (Read and Markopoulos, 2014) provides a comprehensive summary of different methods for evaluating more tractable qualities such as usability, likeability or accessibility, but offers more limited guidance on how to assess learning benefits (Manches et al., 2010).

For evaluation work that does focus on learning, an important consideration is the relationship between the evaluator and the product design. It is understandable that an individual will likely be more content with findings demonstrating the positive impact of their work/product, and this potential for bias may unintentionally influence their methodological approach in at least two key ways. Firstly, in the way in which they define and measure learning and secondly, in their influence of the context in which the technology is evaluated. This chapter proposes that these two aspects are key to considering any evaluation of learning technology for children, and are subsequently examined in more depth.

What we mean by learning with respect to technology

If we are interested in how technology influences learning, it is important to define what we mean by learning. Unfortunately, this is not always clearly communicated in research studies, although, the impression given by many authors, either explicitly (e.g. De Jong et al., 1998) or by implication, is that learning is about acquiring knowledge. However, not only does this introduce new questions about what we mean by 'knowledge' (see Chapter 1), but is likely to sit uncomfortably with more constructionist pedagogical stances arguing that knowledge is constructed rather than transmitted. This definition of learning also frames knowledge as something rather static and independent of the environment – something independent that can be 'acquired'. Such a definition can be contrasted to those working in more recent theoretical paradigms that consider knowledge as distributed across a culturally constituted world (e.g. books), not just within brains. These more recent theoretical paradigms reflect an epistemological shift by arguing that knowledge is something intrinsically bound to a social, cultural and physical context, rather than something that can be extracted, stored and retrieved. For example, in my own work, children's knowledge of mathematics is situated in the tools we provide (e.g. blocks or number lines), cultural practices (e.g. counting together) and the physical actions involving in 'doing mathematics' (e.g. pointing when counting), rather than some decontextualized abstractions laying within children's heads. The significance of this epistemological shift in thinking is the need to consider the social, cultural and physical context in which children demonstrate their thinking.

Activity 11.1

A possible activity to help think about the significance of this paradigm shift is to really observe how we judge what children 'know'. Is it just through the symbols they write on page? What else do we look at? The language they use? Their drawings? How they move their hands when they talk? How engaged they seem?

Different perspectives of knowledge have required changes in how we define learning.

Hutchins offers the following definition of learning: *adaptive reorganization in a complex system* (Hutchins, 1995: 289). By using the term *adaptive,* Hutchins' definition highlights how the value of what is learnt will ultimately depend upon the child's unique world. Learning how to work efficiently with international peers may be highly adaptive to one child's world; learning how to de-contaminate water may reflect another's. Even within a shared culture, perceptions of value may vary depending on what knowledge/skills are considered valuable. For example, individuals may disagree about the importance of knowing how to spell as we move to an environment where nearly all formal writing is digital and can be autocorrected.

Whether 'acquiring' or 're-organizing', definitions of learning share a common feature: learning is about change, and implies some form of positive judgement of that change. When evaluating technologies, we are interested in the role of a particular design in this change: how, and possibly how much, any changes in the child's interaction with the world can be attributed to the design. In trying to understand the role of technology in how children change their thinking/interaction with the environment, we can focus on the *process* of their interaction with the technology or the *outcome* of this interaction.

Process vs. outcome

Methods focusing on the learning process seek to describe what happens when children use technology: Do children appear interested (eye gaze)? Do they stay 'on task'? Do they express themselves in novel ways (e.g. create animated stories?). Are they interacting with peers, and if so, how does the technology feature in their interaction? Do they engage with adults with the technology? Furthermore, we can examine how children change their interaction within tasks; for example, do they change strategy? Do they start answering more questions 'correctly'? Do they explore a range of possibilities or focus on one particular approach? A useful activity is to consider what you would consider evidence that a child seems to be learning. What is notably different from a child who appears *not* to be learning?

An important question is how we can judge whether the way children interact is indicative of learning. Although some measures are predictive of improved outcome measures (e.g. time on task), they tell us little about how the particular technology influences learning. To help address this challenge we can draw upon work describing the value of particular types of interactions. One example is offered by the Decoding Learning report (Luckin et al., 2012), which was commissioned to evaluate evidence for the potential of learning technologies. In order to examine the way technologies have been designed to support learning, the report presents eight types of 'learning themes'. These eight themes are themselves synthesized from a list of seventeen forms of learning acts (forms of interaction), co-developed by one of the authors in previous work (Crook et al., 2011). Rather than advocate a particular theory of learning, the following eight themes offer a language to reflect upon how technology can influence different interactions considered important in learning:

- Learning from experts
- Learning with others
- Learning through making
- Learning through exploring
- Learning through inquiry
- Learning through practising
- Learning from assessment
- Learning in and across settings

The methodological significance of providing frames to describe the process of learning is that they offer a language to examine and analyse children's interaction with technology. For example, how does technology mediate children's interaction across settings (e.g. online learning journals)? How is technology generating opportunities to learn from assessment (e.g. annotating videos)? Or, how does technology present new ways for children to learn from experts (e.g. through virtual simulations)?

Activity 11.2

An interesting activity is to consider how some everyday technologies, such as cameras, video conferencing or search engines, might help some of these learning interactions.

Outcome: Transfer

Focusing on process can therefore tell us much about *how* technology influences interactions that we believe are significant for learning. However, many evaluations seek to know the result, or outcome, of using technology. They want to identify how children can apply what they have learnt in one context (using technology) to another context: *transfer*.

Unfortunately, children find transfer notoriously difficult (Bransford and Schwartz, 1999), where performance degrades over time and for tasks that are less similar to the learning context ('far transfer tasks'). This is methodologically significant because it requires us to critically reflect on when and how we measure the outcome of children's learning with technology. We can predict much greater 'effects' will be found if measuring soon after a task (although there is interesting research suggesting that there are benefits from having a sleep before testing (Drosopoulos et al., 2005)), and for a task that is similar to the learning context. For example, if evaluating a mathematics app where children practise sums, the greatest benefits may be found if measuring soon afterwards on a test involving similar sums – how well children can 'replicate' what they have learnt.

According to Bransford and Schwartz (1999), a problem of many formal assessments is that they focus more on how efficient learners are at replicating what they have learnt. They contrast this with more interpretative aspects of learning that are best demonstrated in more novel contexts. The authors argue that there are relative merits of these two dimensions of learning and transfer, and their work presents their own thinking of how each can be engendered and assessed.

The key methodological implication for evaluating learning technologies is to consider the relationship between the learning task and the task assessing the outcome of this learning experience. It is also important to consider the relationship between the context to which you wish to generalize. For example, when assessing what children have learnt using a mathematics app, there is the context of using the app, the context of assessing what children have learnt (e.g. a paper and pencil test carried out alone at a desk) and the everyday world context that this learning is meant to support (e.g. helping calculate change in a shop). The expression we use to describe the relationship between the assessment task and the everyday context is *ecological validity*.

Therefore, it is important to consider the relationship between the context of the learning experience, the assessment task and the everyday situations which you think the learning experience can support. 'Near transfer' tasks may detect greater effects of the learning activity (because they are similar) but may be a poor indicator of how this learning transfers to everyday contexts. But herein raises a fundamental issue: to what extent do we consider technology itself as part of our everyday contexts?

Activity 11.3

A point of reflection is considering the proportion of tasks where you do or do not use digital technology, for example, communicating with people, writing letters, calculating bills, having fun. How does this proportion vary across people, and across ages? How might this proportion change in the future?

Effects with, and of, technology

In 1990, Salomon (1990) provided a useful lens to reflect on the role of technology between contexts by distinguishing between the 'cognitive effects with computers, whereby one's performance is redefined and upgraded during intellectual partnership with the computer, and effects of computers, whereby such partnership leaves durable and generalizable cognitive residues later on'. Assessing what children have learnt with a particular technology by using an assessment task without this technology assumes that children have developed knowledge that is technology-independent ('cognitive residue'). However, recent epistemological paradigms discussed previously argue that we need to reconsider this relationship between the external (things outside our heads) and internal (things inside our heads). More recent theoretical perspectives argue that cognition is externalized (we use the environment to support thinking), embodied (our thinking is inseparably linked to our prior experiences with the environment) and even extended (we should consider our environment as part of our cognitive system). For example, our knowledge of where our friends are, and details for how to contact them, will often depend on our everyday technologies such as mobiles. This example illustrates our 'intellectual partnership with the computer', a partnership that has arguably continued to grow since Salomon wrote his paper.

It is therefore important to consider differences between the context of any learning activity and the context of where this learning is evaluated, particularly in relation to the role of digital technology. During my final degree exams, I wrote, rewrote and consequently learnt using my computer. But I was not allowed my computer in the exams. Practical issues aside (e.g. my ability to write non-stop for two hours), the assessment task using pencil and paper dramatically changed the nature of the task. And significantly, it changed the nature of the task to one I have not encountered ever since those exams – despite the importance of writing for my career.

When children are learning with technology, we have to be very careful about testing the 'cognitive residue'. Instead, we may want to assess how they develop an intellectual partnership with technology that they can draw upon in future tasks. Learning experiences using and creating multimedia (e.g. showing their understanding of a science concept by creating an animation) may help children later express themselves through these media, in a similar way to how learning from reading/writing may support how they later express themselves through this particular (non-digital) technology. When evaluating children's learning with technology we should always critically reflect upon our assumptions that learning can be demonstrated through other media, e.g. writing, drawing. The most significant benefit of children's experience using a mathematics app may actually be their capacity to use touch-screen devices to solve future numerical problems.

Context of learning

The previous section discussed the need to consider how the context of learning may be different from the context in which such learning is evaluated. This presents the challenge of unpacking what we mean by 'different contexts'. Which factors are important?

The difficulties of examining learning in context due to the complexity of interrelated factors, have long been recognized (O'Donnell, 2004). However, possibly reflecting the more unique ability of digital technology to provide both an artefact and designed responses (interactive activities), the influential role of multiple factors is often downplayed. This is most evident in questions and methodological approaches that isolate the effect of technology, for example, 'Do tablets support learning?' Or 'Will augmented reality transform education?'. Such questions often fail to

Activity 11.4

For example, as you read this chapter, what factors influence what meaning your draw, beyond the quality (or otherwise!) of the writing itself? Are you reading from a book or digital device? Alone or with company? In the morning or evening? Are you tired or hungry? What prompted you to read this chapter (personal choice?)? To what extent do you feel these different factors do, or do not, make a difference to what you are 'learning'?

recognize the dynamic and complex context in which technologies are used. This is useful advice for any researcher reflecting upon their choice of research question. Unfortunately, this does raise a challenge: how do we frame and communicate the context in which a technology is used, given such complexity?

Factors that influence how a technology is adopted into a particular context often echo those that determine *if* the technology is adopted in the first place. In the final report for BECTA's Harnessing Technology strategy (non-departmental public body funded by the UK's Department for Education) colleagues and I identified eight significant factors (Table 11.1) influencing the successful introduction of new technologies.

These factors are evident in much work examining the challenges of introducing digital technology into the classroom. For example, in the *Decoding Learning* report (Luckin et al., 2012), which was commissioned to evaluate evidence for the potential of learning technologies, consideration was given to the key contextual factors influencing particular digital interventions, such as who was there to support learners. To frame the contextual factors, the report drew upon prior research of one of the authors: Luckin (2008). Figure 11.2 illustrates how the success of any intervention will ultimately depend upon a range of resources: people, tools, environment and knowledge and skills, and hence we need to consider how a particular context filters access to these resources. For example, the way that the curriculum filters the types of knowledge and skills that learners are exposed to, as well as the available materials, spaces and human support. A key message from the Decoding Learning report is that innovative digital innovations are less about new technologies and more about novel, and well

Table 11.1 Factors mediating integration of technology into educational practice

Factor	Description
Home–school setting	The relationship between informal (e.g. home, museum) and formal settings (e.g. classroom)
Learning spaces	The design of the space in which technologies may be used
Curriculum flexibility	The extent to which the curriculum can be adapted to accommodate different tools/ideas
Assessment culture	The requirements to obtain and utilize specific assessment information
Leadership	The role of leadership at different levels, within and beyond individual institutions
Teacher skills/confidence	Individual teacher's own skills, attitudes and experiences towards technology
Reliability	The reliability of the technology when used
Appropriation of available tools	The extent to which available tools can be adapted to teaching context

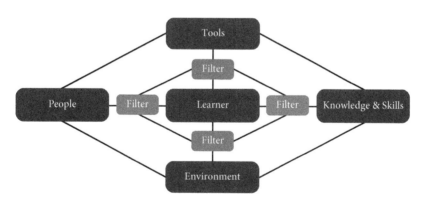

Figure 11.2 Learning context (based on Luckin's *Ecology of Resources*)

considered, ways of using existing digital tools (e.g. using a digital camera for personal inquiry across contexts). The significance of this work for those researching in this field is the need to consider the validity of isolating certain variables within a complex system.

Factors shaping interaction with technology

Research has shown therefore that the way children interact with technology (or whether they interact at all) greatly depends upon a complex range of factors that, according to Plowman (2016) interweave and dynamically unfold within a particular 'context'. So, from a methodological point of view, this presents a challenge – to what extent should a research project try to disentangle the complex web of factors influencing children's interaction with technology? Should we, for example, examine how the digital design evokes parents' own childhood recollections, which may ultimately influence the way they support children? Should an evaluation consider internet speed? What about children's prior relevant experiences? Predictably, the answer depends on the research focus and questions being asked. To gain deeper insight into how a particular technology mediates children's interaction, it may be important to explore a wide range of possible influences, possibly as a detailed case study. While such depth of exploration may not be feasible if working with multiple children, it will still be valuable to frame the key factors influencing children's interactions in order to plan, interpret and communicate any evaluation. Doing so offers the reader a better understanding of the particular conditions of an evaluation, and how these may translate across different conditions, for example, by reflecting on whether their own context offers the same adult or technical support.

Figure 11.3, illustrates three key observable actors in a particular interaction, factors that are articulated in dominant social learning theories (e.g. Vygotsky, 1978). While an adult may not necessarily be present during children's interaction with technology, they will likely have played a key role before and afterwards in accessing, curating and setting up technologies. It is also possible to consider how the design of a particular technology often incorporates the adults' role in the digital feedback given to children (e.g. drawing attention to a particular action; stating whether an answer is correct). The main implication of Figure 11.3 for researchers is to consider the range of factors that will influence how children interact and potentially learn when using technology. Simply measuring what children know before or after interacting with technology may conceal the influence of the factors. Instead, it is possible to observe the dynamic interplay between these factors.

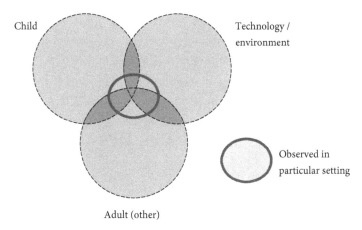

Child

Technology / environment

Observed in particular setting

Adult (other)

Figure 11.3 Considering factors influencing children's interaction with technology

Observing context of interaction

Interaction is multimodal so it is possible to focus on one or several modes such as speech, intonation, gesture, or physical or on-screen actions. In some of our previous research, for example, colleagues and I have focused on the dynamics between children's (aged 0–3 years) and parents' speech, gesture and actions when interacting with tablet devices (Figure 11.4). In this research, we were seeking to better understand how these devices influence parent-child interaction. As well as observing children's interaction with parents (in situ and later from video recordings), we interviewed parents (and older children) and collected questionnaires.

Trying to capture interaction in real-time is challenging. Therefore, it is possible to benefit from a range of recording devices (e.g. camera; microphone) for later inspection. However, it is important to remember how observing or recording individuals is likely to influence their behaviour (although sometimes it is easier to place recording devices so they are easier to forget about, notwithstanding important ethical considerations). There are also the significant limitations of timing – only being able to capture what occurs at the time of data collection, or alternatively set up a particular interaction that is necessarily unnatural. In some of her earlier work, Plowman (2015) addressed this challenge by asking parents to take pictures/videos of children's interaction with technology at the time it was occurring.

Figure 11.4 Dynamic interplay between children's and adults' modes of interaction using technology

Considering factors beyond the observable context

The interaction between a child, adult (other) and technology (and environment) will depend upon a wider range of factors that may not be observable at one particular time. This chapter argues that it is possible to frame the complex range of factors influencing children's interaction with technology in terms of the three actors in a particular interactional context: children, adults (other) and technology (environment). For example, assessment procedures are significant, but these are mediated by the teachers' (or students', for older children) interpretation of these. Similarly, finance (e.g. device cost) is important but this can be considered as a factor sharing what equipment (and teacher development) is available at a particular time. Table 11.2 presents examples of some influential factors.

Table 11.2 is not a comprehensive list of factors, but serves to exemplify factors that may (or may not) shape any given context. As discussed in the previous section, these contextual factors are not simply factors influencing what knowledge children 'acquire' but rather an intrinsic part of what we consider knowledge. For example, children's physical, social and emotional interaction with a tablet may be core elements of what it means to 'read'. Therefore, it is important for any research to consider their epistemological position when collecting data on children's interaction with technology. Are factors such as adult support or battery charging problems seen as mitigating variables, as 'noise'? Or are they considered an important part of the rich, dynamic fabric of activity?

It is possible to explore factors such as those in Table 11.2 through a number of methods such as interviews, surveys, document analysis or observing other tasks. Some factors (e.g. internet access) may be more amenable to examination than others (e.g. cultural attitudes). However, whether or not these factors are explored in a study, we should at least be mindful of their possible role. For example, in one project investigating the potential impact of a new tool for multimodal assessment (assessing portfolios including media such as video) all was well until we learned (almost by accident) of a key challenge: teachers encountered significant issues trying to send large files to external markers. While it could be said that this obstacle falls beyond the context of the children using the technology for learning, the finding was that this obstacle demotivated teachers who then developed negative attitudes towards the technology. At first, they discouraged children's use, and ultimately prevented its use. Such an outcome does seem relevant when evaluating the potential of a technology to support children's learning. In another study evaluating early learning apps for a major media company, we found significant differences in how children were accessing a particular set of screen-based learning games – via a tablet, laptop, or large interactive whiteboard in class. The devices varied substantially in the skills and experiences required to manipulate them, and how they mediated different forms of interaction with adults (e.g. mobile phones are not easy for groups to observe compared to classroom interactive whiteboards).

Table 11.2 Wider factors influencing children's interaction with technology

Overarching factor	Possible significant factors shaping interaction
	Range of ways to physically interact with the device (e.g. touchscreen, titling, moving, linking to other objects via Bluetooth)
	Range of different applications possible on the device (e.g. different apps)
Technology and surrounding environment	Technology set up (and pack away) time (e.g. installing app, charging devices)
	Reliability of technology (e.g. power; internet, errors)
	Physical space to move the technology (inside/outside, at tables/on floors)
	Influence of other tools (e.g. access to paper alongside technology)
	Experience of technology – notably the 'novelty effect' of new designs
	Knowledge/understanding of the core relevant ideas
Children	Experience of content (e.g. recognizing characters)
	Physical dexterity (e.g. ability to double click, trace accurately)
	Perceptions of identity in relation to the activity (e.g. gender)
	Adults' own digital experiences (e.g. their use of social media, their childhood memories)
	Adults' confidence (link to experiences and other factors such as training)
Adult/Others	Beliefs/values in technology (e.g. do they see technology as having a generally positive role; do they see technology as core to the future)
	Beliefs/values in learning area (i.e. do they think the learning area is important; how does the area fit with the curriculum)
	Perceptions of support (e.g. head teachers; parents)
	Relationships with peers (e.g. pride in using technology innovatively)
	Technical support available (both generally and immediately to problem fix in class)

Activity 11.5

Consider any particular learning activity with technology and simply list the range of factors that may influence interaction. How does your list compare to another's? Having written a list, then consider the relationship between your factors, for example, internet reliability and teacher's attitudes, or parental attitudes and children's experiences with different devices.

Activity 11.6

I referred previously to my own research evaluating the potential of tangible technology to support early learning. Ten years after this research, I span out a company from the University developing a set of Tangible blocks to support early numeracy: Numbuko (Figure 11.5).

Numbuko are intelligent blocks that change colour according to the specific number attached in a row, in order to help children to explore and talk about number patterns.

- How would you evaluate Numbuko?
- How would your research differ depending on whether you are a researcher or practitioner?
- As the designer of Numbuko, what would I need to do to minimize my own potential bias if evaluating Numbuko myself?
- Drawing on the key points of this chapter, what methodological issues can you identify if trying to evaluate Numbuko by carrying out a controlled comparison with another early maths product?

Conclusions

Evaluations and research into technology for learning often present technology as having some intrinsic pedagogical value independent of the context in which it is used, resulting in 'technocentric' questions such as 'does [particular device/digital activity] support learning?' The answer to

Figure 11.5 Numbuko blocks (www.numbuko.com)

such questions is: it depends. It depends on the role of many factors that fluidly shape children's interaction with that device/application/activity. And it depends on how you define and measure learning. If defining learning as how a child has adapted to complex system (everyday life), it is necessary to consider the role of those factors across diverse future scenarios, and notably whether the technology under examination plays its own part within those scenarios.

Evaluating if and how technology supports learning is therefore challenging. This chapter presents two fundamental questions that should be considered when interpreting research in this area, namely:

- How is learning being defined? What is the relationship between the context of the learning experience, the assessment task and the range of everyday settings that learning is being generalized to? How does the increasing integration of technology in our lives change these everyday settings?
- What factors played a role when children interacted with the technology? What factors are reported and how significant could they have been? What, potentially significant, factors are not reported? What is the relationship between contextual factors when children interacted with technology, when they were assessed, and the everyday scenarios this learning is intended to benefit?

Chapter key points

- Raising these questions draws attention to the difficulty in addressing seemingly simple questions presented in the form: Does [name of technology] support learning? These questions help explain why evidence is often mixed on the benefits of a particular technology or group of technologies (different contexts/definitions of learning), the dangers of designing studies to confirm what you believe/want to show (select specific contexts/learning tasks) and the significant challenge facing anyone wishing to conduct research in this area.
- Unfortunately, as with much educational commentary, it is often easier to critique than propose guidelines of good practice. While, this chapter aims to highlight why there is much lack of agreement over what constitutes good practice, the following methodological guidelines are offered:

- Be explicit in how you define knowledge and learning. Is learning something you can identify in terms of particular types of interactions, or is it defined by change that can be quantified in some way (including simple 'more' or 'less' statements). Is knowledge considered independent or dependent upon social, cultural and physical dimensions of interaction? Does technology itself play a role in what it means to know in your area of focus? To what extent is your definition of learning shared (including by the 'learner')?
- Be clear and honest about the contextual factors shaping the intervention using technology

As stated by Shattuck: '*The researcher is careful to document the time, commitment and contingencies that are involved in the creation and implementation of the intervention. These are documented so that readers of the research can judge for themselves the possibility of achieving similar – or even better results – from the use of this intervention in their own contexts*' (Anderson and Shattuck, 2012)

- Reflect upon the relationship of the task and context between the learning experience, when this is assessed, and the everyday context to which learning will be generalized. Is the assessment task close to (near transfer) the learning experience, and if so, is this to intentionally capture more replicative rather than interpretative knowledge? What other evidence is there that performance in the assessment task generalizes to everyday contexts (ecological validity)?
- Be clear and honest about the potential for your own bias. Is there value in you finding a particular outcome, and if so, how have you guarded against your unwitting influence on the study design to 'discover' this outcome? Could you have introduced supportive factors in the learning experiences that may not be there later (e.g. technical support, greater adult to child ratios)?
- This chapter argues that these questions are important to consider at some level, whatever your reasons for evaluating technology for children's learning: whether you are trying to analyse learning processes in depth, or simply informing a judgement on whether to purchase the next interesting design.

Recommended reading

Light, D. (2008). Evaluating Educational Technology Interventions: How Do We Know It's Working. Paper presented at the Quest, Bangalore, India.
While focused mainly on the United States, this paper shares over twenty-one years of experience from the Centre for Children and Technology group, demonstrated clear understanding of the challenges of evaluating technology and some of their practical suggestions for how to resolve.

Luckin, R., Bligh, B., Manches, A., Ainsworth, S., Crook, C., & Noss, R. (2012). Decoding Learning: The Proof, Promise and Potential of Digital Education.
I draw upon this report several times in this chapter. The report has been described as a key text for this interested in evaluating learning, and is written in accessible language. The report is long but I would certainly recommend the introduction and discussion chapters.

Plowman, L. (2015). Studying Children's Everyday Uses of Technology in the Family Home. *Interacting with Computers*, 27(1): 36–46.
This paper offers an expert understanding of the challenges of evaluating technology in children's homes and ways to address these challenges.

Rodríguez, P., Nussbaum, M., & Dombrovskaia, L. (2012). ICT for Education: A Conceptual Framework for the Sustainable Adoption of Technology-Enhanced Learning Environments in Schools. *Technology, Pedagogy and Education*, 21(3): 291–315.
This work focuses on successfully integrating technology into schools and builds on research in six countries.

Advanced reading

Bransford, J. D. & Schwartz, D. L. (1999). Rethinking Transfer: A Simple Proposal with Multiple Implications. *Review of Research in Education*, 24 : 61–100. Washington: American Educational Research Association.
This paper is referenced in this chapter and is recommended for those interested in developing their understanding of the complexity of assessing learning, and the issue of transfer. The paper proposes a new approach to assessment that considers how well we can apply our learning in unfamiliar contexts.

Manches, A. (2013). Emerging Technologies for Young Children: Evaluating the Learning Benefits of New Forms of Interaction. *Handbook of Design in Educational Technology*, 37: 425–445.
This book chapter provides more theoretical depth around evaluating more recent technologies that offer more direct, hands-on, interaction.

McReynolds, E., Hubbard, S., Lau, T., Saraf, A., Cakmak, M., & Roesner, F. (2017). Toys that Listen: A Study of Parents, Children, and Internet-Connected Toys. Paper presented at the CHI 2017, Denver, CO, USA.
While it is beyond the remit of this paper to examine the potential risks of technology (including the need to explain why many scare stories can be ignored due to lack of empirical support), a more recent issue that I believe is significant with respect to new technologies, is the issue of toys that capture children's personal data. This conference paper highlights this concern, using examples from recent connected toys.

Radich, J. (2013). Technology and Interactive Media as Tools in Early Childhood Programs Serving Children from Birth through Age 8. *Every Child*, 19(4): 18.
This is the joint position statement on young children technology from the National Association for the Education of Young Children (NAEYC) and the Fred Rogers Center for Early Learning and Children's Media at Saint Vincent College. It is an important text, if only for the fact that many practitioners may draw upon this for guidance. It is interesting to compare the current NAEYC position with previous statements, where more recent work recognizes the role of technology for younger children (<5).

Web links

http://children-and-technology.ed.ac.uk
This will take you to the home page of the Children and Technology group in the School of Education, University of Edinburgh and provides some more information about some of the early technology projects we have worked/are working on, including work evaluating apps for children.

https://www.commonsensemedia.org
This is a good example of a review website providing summary reviews of a range of children's media including apps. It is a good reference to critically reflect on some of the arguments put forward in this paper.

http://www.joanganzcooneycenter.org
This is the home page of the Joan Ganz Cooney Center who have an international reputation for their work on young children and technology.

https://llk.media.mit.edu
This is the homepage of the Lifelong Kindergarten group at Massachusetts Institute of Technology (MIT). As well as the researchers behind the well-known programming environment for children – Scratch (and Scratch Jnr), they have produced many leading projects exploring the potential of playful technology.

Conclusion

The start of any research should have the foundation stones of a theoretical and conceptual framework, ask any Ph.D. examiner, and therefore we started our journey (Chapter 1) within this book with an exploration of this complexity within educational research design. This underpinning of the research process affords the researcher to identify the epistemic driver(s) for their own research questions. It allows the researcher to ask questions that are sometimes missed within the research process, such as 'what is knowledge', 'what counts as knowledge' and 'what assumptions am I making about the nature of knowledge?' These questions, as we have seen within all of the chapters in this book, have been approached in sometimes similar (see Chapters 2, 3 and 7) ways but then approached differently (see Chapters 4, 5 and 8) or even through a mixed approach (Chapter 6). We see how new emergent, speculative and even technological evaluative approaches to research have had to address these epistemic questions (Chapters 9, 10 and 11). Despite the coherence of structure and organization within the book, we have deliberately encouraged authors to retain their own distinctive styles and voices. The commonality running through these chapters is theoretical framing and research design but the distinctiveness of each author's approach to research shines through.

Research is a wonderful process to help us understand the world we live in, a tool to help us build knowledge and potentially enhance experiences. Research, as we have shown, whether it is used comparatively or ethnographically, experimentally or mixed, is an enabling device, for it can be transformative, enlightening, as well as a tool to provide scepticism and critical thought. It is a powerful tool and like all tools it requires us to understand how to use it and when to use it appropriately. The chapters in this book have focused on the different philosophical approaches that are the drivers for when we make design choices. We have attempted within this book to show that there is a stage even before the research question is asked and that is when we should, as researchers, start the research process by interrogating and understanding what our own philosophical assumptions are about the world.

Throughout this book, we have tried to emphasize the importance of understanding knowledge and what an understanding of knowledge means to education research and education research design. Yet, we have not set out to prescribe theoretical stances but instead we have placed an emphasis on understanding distinctive ways of approaching this key aspect of the research process from a rich and varied range of research positions. Each chapter stands on its own but is tethered by the initial chapter that sets up the philosophical questions that initiate research reflections. We have tried to present each chapter so one chapter does not have primacy over others; for example, the case study genre should not be seen as 'more' than experimental or quasi-experimental approaches, collaborative ethnography over comparative design. Each position is equally valid. We have tried to position the book as neutrally as possible and uptake on the differing approaches may depend on the possible positions/stances of the researcher. However, readers may find, as we have, that reading a range of positions, even those diametrically opposed to your starting place, can help the researcher to revisit prejudices and assumptions and to enhance his/her choices and justifications.

We agree with other writers such as Pring (2000) in saying that those that underplay or even dismiss notions of truth, knowledge and reality are misguided. To ignore these essential philosophical notions, which are so important to research (not just in education), is akin to building a house without strong foundations. Without such foundations, the whole edifice might fall. Perhaps some researchers who feel that they are closer to postmodernist traditions feel exempt from the normal etiquette of research, and they feel it does not apply as they are not interested in finding 'truth'. But as we have seen in the chapters here, this belief is simply insufficient. It is perfectly acceptable to deny objective truth and believe that knowledge is constructed or co-constructed and that construction can change minute by minute or even second by second. But not to understand why this is the case is to starve research of its primary core foundation.

One aim of this book has been to emphasize the diversity of possibilities in education research and we have drawn on expertise and experiences from individuals with disparate backgrounds and research stances. We have, of course, not exhausted, by any means, the full range of research approaches that can be taken. But what we have argued here is that there is no one 'right way' to design and conduct education research. Each way is different, and indeed may be at odds with the previous or future chapters, contradicting and challenging the others' approaches. We do not see this as a weakness within the book, but instead as a means of enriching the reader's thinking and reflections on the ways that these different approaches may help us to understand not only where you as a researcher position yourself, but most importantly why you do so. Above all, we hope that learning about these differences will help readers to engage more confidently with possible stances in order to create a strong root system that helps research to flourish.

Obviously, this book is not fully comprehensive in its coverage; there are many areas that we have not written about such as ethics, policy, other ontologies and so forth. We are aware of this and if we had more space, we might have added another chapter or two particularly about the nature of power imbalances and inequity in research but we have limited ourselves to a range of research which are likely to be of relevance: established research approaches within major paradigms (quantitative and qualitative); powerful participatory and collaborative work where boundaries between academic researcher and participants (or consultants) are blurred or almost swept away; and finally research in this exciting digital, technology-driven world which challenge us to think in new ways about how we approach research. Power has been touched on in this book especially in chapters on collaborative ethnography and PAR, but it is important to remember that addressing power relations in research holds significance, especially for those researchers that are trying to co-construct knowledge and/or those that are seeking to understand power, as well as those aiming to disrupt the inequitable power relations that exist in the world today, such as feminist approaches to research. Understanding the power you have as a researcher is something, therefore, that should be part of your ontological underpinning and to ignore it is as equally fallible as failing to understand your own positioning.

Finally, we hope you have been intrigued by the philosophical traditions that have been feeding into this book and that you agree with the authors that the nature of knowledge that underpins education and education research is the key that opens the door to understanding what and why you are asking your research question(s) and how this will shape your future research designs.

Although slightly overused nowadays, we have often used the metaphor of a journey to characterize the research process and have concentrated on those early stages when the researcher must determine what is needed for the adventure ahead. No one can take that first step for you, but it is our hope that this book might aid you in making informed and thoughtful decisions that will sustain you as you begin to explore the research terrain.

References

Adelman, C., Jenkins, D., & Kemmis, S. (1980). Rethinking Case Study: Notes from the Second. *Cambridge Journal of Education*, 6: 139–141.

Agee, J. (2009). Developing Qualitative Research Questions a Reflective Process. *International Journal of Qualitative Studies in Education*, *22*(4): 431–447.

Anderson, T. & Shattuck, J. (2012). Design-based Research a Decade of Progress in Education Research? *Educational Researcher*, *41*(1): 16–25.

Andres, L. (2014). *Designing and Doing Survey Research*. London: Sage.

Arthur, J., Waring, M., Coe, R., & Hedges, L. (2012). *Research Methodologies in Education*. Sage.

Avissar, G. (2012). Inclusive Education in Israel from a Curriculum Perspective: An Exploratory Study. *European Journal of Special Needs Education*, *27*(1): 35–49.

Balen, R., Blyth, E., Calabretto, H., Fraser C., Horrocks, C., & Manby, M. (2006). Involving Children in Health and Social Research: 'Human Becomings' or 'Active Beings'? *Childhood*, *13*(1): 29–48.

Balfour, S. (2013). Assessing Writing in MOOCs: Automated Essay Scoring and Calibrated Peer Review. *Research and Practice in Assessment*, 8: 40–48.

Barbour, S. R. (2014). *Introducing Qualitative Research – A Student's Guide*. London: Sage.

Bartlett, L. & Vavrus, F. (2017). *Rethinking Case Study Research: A Comparative Approach*. London: Routledge.

Basit, T. N. (2010). *Conducting Research in Educational Contexts*. Continuum. London: Bloomsbury.

Bassey, M. (1999). *Case Study Research in Educational Settings*. Buckingham: Open University Press.

Baxter, P. & Jack, S. (2008). Qualitative Case Study Methodology: Study Design and Implementation for Novice Researchers. *The Qualitative Report*, *13*(4): 544–559. Retrieved from http://nsuworks.nova.edu/tqr/vol13/iss4/2.

Bayne, S. (2014). What's the Matter with 'Technology-enhanced Learning'? *Learning, Media and Technology*, 1–16. doi:10.1080/17439884.2014.915851.

Bayne, S. (2015). Teacherbot: Interventions in Automated Teaching. *Teaching in Higher Education*, *20*(4): 455–467.

Bayne, S. & Ross, J. (2013). *The Pedagogy of the Massive Open Online Course (MOOC): The UK View*. the Higher Education Academy.

Bazeley, P. (2009). Integrating Data Analyses in Mixed Methods Research. *Journal of Mixed Methods Research, 3(3)*: 203–207.

Bazeley, P. (2010). 'Computer-Assisted Integration of Mixed Methods Data Sources and Analysis', in A. Tashakkori & C. Teddlie (eds), *SAGE Handbook of Mixed Methods in Social and Behavioral Research*, 2nd edn, 431–467. Thousand Oaks, CA: Sage.

Belfiore, E. & Bennett, O. (2010). Beyond the 'Toolkit Approach': Arts Impact Evaluation Research and the Realities of Cultural Policy-Making. *Journal for Cultural Research, 14(2)*: 121–142. doi: 10.1080/14797580903481280.

Bell, M. (2011). *Promoting Children's Rights in Social Work and Social Care: A Guide to Participatory Practice*. London: Jessica Kingsley Publishers.

Bereday, G. (1964). *Comparative Method in Education*. New York: Holt, Rinehart & Winston.

Berg-Schlosser, D. (2001). Comparative Studies: Method and Design, in N. J. Smelser & P. B. Baltes (eds), *International Encyclopedia of the Social & Behavioral Sciences*, 2427–2433. New York: Pergamon.

Berry, M. (2015). What the OECD report really means. Retrieved from http://edtechnology.co.uk/Article/what-the-oecd- report-really-means.

Bianco, F. & Lecce, S. (2016). Translating Child Development Research into Practice: Can Teachers Foster Children's Theory of Mind in Primary School? *British Journal of Educational Psychology, 86(4)*: 592–605.

Bianco, F., Lecce, S., & Banerjee, R. (2016). Conversations about Mental States and Theory of Mind Development during Middle Childhood: A Training Study. *Journal of Experimental Child Psychology, 149*: 41–61.

Biesta, G. (2007). Why 'What Works' Won't Work: Evidence-based Practice and the Democratic Deficit in Educational Research. *Educational Theory, 57(1)*: 1–22. doi:10.1111/j.1741-5446.2006.00241.x.

Biesta, G. (2010a). Pragmatism and the Philosophical Foundations of Mixed Methods Research, in A. Tashakkori & C. Teddlie (eds), *SAGE Handbook of Mixed Methods in Social and Behavioral Research*, 2nd edn, 95–117. Thousand Oaks, CA: Sage.

Biesta, G. (2010b). Why 'What Works' Still Won't Work: From Evidence-Based Education to Value-Based Education, *Studies in Philosophy and Education, 29(5)*: 491–503. doi: 10.1007/s11217-010-9191-x.

Biesta, G. (2012). Mixed Methods, in J. Arthur, M. Waring, R. Coe & L. Hedges (eds), *Research Methods and Methodologies in Education*, 147–152. Thousand Oaks, CA: Sage.

Bloor, M. & Wood, F. (2006). *Keywords in Qualitative Methods a Vocabulary of Research Concepts*. London: Sage.

Boeren, E. (2015). Surveys as Tools to Measure Qualitative and Quantitative Data, in V. Wang (ed.), *Handbook of Research on Scholarly Publishing and Research Methods*. Hershey: IGI.

Brandom, R. B. (ed.) (2000). *Rorty and His Critics*. Malden, MA: Blackwell.

Branley, D. (2004). Doing a Literature Review, in C. Seale (ed.), *Researching Society and Culture*, 2nd edn, 145–162. London: Sage.

Brannen, J., Filipović-Carter, D., & Hantrais, L. (2011). International Social Research Methods Case Studies.

Bransford, J. D. & Schwartz, D. L. (1999). Rethinking Transfer: A Simple Proposal with Multiple Implications. *Review of Research in Education*, Vol. 24, 61–100. Washington: American Educational Research Association.

Bray, M., Adamson, B., & Mason, M. (2014). Introduction, in M. Bray, B. Adamson & M. Mason (eds), *Comparative Education Research: Approaches and Methods*, 1–16. London: Springer.

Bray, M. & Thomas, M. (1995). Levels of Comparison in Educational Studies: Different Insights from Different Literatures and the Value of Multilevel Analyses. *Harvard Educational Review*, 65(3): 472–491.

British Education Research Association (BERA). (2011). *Revised Ethical Guidelines for Educational Research*. Retrieved from https://www.bera.ac.uk/wp-content/uploads/2014/02/BERA-Ethical-Guidelines-2011.pdf

Bronfenbrenner, U. (1979). *The Ecology of Human Development: Experiments by Design and Nature*. Cambridge, MA: Harvard University Press.

Brooks, R., Te Riele, K., & Maguire, M. (2014). *Ethics and Research in Education*. London: Sage.

Brown, J. (2007). Gender Time and Space: Understanding Problem Behavior in Children. *Children and Society*, 21(2): 98–110.

Brown, J. (2011). Citizens Fit for the 21st Century? The Role of School Design in Facilitating Citizenship in Young People. *Education, Citizenship and Social Justice*, 7(1): 19–31.

Brown, J., Croxford, L., & Minty, S. (2017). *Pupils as Citizens: Participation, Responsibility and Voice in the Transition from Primary to Secondary School*. Funded by Gordon Cook Foundation, University of Edinburgh. Retrieved from http://www.docs.hss.ed.ac.uk/education/creid/Projects/37_i_PupilAsCitizens_FinalRpt.pdf.

Bryman, A. (1988). *Quantity and Quality in Social Research*. London: Unwin Hyman.

Bryman, A. (2004). *Social Research Methods*. Oxford: Oxford University Press.

Bryman, A. (2006). Integrating Quantitative and Qualitative Research: How Is It Done? *Qualitative Research*, 6(1): 97–113.

Bryman, A. (2008). Why do Researchers Integrate/Combine/Mesh/Blend/Mix/Merge/Fuse Quantitative and Qualitative Research?, in M. M. Bergman (ed.), *Advances in Mixed Methods Research*, 86–100. London: Sage.

Burr, V. (2004). *Social Constructionism*. London: Rutledge.

Cammarota, J. & Romero, A. (2011). Participatory Action Research for High School Students: Transforming Policy, Practice, and the Personal with Social Justice Education. *Educational Policy, 25*: 488–506.

Campbell, D. T. & Stanley, J. C. (1963). *Experimental and Quasi-Experimental Designs for Research*. Boston: Houghton Mifflin.

Campbell, E. & Lassiter, L. E. (2015). *Doing Ethnography Today: Theories, Methods, Exercises*. London: Wiley Blackwell.

Caracelli, V. J. & Greene, J. C. (1993). Data Analysis Strategies for Mixed-Method Evaluation Designs. *Educational Evaluation and Policy Analysis, 15(2):* 195–207.

Carr, W. (2006). Philosophy, Methodology and Action Research. *Journal of Philosophy of Education, 40(4)*: 421–435.

Cebula, K., Wishart, J., Willis, D., & Pitcairn, T. (2017). Emotion Recognition in Children with Down Syndrome: Influence of Emotion Label and Expression Intensity. *American Journal on Intellectual and Developmental Disabilities, 122(2)*: 138–155.

Chisholm, R. M. (1966/1977/1989). *Theory of Knowledge* (any of the three editions). Englewood Cliffs, NJ: Prentice Hall.

Christensen, P. & James, A. (2008). Researching Children and Childhood: Cultures and Communities, in P. Christensen & A. James (eds), *Research with Children*. London: Routledge.

Clark-Carter, D. (2004). *Quantitative Psychology Research: A Student's Handbook*. Hove: Psychology Press.

Coffey, A. & Atkinson, P. (1996). *Making Sense of Qualitative Data: Complementary Research Strategies*. London: Sage.

Cohen, L., Manion, L., & Morrison, K. (2007). *Research Methods in Education*. London: Routledge.

Cohen, L., Manion, L., & Morrison, K. (2011). Surveys, Longitudinal, Cross-Sectional and Trend Studies, in *Research Methods in Education*, 7th edn, 261–264. Abingdon: Routledge.

Collins, K. M. T., Onwuegbuzie, A. J., & Johnson, R. B. (2012). Securing a Place at the Table: A Review and Extension of Legitimation Criteria for the Conduct of Mixed Research. *American Behavioral Scientist, 56(6)*: 849–865.

Cook, T. D. (2003). Why have Educational Evaluators Chosen Not to Do Randomized Experiments. *The Annals of the American Academy of Political and Social Science*, 589, 114–149.

Cook, T. D. & Reichardt, C. S. (1979). *Qualitative and Quantitative Methods in Evaluation Research* (Vol. 1). Sage Publications, Inc.

Coolican, H. (2004). *Research Methods and Statistics in Psychology*. Psychology Press. England.

Crede, E. & M. Borrego (2013). 'From Ethnography to Items: A Mixed Methods Approach to Developing a Survey to Examine Graduate

Engineering Student Retention.' *Journal of Mixed Methods Research, 7(1):* 62–80.

Creswell, J. & Plano Clark, V. L. (2007). *Designing and Conducting Mixed Methods Research.* Thousand Oaks, CA: Sage.

Creswell, J. & Plano Clark, V. L. (2011). *Designing and Conducting Mixed Methods Research,* 2nd edn. Thousand Oaks, CA: Sage.

Creswell, J. W. (1995). *Research Design: Qualitative and Quantitative Approaches.* Thousand Oaks, CA: Sage.

Creswell, J. W. (2013). *Qualitative Inquiry and Research Design: Choosing among Five Approaches* (4th edn). London: Sage.

Creswell, J. W. (2015). *A Concise Introduction to Mixed Methods Research.* Thousand Oaks, CA: Sage.

Crook, C., Harrison, C., & Tomas, C. (2011). Learning Acts and the Role of Digital Technology in Achieving Coherence among Them. Paper presented at the *Informing Science & IT Education Conference (InSITE),* Novi Sad, Serbia and Montenegro.

Crotty, M. (1998). *The Foundations of Social Research: Meaning and Perspective in the Research Process.* London: Sage.

Crow, G. (2017). *What are Community Studies?* London: Bloomsbury Academic.

Davis, J., Ravenscroft J. & Bizas N. (2015). Transition, Inclusion and Partnership: Child, Parent and Professional Led Approaches in a European Research Project. *Child Care in Practice, 21:* 3–49.

De Jong, A. J. M, Ainsworth, S., Dobson, M., Van Der Hulst, A., Levonen, J., Reimann, P., Sime, J. A., Van Someren, M., Spada, H., & Swaak, J. (1998). Acquiring Knowledge in Science and Mathematics: The Use of Multiple Representations in Technology based Learning Environments, in M. W. Van Someren (ed.), *Learning with Multiple Representations.* Advances in learning and instruction series, 9–41. Elsevier Science, Oxford.

Della Porta, D. (2008). Comparative Analysis: Case-oriented versus Variable-oriented Research, in D. Della Porta & M. Keating (eds), *Approaches and Methodologies in the Social Sciences: A Pluralist Perspective,* 198–222. Cambridge: Cambridge University Press.

Dellinger, A. B. & Leech, N. L. (2007). Towards a Unified Validation Framework in Mixed Methods Research. *Journal of Mixed Methods Research, 1(4):* 309–332.

Denscombe, M. (2008). Communities of Practice: A Research Paradigm for the Mixed Methods Approach. *Journal of Mixed Methods Research, 2(3):* 270–283.

Denzin, N. K. (1978). *The Research Act: A Theoretical Introduction to Sociological Methods.* New York: McGraw Hill.

Denzin, N. K. & Lincoln, Y. S. (2005). *The Handbook of Qualitative Research.* London: Sage.

Devine, R. T. & Hughes, C. (2016). Measuring Theory of Mind across Middle Childhood: Reliability and Validity of the Silent Films and Strange Stories Tasks. *Journal of Experimental Child Psychology*, 149, 23–40.

Dewey, J. (1929). The Quest for Certainty, in J. Boydston (ed.), (1988), *The Later Works: 1925–1953*, Vol. 4, Carbondale: Southern Illinois University Press.

Drosopoulos, S., Wagner, U., & Born, J. (2005). Sleep Enhances Explicit Recollection in Recognition Memory. *Learning & Memory*, 12(1): 44–51.

Dumontheil, I., Apperly, I., & Blakemore, S. (2010). Online Usage of Theory of Mind Continues to Develop in Late Adolescence. *Developmental Science*, 13(2): 331–338.

Earp, B. & Trafimow, D. (2015). Replication, Falsification, and the Crisis of Confidence in Social Psychology. *Frontiers in Psychology*, 6: 621.

Edwards, R. & Holland, J. (2013). *What Is Qualitative Interviewing?* Research Methods Series. London: Bloomsbury.

Eltiraifi, M. et al. (2017). Alex and Charlie, Whitewater Publishing Ltd. Retrieved from http://www.edinburgh.gov.uk/info/20075/information_for_professionals/383/learning_publications.

Esping-Andersen, G. (1989). *The Three Worlds of Welfare Capitalism*. Cambridge: Polity Press.

Feilzer, M. Y. (2010). Doing Mixed Methods Research Pragmatically: Implications for the Rediscovery of Pragmatism as a Research Paradigm. *Journal of Mixed Methods Research*, 4(1): 6–16.

Feld, S. (1990). *Sound and Sentiment: Birds, Weeping, Poetics, and Song in Kaluli Expression*, 2nd edn. Philadelphia: University of Pennsylvania Press.

Fenger, H. (2007). Welfare Regimes in Central and Eastern Europe: Incorporating Post-communist Countries in Welfare Regime Typology. *Contemporary Issues and Ideas in Social Sciences*, 3(2): 1–30.

Fern, Edward F. (1982). The Use of Focus Groups for Idea Generation: The Effects of Group Size, Group Type, Acquaintanceship, and the Moderator on Response Quantity and Quality. *Journal of Marketing Research*, 19, 1–13 (Winter 1982).

Field, A. (2013). *Discovering Statistics Using IBM SPSS Statistics*. London: Sage.

Field, Les W. (2008). *Abalone Tales: Collaborative Explorations of Sovereignty and Identity in Native California*. Durham: Duke University Press.

Fielding, M. (2004). 'New Wave' Student Voice and Renewal of Civic Society. *London Review of Education*, 2(3), 197–217.

Fine, G. (2003). *Plato on Knowledge and Forms: Selected Essays*. Oxford: Oxford University Press.

Fink, A. (2003). *They Survey Handbook*. Los Angels, CA: The Langley Research Institute.

Fishman, D. (1991). An Introduction to the Experimental versus the Pragmatic Paradigm in Evaluation. *Evaluation and Program Planning*, 14(4): 353–363.

Fletcher-Watson, S., Petrou, A., Scott-Barrett, J., Dicks, P., Graham, C., O'Hare, A., Pain, H., & McConachie, H. (2016). A Trial of an iPad™ Intervention Targeting Social Communication Skills in Children with Autism. *Autism: The International Journal of Research and Practice*, 20(7): 771–782.

Fowler, F. (2013). *Survey Research Methods*. London: Sage.

Franzoni, J. M. (2008). Welfare Regimes in Latin America: Capturing Constellations of Markets, Families, and Policies. *Latin American Politics and Society*, 50: 67–100. doi:10.1111/j.1548-2456.2008.00013.x

Gage, N. L. (1989). The Paradigm Wars and Their Aftermath: A 'Historical Sketch of Research on Teaching since 1989'. *Educational Researcher*, 18(7): 4–10.

Gallacher, L. A. & Gallagher, M. (2008). Methodological Immaturity in Childhood Research?: Thinking through 'Participatory Methods'. *Childhood*, 15: 499–516.

Gettier, E. (1963). Is Justified True Belief Knowledge? *Analysis*, 23: 121–123.

Gibbs, A. (1997). Focus groups. *Social Research Update, 19*. Retrieved from http://sru.soc.surrey.ac.uk/SRU19.html.

Goldacre, B. (2013). *Building Evidence into Education*. London: Department for Education.

Goldacre, B. & Plant, R. (2013). *Department for Education Analytical Review*. Department for Education. Retrieved from https://www.gov.uk/government/publications/department-for-education-analytical-review.

Goldman, A. (1976). Discrimination and Perceptual Knowledge. *Journal of Philosophy, 73*: 771–791.

Goldman, A. (1999). *Knowledge in a Social World*. Oxford: Oxford University Press.

Goodwin, C. J. (2008). Psychology's Experimental Foundations, in S. F. Davis (ed.). *Handbook of Research Methods in Experimental Psychology*. Oxford: Blackwell.

Gough, N. (2012). Complexity, Complexity Reduction, and 'Methodological Borrowing' in Educational Inquiry. *Complicity: An International Journal of Complexity and Education, 9(1)*. Retrieved from http://ejournals.library.ualberta.ca/index.php/complicity/article/view/16532.

Green, J., Charman, T., Mcconachie, H., Aldred, C., Slonims, V., Howlin, P., & Pickles, A. (2010). Parent-Mediated Communication-focused Treatment in Children with Autism (PACT): A Randomised Controlled Trial. *The Lancet, 375(9732)*: 2152–2160.

Greene, J. C. (2006). Toward a Methodology of Mixed Methods Social Inquiry. *Research in the Schools, 13(1)*: 93–98.

Greene, J. C. (2007). *Mixed Methods in Social Inquiry*. San Francisco, CA: John Wiley & Sons.

Greene, J. C. (2008). Is Mixed Methods Social Inquiry a Distinctive Methodology? *Journal of Mixed Methods Research, 2(1)*: 7–22.

Greene, J. C. & Caracelli, V. J. (1997). Defining and Describing the Paradigm Issue in Mixed-Method Evaluation. *New Directions for Evaluation*, *74*: 5–17.

Greene, J. C. & Caracelli, V. J. (2003). Making Paradigmatic Sense of Mixed Methods Practice, in A. Tashakkori & C. Teddlie (eds), *Handbook of Mixed Methods in Social and Behavioural Research*, 91–110. Thousand Oaks, CA: Sage.

Greene, J. C., Caracelli, V. J., & Graham, W. F. (1989). Toward a Conceptual Framework for Mixed-Method Evaluation Designs. *Educational Evaluation and Policy Analysis*, *11*(*3*): 255–274.

Greene, J. C. & Hall, J. N. (2010). Dialectics and Pragmatism: Being of Consequence, in A. Tashakkori & C. Teddlie (eds), *SAGE Handbook of Mixed Methods in Social and Behavioral Research*, 2nd edn, 119–143. Thousand Oaks, CA: Sage.

Guba, E. G. (ed.) (1990). *The Paradigm Dialog*. London: Sage.

Guba, E. G. & Lincoln, Y. S. (2005). Paradigmatic Controversies, Contradictions, and Emerging Influences, in N. K. Denzin & Y. S. Lincoln (eds), *The Sage Handbook of Qualitative Research*, 3rd edn, 191–215. Thousand Oaks, CA: Sage.

Hager, P. & Halliday, J. (2009). *Recovering Informal Learning: Wisdom, Judgement and Community*. New York: Springer.

Hales, D. (2013). Design Fictions an Introduction and Provisional Taxonomy. *Digital Creativity*, *24*(*1*): 1–10. doi:10.1080/14626268.2013.769453.

Hall, J. N. (2013a). Pragmatism, Evidence and Mixed Methods Evaluation. *New Directions for Evaluation*, *138*: 15–26.

Hall, R. (2013b). Mixed Methods: In Search of a Paradigm, in T. Le & Q. Lê (eds), *Conducting Research in a Changing and Challenging World*, 71–78. New York: Nova Science Publishers.

Hamilton, L. (2015). Early Professional Development in the Scottish Context: Pre Service High School Teachers and the Management of Behaviour in Classrooms. *Journal of Teacher Development*, *19*(*3*): 328–343.

Hamilton, L. & Corbett-Whittier, C. (2013). *Using Case Study in Education Research*. London: Sage.

Hammersley, M. (1989). *The Dilemma of the Qualitative Method*. London: Routledge.

Hammersley, M. & Traianou, A. (2007). *Ethics and Educational Research*. London: TLRP. Retrieved from http://www.tlrp.org/capacity/rm/wt/traianou

Harding, S. G. (1987). *Feminism and Methodology: Social Science Issues*. Indiana University Press.

Hart, A., Maddison, E. & Wolff, D. (eds). (2007). *Community-University Partnerships in Practice*. Leicester: National Institute of Adult Continuing Education.

Haviland, M. (2017). *Side by Side? Community Art and the Challenge of Co-Creativity*. New York: Routledge.

Heary, C. M. & Hennessy, E. (2002). The Use of Focus Group Interviews in Pediatric Health Care Research. *Journal of Pediatric Psychology, 27(1)*: 47–57.

Hedges, L. V. (2012), Design of Empirical Research, in J. Arthur, M. Waring, R. Coe & L. V. Hedges (eds), *Research Methods and Methodologies in Education*, 23–30. Thousand Oaks, CA: Sage.

Heron, J. (1996a). *Co-operative Inquiry: Research into the Human Condition*. London: Sage.

Heron, J. (1996b). Primacy of the Practical. *Qualitative Inquiry, 2(1)*: 41–56.

Heron, J. & Reason, P. (1997). A Participatory Inquiry Paradigm. *Qualitative Inquiry, 3(3)*: 274–294.

Hesse-Biber, S. (2015), Mixed Methods Research: The 'Thingness' Problem, *Qualitative Health Research, 25(6)*: 775–788.

Hesse-Biber, S. & Johnson, R. B. (2015) *The Oxford Handbook of Multimethod and Mixed Methods Research Inquiry*. Oxford: Oxford University Press.

Hetherington, S. (2016). *Knowledge and the Gettier Problem*. Cambridge: Cambridge University Press.

Hirschhorn, J. & Altshuler, D. (2002). Once and Again-Issues Surrounding Replication in Genetic Association Studies. *The Journal of Clinical Endocrinology and Metabolism, 87(10)*: 4438–4441.

Holford, J. & Mleczko, A. (2011). *The European Indicator of Adult Participation in Lifelong Learning: The Significance of Interview Questions*. Paper presented at the 41th annual SCUTREA conference.

Holford, J., Riddell, S., Weedon, E., Litjens, J., & Hannan, G. (2008). *Patterns of Lifelong Learning, Policy and Practice in an Expanding Europe*. Vienna: Lit Verlag.

Holmes, J. & Gathercole, S. (2014). Taking Working Memory Training from the Laboratory into Schools. *Educational Psychology, 34(4)*: 440–450.

Howard-Snyder, F. & Neil, F. (2003). Infallibilism and Gettier's Legacy. *Philosophy and Phenomenological Research, 63*: 304–327.

Howe, K. R. (1988). Against the Quantitative-Qualitative Incompatibility Thesis or Dogmas Die Hard. *Educational Researcher, 17(8)*: 10–16.

Howe, K. R. (2004). A critique of Experimentalism. *Qualitative Inquiry, 10(1)*: 42–61.

Hutchins, E. (1995). *Cognition in the Wild*. Cambridge, MA: MIT Press.

Hyatt, Susan B. ed. (2012). *The Neighborhood of Saturdays: Memories of a Multi-Ethnic Community on Indianapolis's South Side*. Indianapolis, IN: Dog Ear Publishers.

Ivankova, N. V. & Kawamura, Y. (2010). Emerging Trends in Utilization of Integrated Designs in the Social, Behavioral, and Health Sciences, in A.

Tashakkori & C. Teddlie (eds), *SAGE Handbook of Mixed Methods in Social and Behavioral Research*, 2nd edn, 581–611. Thousand Oaks, CA: Sage.

Jang, E. E., McDougall, D. E., Pollon, D., Herbert, M., & Russell, P. (2008). Integrative Mixed Methods Data Analytic Strategies in Research on School Success in Challenging Circumstances. *Journal of Mixed Methods Research*, *2*(3): 221–247.

Jerrim, J. (2016). PISA 2012: How do Results for the Paper and Computer Tests Compare? *Assessment in Education: Principles, Policies & Practice*, *23*(4): 495–518.

John, P. & Wheeler, S. (2012). *The Digital Classroom: Harnessing Technology for the Future of Learning and Teaching*. London: Routledge.

Johnson, B. & Christensen, L. (2014). *Educational Research: Quantitative, Qualitative, and Mixed Approaches*. London: Sage.

Johnson, R. B. & Gray, R. (2010), A History of Philosophical and Theoretical Issues for Mixed Methods Research, in A. Tashakkori & C. Teddlie (eds), *SAGE Handbook of Mixed Methods in Social and Behavioral Research*, 2nd edn, 69–94. Thousand Oaks, CA: Sage.

Johnson, R. B. & Onwuegbuzie, A. J. (2004). Mixed Methods Research: A Research Paradigm Whose Time Has Come. *Educational Researcher*, *33*(7): 14–26.

Johnson, R. B., Onwuegbuzie, A. J., & Turner, L. A. (2007). Toward a Definition of Mixed Methods Research. *Journal of Mixed Methods Research*, *1*(2): 112–133.

Johnston, R. B. & Christensen, L. (2014). *Educational Research: Quantitative, Qualitative and Mixed Approaches*, 5th edn, Thousand Oaks, CA: Sage.

Johnston, R. B. & Turner, L. A. (2003), Data Collection Strategies in Mixed Methods Research, in A. Tashakkori & C. Teddlie (eds), *Handbook of Mixed Methods in Social and Behavioural Research*, 297–320. Thousand Oaks, CA: Sage.

Kelly, M. & Ali, S. (2004). Ethics and Social Research, in C. Seale (ed.), *Researching Society and Culture*, 2nd edn, 115–128. London: Sage.

King, M. (2010). Documenting Traditions and the Ethnographic Double Bind. *Collaborative Anthropologies*, *3*: 37–68.

Knox, J. (2014). The 'Tweeting Book' and the Question of 'Non-human Data'. *TechTrends*, *59*(1): 72–75. doi: 10.1007/s11528-014-0823-9.

Kotzee, B. (2013). Introduction: Education, Social Epistemology and Virtue Epistemology. *Journal of Philosophy of Education*, *47*: 157–167.

Kotzee, B. (2016). Learning How. *Journal of Philosophy of Education*, *50*: 218–232.

Kuhn, T. (1967). *The Structure of Scientific Revolutions*. Chicago: The University of Chicago Press.

Kuhn, T. S. (1970). *The Structure of Scientific Revolutions*. Chicago: Chicago University Press.

Landman, T. (2008). *Issues and Methods in Comparative Politics: An Introduction*. London: Routledge.

Larochelle, M., Bednarz, N., & Garrison, J. (1998). *Constructivism and Education*. Cambridge: Cambridge University Press.

Lassiter, L. E. (1995). *The Power of Kiowa Song*. Tucson: University of Arizona Press.

Lassiter, L. E. (2005). *The Chicago Guide to Collaborative Ethnography*. Chicago: University of Chicago Press.

Lassiter, L. E. (2012). 'To Fill in the Missing Piece of the Middletown Puzzle': Lessons from Re-Studying Middletown. *Sociological Review, 60*: 421–437.

Lassiter, L. E., Clyde, E., & Kotay, R. (2002). *The Jesus Road: Kiowas, Christianity, and Indian Hymns*. Lincoln: University of Nebraska Press.

Lassiter, L. E, Goodall, H., Campbell, E., & Johnson, M. N. (eds) (2004). *The Other Side of Middletown: Exploring Muncie's African American Community*. Walnut Creek, CA: AltaMira Press.

Law, J. (2004). *After Method: Mess in Social Science Research*. Psychology Press.

Lawless, E. (1993). *Holy Women, Wholly Women: Sharing Ministries through Life Stories and Reciprocal Ethnography*. Philadelphia: University of Pennsylvania Press. Neighborhood Story Project. 2017. Neighborhood Story Project – Our Stories Told by Us. Retrieved from https://www.neighborhoodstoryproject.org.

Liasidou, A. (2011). Unequal Power Relations and Inclusive Education Policy Making: A Discursive Analytic Approach. *Educational Policy, 25*(6): 887–907.

Likert, R. (1929). *A Technique for the Measurement of Attitudes*. New York: Columbia University.

Lincoln, Y. S. & Guba, E. G. (1985). *Naturalistic Inquiry*. Newbury Park, CA: Sage.

Lincoln, Y. S. & Guba, E. G. (2000). The Only Generalisation Is: There Is No Generalisation, in R. Gromm, M. Hammersley & P. Foster (eds), *Case Study Method: Key Issues, Key Texts*. London: Sage Munchen: De Gruyter Saur.

Lo Lacono, V., Symonds, P., & Brown, D. H. K. (2016). Skype as a tool for qualitative research interviews. *Sociological Research Online, 21*(2): 12. Retrieved from http://www.socresonline.org.uk/21/2/12.html.

Lofland, J., Snow, D., Anderson, D., & Lofland, L. H. (2006). *Analyzing Social Settings: A Guide to Qualitative Observation and Analysis*, revised edn. Belmont, CA: Wadsworth.

Lor, P. (2011). *International and Comparative Librarianship: A Thematic Approach*. Walter de Gruyter, Berlin.

Luck, L., Jackson, D., & Usher, K. (2006). Case Study: A Bridge Across the Paradigms. *Nursing Inquiry, 13*(2): 103–109.

Luckin, R. (2008). The Learner Centric Ecology of Resources: A Framework for Using Technology to Scaffold Learning. *Computers & Education, 50*: 449–462.

Luckin, R., Blight, B., Manches, A., Ainsworth, S., Crook, C., & Noss, R. (2012). *Decoding Learning: The Proof, Promise and Potential of Digital Learning*. London: Nesta.

Lury, C. & Wakeford, N. (2012). *Inventive Methods: The Happening of the Social*. London: Routledge.

Lycan, W. (2006). On the Gettier Problem Problem, in S. Hetherington (ed.), *Epistemology Futures*, 148–168. Oxford: Oxford University Press.

Macfarlane, B. (2009). *Researching with Integrity – The Ethics of Academic Enquiry*. Routledge: London.

Mackenzie, J., Tan, P. L., Hoverman, S., & Baldwin, C. (2012). The Value and Limitations of Participatory Action Research Methodology. *Journal of Hydrology, 474*: 11–21.

MacLure, M. (2006). The Bone in the Throat: Some Uncertain Thoughts on Baroque Method. *International Journal of Qualitative Studies in Education, 19*(6): 729–745. doi:10.1080/09518390600975958.

Manches, A. (2010). The Effect of Physical Manipulation on Children's Numerical Strategies: Evaluating the Potential for Tangible Technology. Unpublished doctoral dissertation, University of Nottingham, Nottingham, UK. Retrieved from http://etheses.nottingham.ac.uk/1372/1/AndrewManchesFinalThesis2010.pdf

Manches, A., Horton, M., & Yarosh, S. (2010). Children's Role in Mobile Interaction Design: Review and Reflection. *International Journal of Mobile Human Computer Interaction, 2*(2): 72–78.

Manches, A., Phillips, B., Crook, C., Chowcat, I., & Sharples, M. (2010). Year 3 Final Report: *Shaping Contexts to Realise the Potential of Technologies to Support Learning*. Nottingham: Capital Report: Retrieved from http://www.lsri.nottingham.ac.uk/capital/Final.

Manches, A., Phillips, B., Crook, C., Sharples, M., Patterson, W., Stokes, E., & Chowcat, I. (2010). Technology and Education: Putting It in context. Nottingham: Capital Report: Retrieved from http://www.lsri.nottingham.ac.uk/capital/Final.

Mannion, G., Sowerby, M., & L'anson, J. (2015). *How Young People's Participation in School Supports Achievement and Attainment*. Edinburgh: Scotland's Commissioner for Children and Young People (SCCYP). Retrieved from http://www.sccyp.org.uk/ufiles/achievement-and-attainment.pdfoxf.

Manzon, M. (2014). Comparing Places, in M. Bray, B. Adamson & M. Mason (eds), *Comparing Education Research: Approaches and Methods*, 97–138. London: Springer.

Manzon, M. & Areepattamannil, S. (2014). Shadow Educations: Mapping the Global Discourse. *Asia Pacific Journal of Education*, 34(4): 389–402.

Marchal, B., Westhorp, G., Wong, G., Van Belle, S., Greenhalgh, T., Kegels, G., & Pawson, R. (2013). Realist RCTs of Complex Interventions–An Oxymoron. *Social Science & Medicine*, 94: 124–128.

Martin, G. N. & Clarke, R. M. (2017). Are Psychology Journals Anti-Replication? A Snapshot of Editorial Practices. *Frontiers in Psychology*, 8(523): 1–6.

Mason, J. (1996). *Qualitative Researching*. London: Sage.

Maxcy, S. J. (2003). Pragmatic Threads in Mixed Methods Research in the Social Sciences: The Search for Multiple Modes of Inquiry and the End of the Philosophy of Formalism, in A. Tashakkori & C. Teddlie (eds), *Handbook of Mixed Methods in Social and Behavioral Research*, 51–89. Thousand Oaks, CA: Sage.

Maxwell, J. A. and Mittapalli, K. (2010). Realism as a Stance for Mixed Methods Research, in A. Tashakkori & C. Teddlie (eds), *SAGE Handbook of Mixed Methods in Social and Behavioral Research*, 2nd edn, 145–168. Thousand Oaks, CA: Sage.

Maxwell, S. E. & Delaney, H. D. (1990). *Designing Experiments and Analyzing Data: A Model Comparison Approach*. Belmont, CA: Wadsworth.

Maxwell, S., Lau, M., Howard, G., Anderson, Norman B., & Kazak, Anne E. (2015). Is Psychology Suffering from a Replication Crisis? *American Psychologist*, 70(6): 487–498.

McArthur, J. (2012). Virtuous Mess and Wicked Clarity: Struggle in Higher Education Research. *Higher Education Research & Development*, 31(3): 419–430. doi:10.1080/07294360.2011.634380.

McCain, K. (2016). *The Nature of Scientific Knowledge. An Explanatory Approach*. Springer.

McGeown, S. (2013). *Quantitative Data Gathering: Questionnaires. Hand-Outs for Students*. Edinburgh: University of Edinburgh.

McKelvie, P. & Low, J. (2002). Listening to Mozart Does Not Improve Children's Spatial Ability: Final Curtains for the Mozart Effect. *British Journal of Developmental Psychology*, 20(2): 241–258.

McMellon, C. & Mitchell, M. (2016). Young Edinburgh Action: Reinvigorating Young People's Participation in Edinburgh. Retrieved from https://www.era.lib.ed.ac.uk/handle/1842/16875

Merriam, S. (1998). *Case Study Research in Education: A Qualitative Approach*. San Francisco, CA: Jossey-Bass.

Merriam, S. (2001). *Qualitative Research and Case study Applications in Education*. San Francisco, CA: Jossey-Bass Publishers.

Mertens, D. M. (2012). Transformative Mixed Methods: Addressing Inequities. *American Behavioral Scientist*, 56(6): 802–813.

Mertens, D. M., Bledsoe, K. L., Sullivan, M., & Wilson, A. (2010). Utilization of Mixed Methods for Transformative Purposes. *SAGE Handbook of Mixed Methods in Social and Behavioural Research,* 2nd edn, 193–214. Thousand Oaks, CA: Sage.

Michael, M. (2012). 'What Are We Busy Doing?' Engaging the Idiot. *Science, Technology & Human Values, 37*(5): 528–554. https://doi.org/10.1177/0162243911428624

Miles, M. B. & Huberman, A. M. (1984). *Qualitative Data Analysis: A Sourcebook of New Methods.* Thousand Oaks, CA: Sage.

Miller, A. (2016). Realism. The Stanford Encyclopaedia of Philosophy (Winter 2016 edition), Edward N. Zalta (ed.). Accessed 2 February 2017. Retrieved from https://plato.stanford.edu/archives/win2016/entries/realism/

Morgan, D. L. (2007). Paradigms Lost and Pragmatism Regained: Methodological Implications of Combining Qualitative and Quantitative Methods. *Journal of Mixed Methods Research, 1*(1): 48–76.

Morgan, M., Gibbs, S., Maxwell, K., & Britten, N. (2002). Hearing Children's Voices Methodological Issues in Conducting Focus Groups with Children aged 7–11 years. *Qualitative Research, 2*(1): 5–20.

Morse, J. M. (1999). The Armchair Walkthrough. *Qualitative Health Research, 9*(4): 435–436.

Morse, J. M. (2003). Principles of Mixed Methods and Multimethod Research Design, in A. Tashakkori & C. Teddlie (eds), *Handbook of Mixed Methods in Social and Behavioral Research,* 189–208. Thousand Oaks, CA: Sage.

Morse, J. M. & Niehaus, L. (2016). *Mixed Method Design: Principles and Procedures.* London: Routledge.

Moser, S. (2002). Observing Differences, Embodying Knowledge: Radical Constructivism Meets Feminist Epistemology. *Cybernetics & Human Knowing, 9*(3–4): 35–54.

Nastasi, B. K., Hitchcock, J. H., & Brown, L. M. (2010). An Inclusive Framework for Conceptualizing Mixed Methods Design Typologies: Moving toward Fully Integrated Synergistic Research Models. *Handbook of Mixed Methods in Social & Behavioral Research,* 305–338.

Niglas, K. (2009). How the Novice Researcher Can Make Sense of Mixed Methods Designs. *International Journal of Multiple Research Approaches, 3*: 34–46.

Niglas, K. (2010). The Multidimensional Model of Research Methodology: An Integrated Set of Continua, in A. Tashakkori & C. Teddlie (eds), *SAGE Handbook of Mixed Methods in Social and Behavioral Research,* 2nd edn, 215–236. Thousand Oaks, CA: Sage.

Noah, H. & Eckstein, M. (1969). *Toward a Science of Comparative Education.* New York: Macmillan.

O'Cathain, A. (2010). Assessing the Quality of Mixed Methods Research: Toward a Comprehensive Framework, in A. Tashakkori & C. Teddlie (eds), *SAGE Handbook of Mixed Methods in Social and Behavioral Research*, 2nd edn, 531–555. Thousand Oaks, CA: Sage.

O'Day, R. & Englander, D. (1993). *Mr Charles Booth's Inquire: Life and Labour of the People in London Reconsidered*. London: Hambledon Press.

O'Donnell, A. M. (2004). A Commentary on Design Research. *Educational Psychologist*, 39(4): 255–260.

O'Reilly, M. & Kiyimba, N. (2015). *Advanced Qualitative Research: A Guide to Using Theory*. London: Sage.

OECD. (2015). *The ABC of Gender Equality in Education: Aptitude, Behaviour, Confidence*. Paris: OECD.

Onwuegbuzie, A. J. & Dickinson, W. B. (2008). Mixed Methods Analysis and Information Visualisation: Graphical Display for Effective Communication of Research Results. *Qualitative Report*, 13(2): 204–225.

Onwuegbuzie, A. J. & Leech, N. L. (2006). Linking Research Questions to Mixed Methods Data Analysis Procedures. *The Qualitative Report*, 11(3): 474–498.

Onwuegbuzie, A. J. & Teddlie, C. (2003). A Framework for Analyzing Data in Mixed Methods Research, in A. Tashakkori & C. Teddlie (eds), *Handbook of Mixed Methods in Social and Behavioral Research*, 351–383. Thousand Oaks, CA: Sage.

Opdenakker, R. (2006). Advantages and Disadvantages of Four Interview Techniques in Qualitative Research. *Forum: Qualitative Research*, 7(4).

Ornstein, M. (2013). *A Companion to Survey Research*. London: Sage.

Panero, M., Weisberg, D., Black, J., Goldstein, T., Barnes, J., Brownell, H., & Winner, E. (2016). Does Reading a Single Passage of Literary Fiction Really Improve Theory of Mind? An Attempt at Replication. *Journal of Personality and Social Psychology*, 111(5): e46–e54.

Park, C. & Jung, D. (2008). *Making Sense of the Asian Welfare Regimes with the Western Typology*, presented at EASP 5th Conference, November 3–4, National Taiwan University, Taipei.

Parker, I. (1998). *Social Constructionism, Discourse and Realism*. London: Sage.

Pashler, H. & Wagenmakers, E. (2012). Editors' Introduction to the Special Section on Replicability in Psychological Science. *Perspectives on Psychological Science*, 7(6): 528–530.

Patton, M. Q. (1990). *Qualitative Evaluation and Research Methods*, 2nd edn. Thousand Oaks, CA: Sage.

Pawson, R. (2013). *The Science of Evaluation*. London: Sage.

Pawson, R. & Tilley, N. (1997). *Realistic Evaluation*. London: Sage.

Peirce, C. S. (1893). Immortality in the Light of Synechism, in N. Houser & C. Kloesel (eds), (1998), *The Essential Peirce: Selected Philosophical Writings*, 1–10. Bloomington: Indiana University Press.

Peña-López, I. (2015). *Students, Computers and Learning. Making the Connection.* Paris: OECD.

Percy-Smith, B. (2010). Councils, Consultations and Community: Rethinking the Spaces for Children and Young People's Participation. *Children's Geographies*, 8: 107–122.

Pereira, M. D. & Vallance, R. (2006). Multiple Site Action Research Case Studies: Practical and Theoretical Benefits and Challenges. *Issues in Educational Research*, 16(1): 67–79. Retrieved from http://www.iier.org.au/iier16/pereira.html

Phillips, D. & Ochs, K. (2003). Processes of Policy Borrowing in Education: Some Explanatory and Analytical Devices. *Comparative Education*, 39(4): 451–461.

Phillips, D. & Schweisfurth, M. (2007). *Comparative and International Education: An Introduction to Theory, Method and Practice.* London: Continuum.

Phillips, D. C. (2005). The Contested Nature of Empirical Education Research (and why philosophy of education offers little help). *Journal of Philosophy of Education*, 39(4): 577–597.

Plano Clark, V. L. & Badiee, M. (2010). Research Questions in Mixed Methods Research, in A. Tashakkori & C. Teddlie (eds), *SAGE Handbook of Mixed Methods in Social and Behavioral Research*, 2nd edn, 275–304. Thousand Oaks, CA: Sage.

Platt, J. (1986), Functionalism and the Survey: The Relation of Theory and Method, *Sociological Review*, 34(3): 501–536.

Plowman, L. (2015). Researching Young Children's Everyday Uses of Technology in the Family Home. *Interacting with Computers*, 27(1): 36–46.

Plowman, L. (2016). Rethinking Context: Digital Technologies and Children's Everyday Lives. *Children's Geographies*, 14(2): 190–202.

Popper, K. R. (1968). *The Logic of Scientific Discovery*, 2nd edn. New York: Harper & Row.

Preissle, J., R. Glover-Kudon, E. A. Rohan, J. E. Boehm, & A. DeGroff (2015). Putting Ethics on the Mixed Methods Map, in S. N. Hesse-Biber & R. B. Johnson (eds), *The Oxford Handbook of Multimethod and Mixed Methods Research Enquiry.* Oxford: Oxford University Press.

Premack, D. & Woodruff, G. (1978). Does the Chimpanzee Have a Theory of Mind? *Behavioral and Brain Sciences*, 1(4): 515–526.

Pring, R. (2000). The 'False Dualism' of Educational Research. *Journal of Philosophy of Education*, 34(2): 247–260.

Pring, R. (2004). *Philosophy of Educational Research.* London: Continuum.

Pritchard, D. (2009). *Knowledge.* Palgrave Macmillan.

Pritchard, D. (2013). Epistemic Virtue and the Epistemology of Education. *Journal of Philosophy of Education*, 47(2): 236–247.

Prout, A. & James, A. (1997). A New Paradigm for the Sociology of Childhood: Provenance, Promise and Problems, in A. James & A. Prout (eds), *Constructing and Reconstructing Childhood: Contemporary Issues in the Sociological Study of Childhood*. A seminal tect on the new Sociology of Childhood.

Punch, K. & Oancea, A. (2014). *Introduction to Research Methods in Education*. London: Sage.

Putnam, H. (2002). *The Collapse of the Fact/Value Dichotomy and Other Essays*. Cambridge, MA: Harvard University Press.

Rabinow, P., Marcus, G. E., Faubion, J. D., & Rees, T. (2008). *Designs for an Anthropology of the Contemporary*. Duke University Press.

Raffe, D. (2011). *Policy Borrowing or Policy Learning? How (not) to Improve Education Systems – Briefing 57*. Edinburgh: Centre for Educational Sociology.

Ragin, C. (1987). *The Comparative Method. Moving beyond Qualitative and Quantitative Strategies*. Berkeley, Los Angeles: University of California Press.

Read, J. C. & Markopoulos, P. (2014). *Evaluating Children's Interactive Products*: ACM.

Reason, P. & Bradbury, H. (2001). *Handbook of Action Research: Participative Inquiry*, Thousand Oaks, CA: Sage.

Reeves, B. D. (2009). *Leading Change in Schools: How to Conquer Myths, Build Commitment and Get Results*. Alexandria: Association for Supervision and Curriculum Development.

Reichardt, C. S. & Cook, T. D. (1979). Beyond Qualitative versus Quantitative Methods, in T. D. Cook & C. S. Reichardt (eds), *Qualitative and Quantitative Methods in Evaluation Research*. Beverley Hills, CA: Sage.

Reichardt, C. S. & Rallis, S. F. (1994). Qualitative and Quantitative Inquiries Are Not Incompatible: A Call for a New Partnership. *New Directions for Program Evaluation, 61*: 85–91.

Remington, B., Hastings, R. P., Kovshoff, H., Degli Espinosa, F., Jahr, E., Brown, T., & Ward, N. (2007). Early Intensive Behavioral Intervention: Outcomes for Children with Autism and Their Parents after Two Years. *American Journal on Mental Retardation, 112*(6): 418–438.

Rescher, N. (2000). *Realistic Pragmatism: An Introduction to Pragmatic Philosophy*, Albany: State University of New York Press.

Richards, L. (2005). *Handling Qualitative Research Data: A Practical Guide*. London: Sage.

Riddell, S., Markowitsch, J., & Weedon, E. (2012). *Lifelong Learning in Europe: Equity and Efficiency in the Balance*. Bristol: Policy Press.

Ridenour, C. S. & I. Newman (2008). *Mixed Methods Research: Exploring the Interactive Continuum*, Carbondale: Southern Illinois University Press.

Robson, C. (2011). *Real World Research*. Chichester: John Wiley & Sons.

Romich, J. L. (2006). Randomized Social Policy Experiments and Research on Child Development. *Journal of Applied Developmental Psychology*, *27*(*2*): 136–150.

Rosenthal, R. & Rosnow, R. L. (2009). *Artifacts in Behavioral Research*: Robert Rosenthal and Ralph L. Rosnow's classic books. New York; Oxford: Oxford University Press.

Ross, J. (2017). Speculative Method in Digital Education Research. *Learning, Media and Technology*, *42*(*2*): 214–229. doi:10.1080/17439884.2016.1160927.

Ross, J. & Collier, A. (2016). Complexity, Mess and Not-Yetness: Teaching Online with Emerging Technologies, in Veletsianos, G. (ed.), *Emergence and Innovation in Digital Learning: Foundations and Applications*. Athabasca University Press.

Ross, J. et al. (in press). Artcasting, Mobilities, and Inventiveness: Engaging with New Approaches to Arts Evaluation, in L. Ciolfi et al. (eds), *Cultural Heritage Communities: Technologies and Challenges*. London: Routledge.

Royce, J. (1891). Is There a Science of Education? *Education Review*, 1 January 1891.

Ryde, G. C., Booth, J. N., Brooks, N. E., Chesham, R. A., Moran, C. N., & Gorely, T. (Under review). The Daily Mile: What Factors Are Associated with Its Implementation Success? Submitted to *PLOS One*.

Saar, E., Ure, O. B., & Holford, J. (2013). *Lifelong Learning in Europe: National Patterns and Challenges*. Cheltenham: Edward Elgar.

Sadoff, S. (2014). The Role of Experimentation in Education Policy. *Oxford Review of Economic Policy*, *30*(*4*): 597–620.

Salomon, G. (1990). Cognitive Effects with and of Computer Technology. *Communication Research*, *17*(*1*): 26–44.

Sandelowski, M. (1996). Using Qualitative Methods in Intervention Studies, *Research in Nursing and Health*, *19*(*4*): 359–364.

Sanders, E. B.-N. & Stappers, P. J. (2014) Probes, Toolkits and Prototypes: Three Approaches to Making in Codesigning. *CoDesign*, *10*(*1*): 5–14.

Sani, F. & Todman, J. (2006). Experimental Design and Statistics for Psychology: A First Course. Oxford: Blackwell.

Sapford, R. (2007). *Survey Research*. London: Sage.

Saris, W. & Gallhofer, I. (2007). *Design, Evaluation and Analysis of Questionnaires for Survey Research*. Hoboken: Wiley.

Schrag, F. (1992). In Defence of Positivist Research Paradigms. *Educational Researcher*, *21*(*5*): 5–8.

Schwartz-Shea, P. & Yanow, D. (2012). *Interpretative Research Design – Concepts and Processes*. London: Routledge.

Seale, C. (2004). Validity, Reliability and Quality of Research, in C. Seale (ed.), *Researching Society and Culture*, 2nd edn, 71–84. London: Sage.

Seale, C. (2007). Quality in Qualitative Research, in C. Seale, G. Gobo, J. Gubrium & D. Silverman *Qualitative Research Practice*. London: Sage.

Sellitz, D., Wrightsman, L., & Cook, S. (1976). *Research Methods in Social Relations*. New York: Holt, Rinehart & Winston.

Selwyn, N. (2012) Ten Suggestions for Improving Academic Research in Education and Technology. *Learning, Media and Technology, 37*(3): 213–219.

Selwyn, N. (2016). Minding Our Language: Why Education and Technology Is Full of Bullshit … and What Might Be Done about It'. *Learning, Media and Technology, 41*(3): 437–443.

Sheller, M. & Urry, J. (2016). Mobilizing the New Mobilities Paradigm. *Applied Mobilities, 1*(1): 10–25.

Silverman, D. (2010). *Doing Qualitative Research*. London: Sage.

Simons, D. (2014). The value of direct replication. *Perspectives on Psychological Science, 9*(1): 76–80.

Smith, J. K. & Heshusius, L. (1986). Closing Down the Conversation: The End of the Quantitative-Qualitative Debate among Educational Inquirers. *Educational Researcher, 15*(1): 4–12.

Sosa, E. (1991). *Knowledge in Perspective*, Cambridge: Cambridge University Press.

Spatig, L. & Amerikaner, L. (2014). *Thinking Outside the Girl Box: Teaming Up with Resilient Youth in Appalachia*. Ohio University Press.

St Pierre, E. A. (2015). Practices for the 'New' in the New Empiricisms, the New Materialisms, and Post Qualitative Inquiry. *Qualitative Inquiry and the Politics of Research, 10*: 75.

Stake, R. E. (1995). *The Art of Case Study Research*. Thousand Oaks, CA: Sage.

Stake, R. E. (2000). The Case Study Method in Social Inquiry, in R. Gromm, M. Hammersley & P. Foster (eds), *Case Study Method: Key Issues, Key Texts*, 19–26. London: Sage.

Stake, R. E. (2006). *Multiple Case Study Analysis*. London: The Guilford Press.

Stake, R. E. (2010). *Qualitative Research Methods: Collecting Evidence, Crafting Analysis, Communicating Impact*. Oxford: Wiley-Blackwell.

Steup, M. (2005). Contextualism and Conceptual Disambiguation. *Acta Analytica, 20*: 3–15.

Symonds, J. E. & Gorard, S. (2010). Death of Mixed Methods? Or the Rebirth of Research as a Craft. *Evaluation & Research in Education, 23*(2): 121–136.

Tashakkori, A. & Creswell, J. (2007). The New Era of Mixed Methods. *Journal of Mixed Methods Research, 1*(1): 3–7.

Tashakkori, A. & Teddlie, C. (1998). *Mixed Methodology: Combining Qualitative and Quantitative Approaches*, Thousand Oaks, CA: Sage.

Tashakkori, A. & Teddlie, C. (2003). The Past and the Future of Mixed Methods Research: From 'Methodological Triangulation' to '*Mixed Methods*

Designs'. Handbook of Mixed Methods in Social and Behavioral Research. 671–701.

Tashakkori, A. & Teddlie, C. (2008). Quality of Inferences in Mixed Methods Research: Calling for an Integrative Framework, in M. M. Bergman (ed.), *Advances in Mixed Methods Research*, 101–119. London: Sage.

Tashakkori, A. & Teddlie, C. (2010). Current Developments and Emerging Trends in Integrated Research Methodology, in A. Tashakkori & C. Teddlie (eds), *SAGE Handbook of Mixed Methods in Social and Behavioural Research*, 2nd edn, 803–826. Thousand Oaks, CA: Sage.

Teddlie, C. & Tashakkori, A. (2003) Major Issues and Controversies in the Use of Mixed Methods in the Social and Behavioural Sciences, in A. Tashakkori & C. Teddlie (eds), *Handbook of Mixed Methods in Social and Behavioural Research*. Thousand Oaks, CA: Sage Publications.

Teddlie, C. & Tashakkori, A. (2009). *Foundations of Mixed Methods Research: Integrating Qualitative and Quantitative Approaches in Social and Behavioural Sciences.* Thousand Oaks, CA: Sage.

Teddlie, C. & Tashakkori, A. (2010). Overview of Contemporary Issues in Mixed Methods Research, in A. Tashakkori & C. Teddlie (eds), *SAGE Handbook of Mixed Methods in Social and Behavioural Research*, 2nd edn, 1–41. Thousand Oaks, CA: Sage.

Theisen, G. & Adams, D. (1990). Comparative Education Research, in R. Thomas (ed.), *International Comparative Education*, 277–300. Oxford: Pergamon Press.

Thomas, G. (2011). *How to do Your Case Study.* London: Sage.

Thorp, L. (2006). *The Pull of the Earth: Participatory Ethnography in the School Garden.* W. AltaMira Press, Lanham.

Tisdall E. K. M., Davis J. M., & Gallagher, M. (2009) *Researching with Children and Young People: Research Design, Methods, and Analysis.* Los Angeles; London: Sage.

Torche, F. (2011). The Effect of Maternal Stress on Birth Outcomes: Exploiting a Natural Experiment. *Demography*, 48(4): 1473–1491.

Tracy, S. J. (2010). Qualitative Quality: Eight 'Big-Tent' Criteria for Excellent Qualitative Research. *Qualitative Inquiry*, 16(10): 837–851.

Trimmer, J. F. (2006). Teaching and Learning Outside and Inside the Box. *Peer Review 8*(2): 20–22. Walnut Creek, CA: AltaMira Press.

Tsakalou, D. (2014). *Exploring the Construction of Inclusive Educational Communities in Greece: Case Studies of Secondary Schools.* Unpublished Ph.D. thesis. Edinburgh: The University of Edinburgh.

Turkle, S. (1997). Computational Technologies and Images of the self. *Social Research.* 64(3): 1093–1111.

United Nations (1989). Convention on the Rights of the Child. Retrieved from http://www.ohchr.org/EN/ProfessionalInterest/Pages/CRC.aspx

Valliant, R., Dever, J., & Kreuter, F. (2013). *Practical Tools for Designing and Weighting Survey Samples*. New York: Springer.

Veletsianos, G. (2010). *Emerging Technologies in Distance Education*. Athabasca University Press. Retrieved from http://www.aupress.ca/index.php/books/120177.

Vygotsky, L. (1978). *Mind in Society: The Development of Higher Psychological Processes*. Cambridge: Harvard University Press.

Walker, R. (2011). 'Design-based Research: Reflections on Some Epistemological Issues and Practices, in L. Markauskaite, P. Freebody & J. Irwin (eds), *Methodological Choice and Design: Scholarship, Policy and Practice in Social and Educational Research*. Dordrecht: Springer Science & Business Media, 51–56.

Whitely, B. E. & Kite, M. E. (2013). *Principles of Research in Behavioural Science*. New York: Psychology Press.

Whitty, G. & Wisby, E. (2007). Whose Voice? An Exploration of the Current Policy Interest in Pupil Involvement in School Decision-Making. *International Studies in Education*, *17*(3): 1–30.

Wilkie, A., Michael, M., & Plummer-Fernandez, M. (2015). Speculative Method and Twitter: Bots, Energy and Three Conceptual Characters. *The Sociological Review*, *63*(1): 79–101.

Wilson, V. (1997). Focus Groups: A Useful Qualitative Method for Educational Research? *British Educational Research Journal*, *23*(2): 209–224.

Wong, G., Greenhalgh, T., Westhorp, G., & Pawson, R. (2012). Realist Methods in Medical Education Research: What Are They and What Can They Contribute? *Medical Education*, *46*(1): 89–96.

Wood, D., Bruner, J., & Ross, G. (1976). The Role of Tutoring in Problem Solving. *Journal of Child Psychology and Psychiatry*, *17*(2): 89–100.

Woolley, C. M. (2009). Meeting the Mixed Methods Challenge of Integration in a Sociological Study of Structure and Agency. *Journal of Mixed Methods Research*, *3*(1): 7–25.

Yazan, B. (2015). Three Approaches to Case Study Methods in Education: Yin, Merriam, and Stake. *The Qualitative Report*, *20*(2): 134–152. Retrieved from http://nsuworks.nova.edu/tqr/vol20/iss2/12

Yin, R. (2003). *Case Study Research: Design and Methods*, 3rd edn. London: Sage.

Yin, R. (2014). *Case Study Research: Design and Methods*, 6th edn. London: Sage.

Young, F. (2008). *Bringing Knowledge Back In: From Social Constructivism to Realism in the Sociology of Education*. Oxon: Routledge.

Zagzebski, L. (2004). Epistemic Value and the Primacy of What We Care About. *Philosophical Papers*, *33*: 353–376.

Web links
www.cls.ioe.ac.uk/ncds
www.cls.ioe.ac.uk/BCS70

Websites:

Chapter 1
Socialtheoryapplied.com
Stanford Encyclopedia of Philosophy
National Centre for Research Methods
https://www.ncrm.ac.uk/

Chapter 2
datasets for secondary data analysis
www.cls.ioe.ac.uk/ncds
www.cls.ioe.ac.uk/BCS70

Chapter 3
Education Endowment Foundation
https://educationendowmentfoundation.org.uk/
https://ies.ed.gov/ncee/wwc/
British Psychological Society: Origins
http://origins.bps.org.uk/
The Reproducibility Project
https://osf.io/ezcuj/wiki/home/

Chapter 6
An Overview of Mixed Methods Research
Nora Jacobson, University of Wisconsin
http://videos.med.wisc.edu/videos/33600
William T Grant Foundation Mixed Methods Resources
http://wtgrantmixedmethods.com

Chapter 7
http://www.oecd.org/pisa/
http://www.tandfonline.com/toc/cced20/current

Chapter 8
Collaborative Anthropologies: http://coll-anth.anth.ubc.ca/

Imagine – Connecting Communities through Research:
http://www.imaginecommunity.org.uk
Neighborhood Story Project: https://www.neighborhoodstoryproject.org
A New Orleans neighborhood-based program emphasizing collaborative ethnography.

Chapter 9
United Nations (1989) Convention on the Rights of the Child, retrieved 2 June 2017 from http://www.ohchr.org/EN/ProfessionalInterest/Pages/CRC.aspx

Chapter 10
http://nearfuturelaboratory.com
http://www.gold.ac.uk/unitofplay/research/speculation/

Chapter 11
http://childrenandtechnology.ed.ac.uk
https://www.commonsensemedia.org
http://www.joanganzcooneycenter.org
https://llk.media.mit.edu

Index